Michael Barry

HOMAGE TO AL-ANDALUS
The Rise and Fall of Islamic Spain

Andalus Press

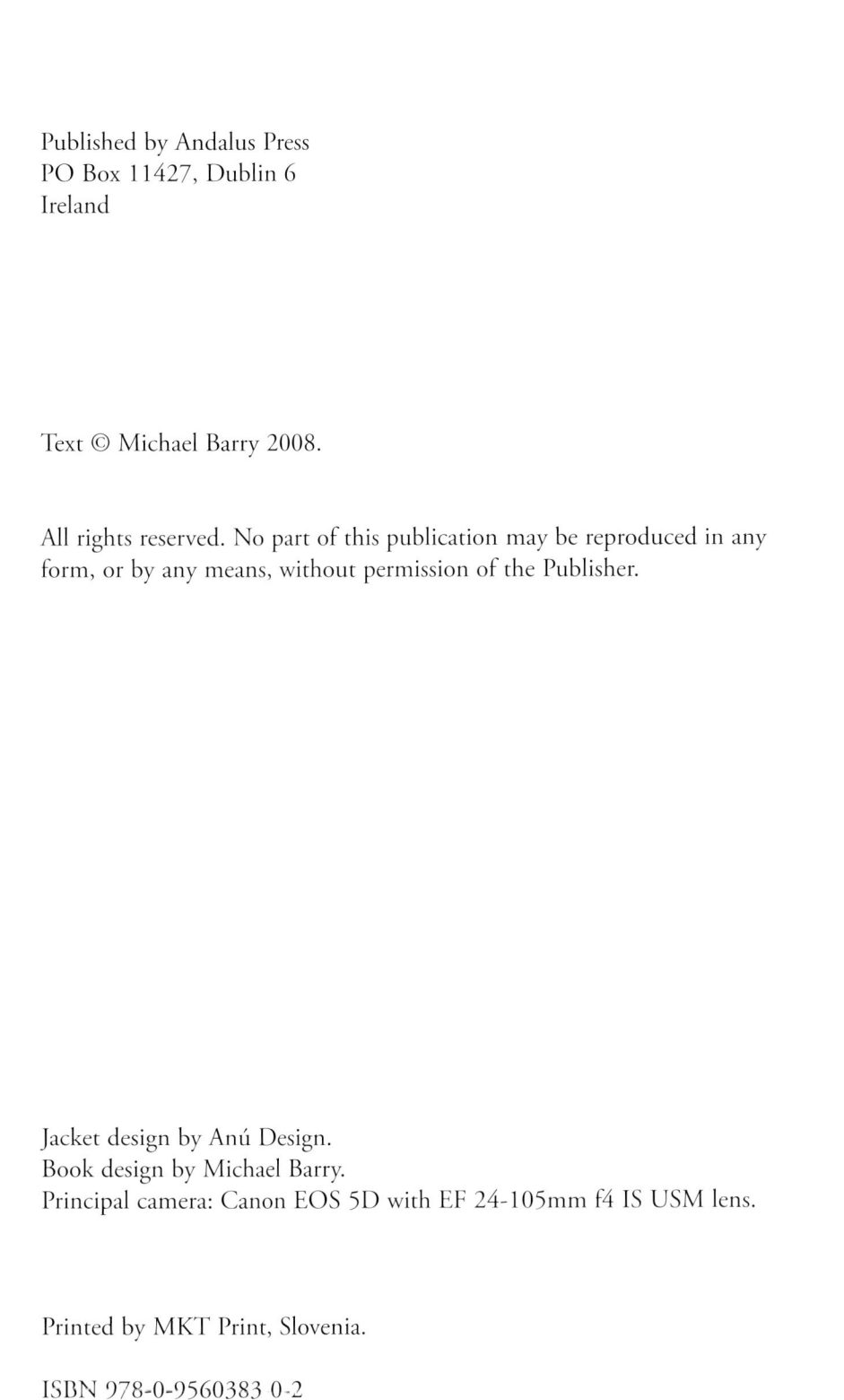

Published by Andalus Press
PO Box 11427, Dublin 6
Ireland

Text © Michael Barry 2008.

All rights reserved. No part of this publication may be reproduced in any form, or by any means, without permission of the Publisher.

Jacket design by Anú Design.
Book design by Michael Barry.
Principal camera: Canon EOS 5D with EF 24-105mm f4 IS USM lens.

Printed by MKT Print, Slovenia.

ISBN 978-0-9560383 0-2

Contents

Acknowledgements		5
Introduction		7
Chapter 1	The Beginnings	9
Chapter 2	Conquest and Consolidation	21
Chapter 3	The Turbulent Umayyad Years	39
Chapter 4	The Caliphate	69
Chapter 5	The Taifas	113
Chapter 6	The Almoravids and the Almohads	141
Chapter 7	Nasrid Granada	177
Chapter 8	Moriscos and Expulsion	215
Glossary, Illustrations		251
Bibliography		252
Index		254

For Olivia Alexandrine Barry

Acknowledgements

My sincere thanks are due to the following :

Museums in Spain were very helpful in providing photographs of artefacts which illustrate the sublime artistry and craftsmanship dating from the times of al-Andalus. These include the Museo del Ejercito, Madrid; Museo de Teruel; the Museo Arqueológico Nacional of Madrid; Museo de Huesca; the Patrimonio Histórico-Artístico del Senado; Archivo General de Simancas and the Fundacion Bancaja. The following museums and locations kindly allowed me to use photographs: Conjunto Arqueológico Madinat al-Zahra; Museo Arqueológico Provincial de Badajoz; Palacio de la Aljafería, Zaragoza; Real Alcázar, Seville; Museo de Zaragoza, as well as the Patronato de la Alhambra y el Generalife and the Capilla Real in Granada. The staff in the Alcazaba, Málaga; Sinagoga del Tránsito, Toledo; Toledo and Seville Cathedrals and the Palau Comtal, Cocentaina were helpful in facilitating me to take photographs.

 The Victoria and Albert Museum was helpful in allowing access to photographs from their collection. Kimberly Henrikson of the admirable ARTstor initiative associated with Metropolitan Museum in New York gave me considerable assistance in gaining access to images.

 Señor Iglesias, of the Catedral de Córdoba, kindly facilitated my entry to the Mihrab of the Great Mosque. Andrés García, of the Conjunto Arqueológico Madinat al-Zahra, assisted me with details of nearby monuments. Michael Forde, helpful with advice, accompanied me on a visit to see the Islamic monuments of Córdoba. José Barasona of Córdoba kindly showed me and Michael the Aqueducto of Valdepuentes (which served the nearby palace-city of Madinat al-Zahra) and then showed us the private jewel that is the fourteenth-century Monastery of San Jerónimo de Valparaíso.

 Frank Twomey gave insightful advice on photographic matters, as did Brendan Fitzpatrick. Declan Lyons and Dermot O' Doherty were a source of useful ideas. Kevin McCaughan assisted me at various stages. The de Linares family gave invaluable help with navigating *el mundo español*. Antonio de Linares in particular was instrumental in guiding me around many obstacles. Paul Spaine assisted me in preparation of the maps. I am grateful for the advice of Elaine Wright of the Chester Beatty Library, Dublin.

 Two people who put in a major effort were Tony Mc Gettigan and Daltún O' Ceallaigh. They contributed to the final edit of this book and read the proofs assiduously and in forensic detail. Any errors are mine.

 My final and most important thanks go to Veronica Barry. This book would not have seen the light of day without her efforts. She was a travelling companion on my forays to Spain. My muse, and an understanding one, she provided ideas and guidance, as well as the hard work of the final edit.

Introduction

It was June in southern Andalucía. As we walked along the dusty track through remote hills, a cluster of old buildings appeared on a promontory. No roofs, just the outline of stone walls. Shards of red brick lay around among the surrounding bushes. A few trees provided welcome shade. What was this? It was a small fortification from the time of al-Andalus, a waypoint on a mule track from the Mediterranean coast. Intrigued, I resolved to find more information on that era. I later travelled through Spain and saw the wonderful legacy: the exquisite detail of the Alhambra; the unique ambience of the Great Mosque in Córdoba and more. I looked for a book that would tell the story. However, apart from a few volumes, mainly of academic bent, there was no information at this level, complete with full illustration. Driven by a growing fascination I decided to fill the gap. Here is the story of al-Andalus, from A to Z, set out in an accessible form.

Once I had begun my research, I realised that there was an intriguing historical connection with my native West Cork in Ireland: a village, not more than ten kilometres from where I grew up, had suffered, at least in part, due to the aftermath of the fall of al-Andalus. Baltimore was sacked in 1631 by Barbary pirates and over a hundred souls were taken into slavery. Piracy in the Maghreb expanded enormously after the expulsion of the Moriscos from Spain. Many of the Moriscos became pirates and even established a pirate republic in Salé, in (present-day) Morocco.

My story starts with the Iberian Peninsula before the invasion in AD 711. The rise of the new successful religion of Islam and the resultant conquest of the Peninsula is sketched out. Any resistance of the original inhabitants was extinguished, save that of a tiny part of the north.

Turbulence and conflict marked the early years of al-Andalus, at that time a far-flung provincial outpost of the Umayyad Caliphate based in Damascus. Then, in a twist of fate, as the ruling family of the Caliph was overthrown and massacred, a survivor of this massacre managed to seize independent power in al-Andalus. Over the 250 years that followed, the Umayyads in al-Andalus developed a society that was sophisticated, learned and technologically advanced.

And it came about that, in the southern extremities of Europe, brilliance flamed, all the more luminous when set against the reigning obscurity and backwardness of the rest of the continent. A new society was forged, based on an Islamic foundation and using the Arabic language. It melded together the Arab and Berber invaders and the original Hispano-Iberian inhabitants of the Peninsula. In those times, Islam was supremely adaptable in terms of taking the best of architecture, learning and science and coming up with a new and enhanced derivation.

By the middle of the tenth century, Córdoba was to the forefront, rivalled only by Constantinople and Baghdad. Córdoba had mosques, bathhouses, public lighting, sanitation, water supply and libraries. It had sumptuous palaces, advanced craftsmanship and produced luxury goods such as silks and jewellery. It had no rival in the unsanitary, cramped, small capitals of Northern Europe.

The Umayyad Caliphate fell apart at the beginning of the eleventh century. A mass of statelets (the taifas) emerged and began to devour each other. Seizing their opportunity, the Christian kingdoms in the north of Spain began to dominate, expand and extract huge amounts of money from the disparate taifas.

The fall of Toledo in 1085 prompted the takeover of al-Andalus by Islamic fundamentalists from the Maghreb - the Almoravids. In time, they were overthrown by a new fundamentalism that was manifested by the Almohads. Despite the rigour of the Almohads, there was still appreciation of literature, art and architecture. The brilliance of al-Andalus shone on the Maghreb where Andalusi technology, art and architecture flowed southwards, a heritage that remains today. A by-product of the fall of Toledo to the Christians was the start of a process that became immeasurably beneficial to western civilisation. An enlightened Archbishop of Toledo encouraged scholars to come from afar and translate the trove of books in Arabic that was found there. From then on the advanced learning in al-Andalus (which had been built on that of the east and earlier Greek works) was unlocked and disseminated throughout the Christian countries to the north. Europe, in turn, was able to use these Andalusi advances as the foundation for later developments in science and philosophy in the run-up to the Renaissance.

The decline of the Almohads in the mid-thirteenth century went hand-in-hand with a massive conquest of territory by the Christian kingdoms, ending with Islamic rule being restricted to a sliver of the Peninsula, the Kingdom of Granada, in what is more or less present-day Andalucía. Nevertheless, the brilliance continued, particularly with the sublimity of the palace-city of the Alhambra. The shine was taken off the brilliance in the last painful hundred years, after the fall of Granada in 1492, when the remaining Muslims were firstly converted forcibly and then summarily expelled.

Al-Andalus forms an illustrious part of the history of Islam. It is also part of the Spanish heritage. The Spanish language has inherited a legacy of several thousand words dating from the Arabic of al-Andalus. The placenames across the country - towns, rivers and districts - are an indelible reminder of the time when Arabic was the dominant language. The present day irrigation systems in Spain are evidence of the technology of that time. The learning and literature, science, mathematics and medicine were incorporated into European thought and practice. Through the prism of the Mudéjar style can still be seen the glory of Andalusi architecture and decoration.

Spain today is a vigorous modern country. It has shaken off the shackles of Francoism, although still has to fully exorcise the demons of the Civil War. It is no longer the intolerant mono-faith country that emerged from the Inquisition, in parallel with the expulsion of the Jews and the Muslims. To me, Spain is certainly is a more interesting country as a result of its heritage from al-Andalus. With all its rich culture, Spain has *duende*. Enjoy this book.

Chapter 1
The Beginnings

Back in distant time the earth was created. Rocks formed and water covered the land. Over the millennia, strata lifted and dipped, the seas receded. The outlines of the present-day land masses started to emerge. On the south-west tip of present-day Europe a long land mass appeared, at one stage connected to the African continent. As there is no permanency in the Earth's structure, in time the Atlantic broke through into the Mediterranean basin, cutting that land link between Europe and Africa. It has been speculated that the ensuing inundation resulted in the great flood of biblical times. This land mass, the Iberian Peninsula, separates the Atlantic ocean and the Mediterranean sea. A peninsula gains many benefits from engaging with the seas around it. The inhabitants of this Peninsula have indeed done this decisively, particularly when they explored and discovered new lands. The seas bring settlers and trade. However, a peninsula is vulnerable and Iberia was at various times buffeted, devastated and enhanced by invaders from the surrounding seas.

In this book we are going to explore one wave of invaders, radically different in every sense to any that went before, who conquered the Peninsula rapidly and stayed for nine hundred years. These Muslim invaders left a rich legacy which still has reverberations today. But first it is worthwhile to look at what preceded them. We will briefly look at the early peoples who settled in the Peninsula. We take particular account of the Roman era, as that impacted on all subsequent epochs. The Visigoths, conquered by the Arab invaders in 711, are also important because the seeds of Christian Spain emerged from a besieged remnant of their kingdom.

First we look at the physical features of the Iberian Peninsula, which influenced the pattern of conquest and settlement. The Peninsula is roughly shaped as a rectangle, with a distance from north to south of more than 800 kilometres. The Pyrenees mountain range forms its neck, dividing it from France. The Meseta Central is the defining element of the Peninsula's geography. A generally treeless plateau, with an average height of around 700 metres, it is bounded by several mountain systems. One is the Cordillera Cantábrica to the north. To the northeast lies the Sistema Ibérico. In the north the river Duero rises in Soria province, flows south, then west to emerge at Porto on the Atlantic. Another northern river is the Ebro which flows south-east to the Mediterranean. To the south-east lie the mountains of the Baetic Cordillera which commence just

Left. Many of the northern rivers that flow through the Meseta Central of the Iberian Peninsula pass through deep gorges and much is unnavigable.

beyond Gibraltar and run parallel to the Mediterranean coast towards Murcia and Valencia. Included here is the Peninsula's highest mountain (Mulhacén, at 3481 metres) in the Sierra Nevada. The major river of the south, the Guadalquivir, flows south-west through fertile low-lying lands past Córdoba and Seville and on to the Atlantic.

The first of the human species to settle in the Peninsula is thought to have reached there by two routes, one coming directly north from Africa across the strait. The other was in a long loop up from Africa, around the east of the Mediterranean, then towards the west and south to the Peninsula. Remains of early modern humans can be seen in Palaeolithic paintings in Cantabrian caves dating from as early as 25,000 BC. By around 6000 BC the techniques of cereal growing and domestic husbandry had been established in the Peninsula, representing the evolution to the Neolithic period. The remains of the settlement of los Millares (Almería) from around 3200 BC, with its stone fortifications and evidence of copper smelting, are an example of the transition from the Neolithic to the Bronze Age, which emerged from around 2000 BC. The Celts ranged over much of Europe from the second millennia before Christ and settled in the north and west of the Peninsula. In the centre of the Peninsula there emerged an amalgam of the Celts in the north and the Iberians in the south, called the Celto-Iberians.

As the techniques of ship building and navigation improved, traders increasingly arrived. One of the principal attractions was the mineral wealth of the

Below. Mulhacén is named after one of the last of the Nasrid rulers of Granada, Muley Hacén. Part of the Sierra Nevada, it is the highest mountain, at an altitude of 3481 metres, on the Iberian Peninsula.

Peninsula. The Phoenicians arrived around 800 BC. These merchants of the Levant built up a healthy trade and established settlements in the mineral-rich south. It was recorded that in 700 BC the volume of silver extracted from the Rio Tinto mine in the Sierra Morena was so great that the market price of the metal fell rapidly in the Assyrian empire. Phoenician settlements in the Peninsula included Gadir (Cádiz), Malaca (Málaga), Carmo (Carmona) and Sexi (Almuñécar). The Greeks in turn founded colonies in the north-east such as those at Rhode (Rosas) and Emporion (Ampurias). The native Bronze Age inhabitants of the eastern and southern Peninsula gradually absorbed the culture of the Phoenicians and the Greeks. The term Iberia began to be used in classical writings and an Iberian civilization developed, with urban settlements incorporating aspects of Greek and Phoenician life.

As the Babylonians subjugated Phoenicia in the sixth century BC the Phoenician colonies and their trade went into decline. By the fourth century BC, the North African state of Carthage filled the vacuum. A major Carthaginian trading colony was founded in Elvissa (Ibiza). Propelled by rivalry with the other Mediterranean power, Rome, the Carthaginians began a course of imperial expansion. Under Hamilcar Barca, they invaded and conquered the southern part of the Iberian Peninsula and founded Cartago Nova (Cartagena) in 228 BC.

The Second Punic war between Carthage and Rome was sparked by an attack by the Carthaginian general Hannibal on the town of Saguntum (present-day Sagunto) in 219 BC, then under Roman protection. The Carthaginian war effort was strongly sustained by troops as well as by silver from the Peninsula. Hannibal made his epic journey to Italy, setting out from Iberia to France and over the Alps. To deny him the possibility of reinforcements, the Romans sent troops to Iberia in 218 BC and finally defeated the Carthaginians there in 207 BC. Across the Mediterranean, the war continued and the Carthaginians were eventually defeated in 202 BC. In Iberia, the Romans by now controlled the eastern coast and the hinterland of the river Baetis (Guadalquivir). They continued to fight the native tribes and slowly expanded their zone of influence. The Roman conquest continued and, by 19 BC, they captured Cantabria and now controlled the Peninsula. They found it difficult to subdue the Cantabrians and the Basques, an experience also encountered by later invaders. The Romans did not build major roads in those parts; rather they constructed fortresses to control the passes.

Roman Hispania was divided into three provinces, Tarraconensis, with its capital in Tarraco (Tarragona), encompassed the north. Baetica (very roughly present-day Andalucía) had its capital in Corduba (Córdoba). Lusitania (roughly most of present-day Portugal and parts of Extremadura) had its capital at Agusta Emerita (Mérida). During the first 400 years after Christ, Hispania formed a flourishing and productive part of the Roman Empire. Colonial settlements were founded across the Peninsula, planted with Roman citizens and soldiers. Hispania's mines were intensively worked and mineral exports such as gold, silver, copper and lead made a valuable contribution to the imperial econo-

Above. The Roman bridge crossing the river Guadiana at Mérida in Extremadura. The bridge is 792 metres long and has sixty arches. Its construction dates back to the city's founding in 25 BC, as Agusta Emerita, capital of the Roman province of Lusitania.

my. There was a strong agricultural sector, with exports of wool, olive oil and wine. Particularly appreciated and much to the Roman taste was *garum* (a piquant fish sauce made from marinated tuna and mackerel) which was produced in such locations as Bolonia (near Tarifa) and Málaga.

To paraphrase the old joke; what did the Romans do for Spain? The list is long and the centuries of Roman presence still strongly resonate in the Spain of today. They brought the advanced technology of the age. In agriculture they established irrigation, efficient cultivation and introduced new plants. They also introduced effective administration and law. They laid down an essential communication network of roads and bridges. Reflecting the prosperity of Hispania, they built cities, with public buildings such as fora, temples, amphitheatres and basilicas. Cities had drainage systems, water supplies and public baths. The bridges at Mérida and Córdoba, aqueducts at Segovia, Mérida and Tarragona, the city at Itálica (near Seville) are among some of the many outstanding Roman remains. For most of its existence Hispania was largely a peaceful and prosperous region. It also fully participated in the affairs of the Empire and contributed outstanding leaders and philosophers. The philosopher Seneca came from Córdoba. The Emperors Trajan and Hadrian both came from Itálica.

By the end of the Roman era the Romans had generally absorbed the native population into their society and language. Latin was implanted in the Peninsula. This language of these colonizers was probably to have the most fundamental impact on the later development of the Spanish language. The com-

Right. Morning at the Aqueducto de los Milagros at Mérida. This 830 metre-long aqueduct, was built around the beginning of the first century AD. It brought water to the Roman city and its slender arches of granite and brick construction reach a maximum height of twenty-five metres.

Below. Section of Roman road at Mérida. Good communications were important for the Roman Empire. The Romans built an extensive network of strategic roads across the Peninsula. Mérida was an important communications hub. Here was the intersection of the north-south road across Hispania (called the Silver Road) and routes to Lisbon, Toledo and Córdoba.

mon dialect of the Roman soldiers was to migrate and be transformed into a romance dialect that formed the principal basis of today's Spanish. The legacy of the Romans was little diluted by the later Visigoths, who took up Roman customs and practices. Christianity spread to the Peninsula by the second century AD. By the fourth century Christian communities and bishoprics had been established across the Peninsula. Many thousands of Jews settled in Hispania, as part of their diaspora around the Empire following the crushing of revolts in Judea, starting from the first century AD.

By the end of the third century the Roman Empire was in decline. On the borders Germanic tribes were on the move. Pushed by tribes to the east and driven by worsening climatic conditions, they were searching for more fertile and habitable lands. The Visigoths had been an agricultural tribe in the area that is now Romania. When attacked by the Huns they had moved across the Danube. The Emperor Valens allowed them to settle in Roman lands. They turned against Valens and defeated his army in a decisive battle at Adrianople in AD 378. After this shock to the empire the Visigoths were given land to settle in the Balkans, being considered as *federates*, or military allies, and with obligations to defend the border.

In 395 the Roman Emperor Theodosius split the Roman Empire. He assigned the eastern and the western sections to each of his sons respectively. The rivalry which developed between the two sections further weakened the empire. The Visigoths wandered south and invaded Italy. They penetrated as far as Rome, which they sacked in 410. In the meantime, other Germanic tribes, under pressure from the Huns, crossed the Rhine frontier of the weakened Empire. They made their way southwards through Gaul and invaded the northwest of Hispania in 409, entering through the western Pyrenees. The invading tribes ranged far and wide over Iberia. The Hasding Vandals and the Suevi occupied Galicia. The Alans occupied part of Lusitania and extended across to Carthago Nova (Cartagena). The Siling Vandals continued southwards to Baetica.

Fresh from the sack of Rome, the Visigoths moved westwards towards southern Gaul. By now partly romanised, the Visigoths alternated between being enemies and allies of the Romans. The Roman Emperor wished to play the Visigoths off against the invaders of Hispania. They duly obliged, entering Iberia and attacking the Germanic tribes there who were put to flight. The Visigoths returned to the north. In recognition of their efforts, the Roman Emperor Honorius authorized them to settle in southern Gaul in 418.

The other tribes expanded once more, filling the vacuum created by the departure of the Visigoths. The Hasding Vandals settled in Baetica. Continuing their wanderings, they crossed to North Africa in 429 and conquered the Roman province there. In these febrile times the Visigoths switched again to being enemies of the Romans. Under Euric (466-484) they set up an independent kingdom in southern Gaul, with a capital in Toulouse. It extended into the Peninsula and included Tarraconensis, and across to Lusitania. Another Germanic tribe, the Franks, moved on southern Gaul at the beginning of the sixth century and pushed the Visigoths southwards. These now set up their kingdom in Hispania, with an adjunct in southern Gaul. The Visigoths were primarily military leaders and the underlying layers of the newly conquered society continued to be strongly Roman. Roman administrators still carried out their duties under the new rulers.

The Byzantine (in effect, the eastern Roman) Empire harboured ambitions to recapture the territory of the old Roman Empire. During the sixth century, under the energetic Emperor Justinian, it re-asserted its imperial power and recaptured the coast of North Africa. It followed this by seizing the southern Iberian coast, from the Algarve across to Cartagena. The coming to power of Leovigild, in 568, marked the rise of a strong ruler in the Visigothic kingdom. He began a process of consolidation of the kingdom. He based himself in

Above. Roman mosaic of a bear. Museo de Zaragoza.

Left. King Leovigild (568-586). A strong and dynamic ruler, he consolidated the Visigothic kingdom across the Iberian Peninsula.

Right. The Visigothic royal crown of Receswinth (from the treasure of Guarrazar). Archivo Fotográfico, Museo Arqueológico Nacional, Madrid.

Below. Visigothic altar base with frieze of simple geometric designs. Cathedral of Córdoba.

Toledo and took on the trappings of Roman imperial rule, taking a crown, sceptre and throne. He moved against the enemies on the frontiers and attacked the Byzantines and the Suevi. He overcame a revolt by his son Hermenigild, defeating him in 584. One year later Leovigild defeated the Suevi, thus eliminating their kingdom. By Leovigild's death in 586, the Visigothic kingdom was well entrenched across the Peninsula, except on the Cantabrian coast and along the Mediterranean from where the Byzantines were dislodged in 624.

The Visigoth organisation reflected their migratory origins. Many local noblemen, including dukes and counts, were land-owning magnates. These commanded local armed followers, with loyalty being to their noblemen, as opposed to a king. There was no central dynastic structure. The king was elected from among the ranks of noblemen. As it turned out this was not a stable arrangement and gave rise to factions and intrigue. The life of a Visigoth monarch often ended in murder. The economy had significantly declined from the glory days of Hispania. Agricultural production was much lower and there was a move to more basic agricultural activity. While there was some continuing trade with the outside world, it was a more inward-looking economy and did not have the trade and market opportunities that had been afforded by the Roman Empire. Mining declined but there was continued production of metals mainly for the local market.

The Germanic population of Hispania was small. It has been estimated that it amounted to up to one-tenth of the population of the Peninsula, which one account states as being five million people. There was by now quite an ethnic mix in the Peninsula – it included Celts and Celto-Iberians, overlaid with Greek, Carthaginian, Roman and of course, Visigoths. Nor should we forget the Basques, who continued to fiercely assert their independence. It is probable that the main language in use was Latin, in continuity from the times of Hispania. This was used in legal and other documents.

The Visigoths, by the time they arrived in the Peninsula, were believers in Arian Christianity (the belief that Christ was not divine). At that time in Hispania, Catholic Christianity had been well established among the Hispano-Romans. Leovigild was very much of the Arian tradition and, along with his efforts to consolidate his kingdom, was proactive in suppressing Catholicism. The conversion of Leovigild's son and successor Recared to Catholicism marked a great advance for that religion in becoming the established church. The church, with its Hispano-Roman origins, was to play a strong supportive role for the Visigothic kings and it provided a centralising bond for the kingdom. The series of church councils, which were held regularly in this period, were important events in managing not only religious affairs but also in setting down the parameters for the monarchy and in supporting the king and his administration.

A strong current of anti-semitism was an unfortunate feature of the Visigothic state and its church allies. As previously mentioned, Jews had been present in the Peninsula since the first century AD. Laws were passed discriminating against the Jews and requiring them to convert to Christianity, (a precursor of what happened in the Peninsula to the Jews and Moriscos around a millennium later). Anti-semitism was not unique to the Peninsula; it was a strong and continuing feature of the early medieval Christian kingdoms of the west and the Byzantine Empire. From the sixth century onwards repeated decrees were issued against the Jews in the Peninsula. The continuing waves of repression indicated that the decrees had not been implemented successfully. King Egica's decree of 694 represented a new low point: Jews were to be deprived of their property and enslaved.

As the Visigothic kingdom was consolidating across the Iberian Peninsula in the seventh century, on another peninsula, a man of destiny emerged. The Prophet Muhammad was born in Mecca, in the Hijaz region of the Arabian Peninsula, around AD 570. He was to create a religion which was to have resounding consequences for the world. At that time the Middle Eastern world was under the domination of the Byzantine and the Sassanian (Persian) Empires. Mecca was an important commercial centre at the intersection of many trade routes. It was a centre of pilgrimage also, where pilgrims travelled to the city's pagan shrine called the Kaaba.

The people of the Arabian Peninsula generally lived a life of nomadic pastoralism although there were urban centres and some settled farmers. The basic unit of society was that of the tribe. Tribes formed a close bond, providing protection and security for their kinsmen. It was an egalitarian society and there were reciprocal obligations to assist fellow tribesmen when in trouble. These tribes had a strong tradition of raiding and carrying off booty such as valuables, animals and captives. Tribes usually also included external adherents, amongst

Above. Visigothic stone carving. This fine example is in the Museo Arqueológico Provincial de Badajoz.

whom were craftsmen, freedmen and slaves. A strong pride and code of honour permeated tribal culture. One expression of this was through the oral tradition of poetry.

Muhammad was a minor member of one of the leading families in Mecca and his early years were difficult: he was orphaned from an early age. As he grew older he took part in trading expeditions through Arabia. A thoughtful and charismatic personality, he began to ponder on religious and moral questions. It is written that, at the age of forty, he had a vision where the Angel Gabriel disclosed to him that he was God's messenger. He began to preach, based on the revelations and started to gain followers. Muhammad's new religion was a monotheistic one. It holds that he was the last in a line of prophets including Abraham, Moses and Jesus. People who believed in these prophets, such as Christians and Jews, were regarded as 'people of the book'. Mohammed set down a sequence of revealed messages in the holy book of Islam, the Koran. The core of the religion consisted of the five pillars: public profession of God and Muhammad as his messenger; prayer; giving of alms; fasting during Ramadan and pilgrimage to Mecca. *'Islam'* in Arabic means 'surrender' to Gods message. *'Muslim'* means one who has surrendered thus.

In the following years Muhammad and his followers came under pressure from the local leaders of Mecca. They moved to Yathrib (Medina) in AD 622, which is the start-date of the Islamic calendar. There Muhammad took command and developed a society which was to be a model for later Islamic rule and organisation. There were ongoing attacks from the Meccans and local tribes but the Muslims retaliated successfully and expanded their control. Muhammad returned to a subjugated Mecca in 630 and there inaugurated the Kaaba as an Islamic shrine. By the time he died in Medina in 632, most of the tribes in the Arabian Peninsula had acknowledged him as their principal leader.

Muhammad's successor, Abu Bakr, was related to him through marriage. Elected by the leaders of the community, he acted as *Caliph (*or successor of the Messenger of God). A caliph exercised both temporal and spiritual authority. Under Abu Bakr and subsequent caliphs, Islamic armies continued to expand outwards and mounted numerous raids in the region. These armies ranged afar and wrested land from the Byzantines and Sassanians, weakened from their recent war with each other. The initial expansion was to the north and east. Most of Byzantine Syria and Sassanian Iraq was seized by 637. By 642 northern Syria and Iraq were captured, as was Egypt. From Egypt, the Islamic forces thrust further west through North Africa after 647. Moving through Libya, they mounted raids in (modern day) Tunisia.

The new mix of religion and state proved to be an exhilarating success. Fully in tune with the tribal lifestyle of the Arabs, the religion brought an overall cohesion to their community which superseded tribal loyalties. They now had one God and unified laws. The Islamic state turned out to be a powerful military machine which was able to defeat the surrounding superpowers. The expansion was made under the banner of Islam but it was also driven by political and economic factors. The fruit of all this was a gratifying windfall of new territory

Left. A Koran manuscript. It is attributed to the Nasrid period of al-Andalus and dates from the thirteenth or fourteenth century. Metropolitan Museum of Art, New York.

and riches. In addition to the military power that they mustered, the conquerors also utilised a winning technique. They treated the conquered peoples in a relatively benign manner, thus reducing the potential for resistance. Christians or Jews (people of the book) were allowed to continue to practise their religions, albeit with payment of a tax. Pagans had to convert but this did not seem to present a problem. As we see later, this sensible approach to the conquered was to be one of the factors that contributed to the rapid conquest of the Visigothic kingdom.

The momentum of western expansion was halted as a result of the civil war, which broke out when Uthman, the third Caliph, was murdered in 656 by rebels. Following internecine battles, Muawayia, Governor of Syria and member of a leading family, the Umayyads, was proclaimed Caliph in 661. Thus began the dynasty of the Umayyads which proved very successful over the next hundred years. The seat of the caliphate was now moved to Damascus, reflecting that the centre of gravity had shifted from Medina towards Egypt, Iraq and Syria. As Umayyad society developed and grew (684-750), the form of the Islamic state and society began to change and mature. An Islamic aristocracy began to emerge. Provincial governors were appointed to control the increasingly far-flung regions. The army was reorganised into a professional body with more efficient organisation. The growing need for manpower to fight for and garrison the new territories was met by the inclusion of recently conquered local troops in the armies, led by an Arab military elite.

While the initial society was tribal and military, a civilian Islamic social order began to emerge. Islamic literature and law developed as part of the communal and cultural life of the cities. Societies on the rise and with increasing wealth reflect this by constructing new and grander buildings. The new Islamic empire was no exception and construction was begun on many new buildings. These

Right. A view of the Strait of Gibraltar. The Strait lies between the Rif mountains of Morocco, in the background and Gibraltar in the foreground to the right.

proclaimed the prestige and importance of the new religion and political authority. They were inspired by traditional architectural styles which included Roman, Byzantine and Sassanian.

The Umayyad caliphs had as councillors many well educated Christian Syrians, with Byzantine roots. One source suggests that the drive along the North African coast (and north to the Iberian Peninsula and Gaul) was motivated by their wish to recreate the Mediterranean world of the old Roman Empire. Whatever the motivation, the expansion through North Africa recommenced with vigour. In 669, Uqba bin Nafi al-Fihri, commanding an army of Arab horsemen and Berber soldiers, recruited in Libya, moved westwards. Tunisia was captured by 670. He founded Kairouan which developed into the administrative centre of the region which in a few decades became the province of Ifriqiya.

Westward expansion continued in 681, when Uqba ranged across much of present-day northern and middle Morocco and reportedly reached the Atlantic Ocean. Uqba was killed by Berber tribes while on his return journey. The Berbers offered stiff resistance and now pushed the Arab invaders back towards Libya. The Arabs responded with new onslaughts against the Berbers and, against stiff resistance, they recaptured Kairouan. By 698 the Arabs ended the Byzantine presence in North Africa when they captured the enclave of Carthage.

Who are the Berbers, a people that will feature strongly in the story of al-Andalus? They are located in the mountains, deserts and plains of North Africa, particularly in Morocco, Algeria, and Tunisia. The name is drawn from '*barbara*', the term the Romans gave to all barbarians. A Mediterranean race, many have light skin. Some are farmers, others are nomads. Of an independent nature and strong defenders against invaders, they maintained their independence in many parts of the Rif and Atlas mountains until the twentieth century. They have a basic clan structure and the clans are combined into an overall tribe. There are several principal groups, each with its own dialect. The Berbers still maintain their distinctive cultures in present-day North Africa.

Musa bin Nusayr was appointed Governor of Ifriqiya at the beginning of the eighth century. His father was a freedman of the Umayyads and had been head of the bodyguards of the Caliph Muawayia in Damascus. Musa pushed west and occupied Tanjah (Tangier), thus completing the Arab occupation of the North African coast. The rolling form of conquest employed by the Arab armies involved the incorporation of the conquered peoples into the armies, thus making them available for the next phase of conquest. In the conquest of North Africa, the Berbers had proved to be formidable opponents. Yet the formula of incorporation was to work with the Berbers as elsewhere. It is interesting to look at the antecedents of Tariq bin Ziyad, Musa's deputy, appointed in charge of newly captured Tangier since 710. A freedman of Musa, he was of Berber origin, from Libya, which had been conquered since the middle of the seventh century and was likely to be a second generation Muslim. So, as the Arab armies rolled through North Africa, there occurred in turn a process of assimilation of the local Berbers into the new order and religion, thus creating potential reserves for the ongoing conquest. So, the army that invaded the Iberian Peninsula was predominantly Berber.

Whither the conquest? Whether it was driven by a possible empire-creating strategy from the Caliph's councillors in Damascus, or purely based on immediate opportunism, the answer lay to the north. Further conquest to the south offered the likelihood of strong resistance from the formidable local tribes, as well as the prospect of arid and less inviting terrain. To the north lay the more fertile lands of the Iberian Peninsula, still experiencing the (albeit diminished) afterglow of the former prosperity of Roman Hispania. It is likely that the Arabs would have gathered some information on the characteristics of the Visigothic kingdom (and perhaps on the brittle frailty of its royal and military organisation) and cast on this the appraising eye of an experienced conqueror. The fourteen-kilometre distance across the Strait was not a long sea journey for these land-based warriors and did not pose an insurmountable obstacle. So, as the new conquerors consolidated their hold on the new territories and contemplated the bays and mountains of the Iberian Peninsula, it was a logical decision that the momentum of conquest was channelled northwards.

Chapter 2
Conquest and Consolidation

On the Iberian Peninsula, life continued at its normal pace in the Visigothic kingdom. In 703 Witiza succeeded his father King Egica. However, on Witiza's death in 710, the succession by his son Agila did not go smoothly. Another contender for power emerged and conflict erupted. Agila, who had been given governorship of Narbonne by his father, only obtained the allegiance of Septimania and Tarraconensis in the north-east. The other contender, Roderic, *dux* of Baetica, gained support in the rest of the kingdom. Thus the scene was set for the cathartic events that were about to erupt.

For such a significant historical event as the invasion, with implications for the western and Islamic worlds, little reliable detail exists. We look now at the generally accepted facts and there is enough information to infer in broad terms how the key events unfolded. As we have seen, in the course of the Islamic expansion along western North Africa, Musa bin Nusayr, the Governor of Ifriqiya had negotiated with the Berber tribes on the way and secured their submission to the new faith. Having reached the Atlantic coast at Tangier, he established control as far south as the Dra'a valley in present-day Morocco. Musa was now able to look north and think of invasion. The Visigothic kingdom in the north, with its perceived riches and fertile terrain, obviously presented a more attractive prospect than expansion to the more arid south. It is most likely that news of the discord in the Visigothic kingdom reached the Arabs and encouraged them as they planned and organised their invasion army. Perhaps this was the tipping point that set the invasion in train.

The incursions to the south of the Peninsula by the Arabs in 710 were most likely exploratory raids. One of these was led by a Tarif bin Malluq (whose name is remembered in that of the town of Tarifa). The invasion proper began in 711 when an army led by Tariq bin Ziyad, freedman of Musa and Governor of Tangier, sailed across the Strait from North Africa and invaded the Peninsula. They landed at the point dominated by a prominent rock, which was called Calpe (now known as Gibraltar). The invading army was led by a core of Arab warriors but was predominantly made up of Berber soldiers. Many accounts, written centuries afterwards, have described how the Arabs had been requested to invade by the Agila faction of the Visigothic succession. Some tell of support for the invasion by a Visigothic Count Julian who, it was written, ruled in Septa (Ceuta). Count Julian has captured the imagination of these chroniclers. He has

Left. The invaders, led by Tariq bin Ziyad, landed at this promontory, known in Roman times as Calpe, in AD 711. He is remembered in the place name, Jebel Tariq or Gibraltar.

been described in one account as a Byzantine exarch or governor. Another, which has entered folklore, is the story that Roderic had raped Julian's daughter and Julian then induced the invasion out of revenge.

Back to the dynamic of the invasion. Roderic was campaigning in the north against the Basques when he received news of the Arab offensive. One pauses to wonder about the capability of the Visigoth leadership to gather intelligence and assess risks. They must have known of the danger that had arisen when a successful conquering army had arrived a few kilometres to the south of the Peninsula. The exploratory raids across the straits would have given an indication of the threat of invasion. Assuming Roderic was a rational man, the challenge from the Basques must have been a severe one, to cause him to head north. In any case he had to break off the campaign and return with his army to face the invaders. His army met the Arab one in the south where it was defeated. Roderic disappeared, assumed to have been killed. The 'Chronicle of 754', an account written four decades later by a Christian priest, refers to this as occurring in 712 and located in the 'Transductine Promontories'. Transducta is probably present-day Tarifa. The location of the battle has been described at various locations including near the river Guadalete which flows into the Gulf of Cádiz. Another account gives a location near Barbate at Lake Janda (into which flows the river Barbate). Near Vejer de la Frontera, it is a mere thirty-five kilometres to the north-west of Tarifa and probably fits within the 'Transductine' description. In this scenario Tariq deployed part of his army on the flanks of the lake and the other on the heights of the Sierra de Retín. Roderic approached from the north. The Visigoth troops were decisively defeated and fled northwards, spreading terror and despair. Irrespective of the actual location, the most important fact is that the Arabs triumphed over the Visigothic army and eliminated their king.

Again, there are several accounts of the movements of Musa, Governor of Ifriqiya and Tariq's superior. One of these is that he led another invading army, landing near Cádiz. The Arab-led armies rapidly advanced northwards. Toledo

Right. 'Don Rodrigo en la Batalla de Guadalete' by Marcelino de Unceta y López, Museo de Zaragoza.
King Roderic and his Visigoth army were decisively defeated in 712 by the Muslim invaders at a location possibly located at Barbate to the northwest of Tarifa.

was captured by Musa. Some of the Visigothic aristocracy there were put to death. The capture of Toledo marked another decisive point of the invasion. The Visigothic kingdom had now lost both its leader and its capital. The weak bonds of the realm disintegrated and the Arabs met with little further resistance. Musa continued northwards and is reported to have reached the strategic centre on the Ebro, Zaragoza.

Military expansion continued throughout the Peninsula. The network of roads laid down by the Romans was a boon for the invaders, providing easier access through the difficult terrain. As they entered regions, the Arabs adopted a pragmatic approach. If a local leader submitted to them they would conclude a treaty on favourable terms. There is a record of a generous treaty being made with Teodomir, *dux* (lord) of Murcia on the east coast, whose territory, subsequently known by the Arabs as Tudmir, covered the areas around Lorca, Elche and Cartagena. Teodomir was allowed to continue as ruler, while acknowledging the suzerainty of the Arabs. The people were allowed to continue to practise their religion but had to pay a special poll tax. Other similar treaties awarded autonomy in locations such as Braga and Zaragoza.

The Tudmir treaty was made in 713 with Musa's son Abd al-Aziz who was appointed Governor of al-Andalus. Musa had been recalled to Damascus by the Caliph at the end of 712, reportedly in some disfavour. Musa's deputy Tariq also fades out of history, with no further record of his activities. However, this highly successful invader and occupier is appropriately remembered in the name for Gibraltar (*Jebel Tariq* or Tariq's mountain), a piece of real estate that has endured many attacks and, in contemporary Hispanic eyes, ongoing occupation.

Abd al-Aziz in turn came to an unfortunate end. It is reported that he toyed with the idea of an independent kingdom in the Peninsula, with himself as king. He supposedly had been seen wearing a Visigothic crown. He had also married Egilona, the widow of Roderic. To marry the widow of the vanquished was a

Left. The marshes of Lake Janda, near Barbate, with the Sierra de Retín in the background. The defeat of King Roderic and his Visigothic army may have occurred here.

Below. The mountains in the north of the Iberian Peninsula, misty, steep and rugged, proved unpalatable to the Arab-led invaders. The frontiers became established to the south of these mountains.

custom of the times. Up to now, the territories captured by the Arabs had been mere regions of Empires, such as those of the Byzantines. The prospect of an intact Visigothic kingdom may have seemed attractive to Abd al-Aziz and the Caliph in Damascus was far away. Unimpressed by Aziz's kingly ambitions, his followers murdered him in Seville in 715.

By 720 most of the Peninsula had been conquered, with the exception of the mountainous regions of Cantabria and the Pyrenees. The invaders began to assimilate, consolidate and organise their new territories. Reflecting the concept of Islamic rule as being based on religious and temporal matters, *qadis* or religious judges were assigned to serve across the Peninsula. The *qadis*, as well as having a religious role, carried out judicial and administrative duties. One of the primary functions was to collect taxes. The lands of the defeated king and those Visigothic lords who had been killed were taken for the benefit of the conquerors. Those Christian communities that had surrendered by treaty were allowed to administer themselves.

The Visigothic capital, Toledo, is in the centre of the Peninsula. Córdoba became the capital a few years after the invasion. The move there demonstrated

Right. The Iberian Peninsula in the early eighth century, after the conquest.

a southwards shift in the centre of gravity of the new political structures. Córdoba held many advantages for the Arab governors. Located in the fertile Guadalquivir valley, it offered a route to the equally fertile lands in the Levante (around Valencia). Roman roads led to the north and others to the south and west. Closer to the coast than Toledo, it presented easier access to the Mediterranean and in turn to Damascus and the Caliph.

The Arabs called their new territory on the Iberian Peninsula 'al-Andalus'. There are several theories on its origin. One is that 'al-Andalus' comes from the Arabic version of a Visigothic name for Baetica. The land was divided into lots which were allocated to the lords after the Visigothic conquest and was so described in various accounts. 'Land-lot' in the gothic language is *'landa-hlauts'*, which, spoken in Arabic with the definite article could be said as 'al-Andalus'. Another theory is that the name is a permutation of the Berber for 'land of the Vandals,' which people made a brief and much earlier passage through the area in the fifth century before migrating to North Africa.

The civil war in the Visigothic kingdom in 711 had been advantageous to the Arab invaders and now a similar opportunity presented itself in the north. A civil war broke out in the Frankish kingdom in 715. An Arab army crossed the Pyrenees at the eastern end and took Narbonne in 720. The momentum of the recent, extraordinary and successful expansion had clearly not yet died. In addition, there was the lure of a continuing supply of booty. These were probably the main driving forces for expansion, rather than any world view of a Greater (Islamic) Mediterranean. However, raiding France was to prove a more difficult exercise than the previous conquest. In an attack on Toulouse in 721, the Arabs suffered a reverse. They were defeated and their Governor al-Samh was slain.

Left. Rulers of the world, as seen by the Umayyads: fresco showing the rulers of India, China, Ethiopia, Persia, Byzantium and Iberia. King Roderic of the Visigoths is among those depicted. Much deteriorated, this painting is in the early eighth-century desert palace at Qasr Amra in Jordan.

They continued to make further incursions and in 725 sacked Autun in Burgundy. In 732 the Arab army ranged northwards through France, defeated the Duke of Aquitaine at Bordeaux and continued to the north. They reached Poitiers where they were defeated by the leader of the up-and-coming Carolingian dynasty, Charles Martel, whose aid had been requested by the Duke of Aquitaine. Poitiers has been described as signifying the end of the Arab expansion in France but in reality, they continued raiding in Provence for the rest of the decade.

Why did the northward momentum of the Arabs come to a stop? Simple logistics may provide one answer: the Islamic empire was primarily a land-based power and the army in France was at the end of a long supply chain. From Córdoba to Poitiers is nearly 1,100 kilometres. Córdoba to Damascus by land through North Africa is around 5,000 kilometres. Another possible reason was lack of manpower. Previously, as the Arab army advanced through North Africa, it managed to conquer the Berbers and in time absorb them into the army, continuing with even more force onto the next conquest. The Iberian Peninsula proved to be different. The social and religious makeup of the peoples of the former Visigothic kingdom did not lend itself to their rapid conversion or absorption into the conquering army. The newly conquered fertile lands attracted members of the army and its numbers were reduced as soldiers settled around the Peninsula. The extraordinary power and impetus of the conquerors at last

Right. The Umayyad palace at Qasr Amra in Jordan. It consists of an audience hall, covered by barrel vaults, as well as a bathing area. Now surrounded by desert, this was once a well-irrigated location, with luxuriant vegetation.

had begun to run out of steam. Over-extended, they met an equally powerful force in France and came to a halt.

Before the Visigoths fade out of our narrative, it is worth asking why their State fell so quickly to a society that was arguably, at that time, less developed than itself? The converse is: what was the magic formula that allowed the Arabs such success? The Visigothic State had some strengths. It had been gaining in sophistication and had the advantage of the Germanic warrior heritage. With the support of the Church, it had built a State based (however imperfectly) on the solid foundations of the old Hispano-Roman institutions and administration and had incorporated a lot of Roman practices. However, there were structural weaknesses. Even though bolstered by the Church, the kings did not have full or effective control. It was difficult to raise a central army, as the local magnates or noblemen controlled the gathering of their armed followers. The kingdom's economy was much less powerful than in Roman times. Agriculture and commerce were weak. Building and maintenance of infrastructure such as bridges, roads and fortresses had been generally neglected. The civil war, which broke out in 710, weakened a fragile State. There was geographical vulnerability also. The southern coast was exposed and there were good landing points along its shores. The difficulties of a sea crossing were at their minimum at the Strait, a mere fourteen kilometres wide at its narrowest point. In addition, reinforcements from North Africa could easily be availed of by the invaders.

Finally, the Arabs proved to be powerful opponents. Over the previous seventy years or so the Arab armies had been steadily battling and capturing territory. While the Visigoths had the proven experience of fighting among themselves and with the Basques on the frontier, this was not quite in the same league as that of the Arabs, who had honed their battle skills on the tough campaigns through North Africa. Some of the Berber troops had also inherited experience

Above. Early Umayyad religious rigour was not absolute: the frescoes of Qasr Amra include unrobed female figures. Here, in the tepidarium of the baths, three nude women are depicted .

from the earlier battles with the Arabs. In addition to the 'stick' (manifested by the sword) there was also the 'carrot.' As the Islamic invaders entered a local region, if no resistance was offered, the people would be spared and local rule could continue, including the practice of their religion. It was at the beginning that the decisive moment occurred. When the Visigoth army was defeated in the initial battle, together with the loss of the King, it proved to be a mortal blow. The Visigothic kingdom did not have the strength, resilience and organisation to withstand the capture of its capital and the rest of the Peninsula by the experienced and effective Arab invading forces.

As their kingdom evaporated under the onslaught of the Arab invaders, and the Visigoths disappear from the narrative, what was the Visigoth legacy? It's an important question in the context of the history of the Peninsula. The Visigothic Christian heritage and its legal system were to form the foundation on which the later Christian kingdoms were built. The Visigoths had absorbed Roman traditions over the centuries and in Hispania, they used Latin in decrees and on their coinage. They left few words of their own language in present day Spanish. A word with an original root of Germanic 'ing' like *abolengo* (ancestry) is one of the few examples of Spanish words of gothic origin.

A pleasing, if modest, legacy of the Visigoths is that of the architectural remains which can be seen across the Peninsula. These are mainly churches, for example the seventh-century churches of San Juan de Baños (Palencia Province), and San Pedro de la Nave (Zamora Province). Constructed in dressed stone, they use the horseshoe arch. The Visigoths made use of the Roman classical style, including stone columns with capitals decorated with acanthus and other leaves. However, the workmanship on the stonework and carving is generally not of the same quality as that of its Roman predecessors. The Arabs were subsequently influenced by the Visigothic and classical style of architecture. There is controversy over who actually introduced the horseshoe arch, but whatever its origins, it is a fact that in building work across al-Andalus (and latterly in the Maghreb), the Islamic architects embraced and enhanced this form of arch.

One important legacy of the Visigoths was passed on through the person of a northern noble called Pelayo, who was the founder of the first of the Christian kingdoms which eventually prevailed on the Peninsula. A shadowy figure in history, it appears he defeated a Muslim force around 718 at Covadonga, near Oviedo, in the eastern foothills of the Picos de Europa. This skirmish has subsequently been developed into a major religious and legendary event and is considered by some as the start of the Reconquista. There is an elaborate shrine, church and statuary at Covadonga. One legend has it that the Blessed Virgin appeared to Pelayo before the battle and helped him win. The name 'Covadonga' was sufficiently inspirational to the Spanish Falangists to be used as a code word during the run up to the rebellion against the Republic in 1936.

At the time, the battle of Covadonga was most likely a local encounter, driven by a noble fighting for self-preservation and the conservation of his way of life from the threat of domination and an alien culture. The resistance was very much in line with the tradition of independence in those northern mountains, brought to its apogee by the Basques, of resisting any foreign invader, including the Romans and the Visigoths. The Arabs, in turn, were possibly overextended and were advancing through difficult mountainous terrain. This land of high mountains, with rugged tops, damp misty forests at lower levels and frequent rain, would not have been familiar or attractive to most of the Arabs nor to the Berber troops. In any event, the defeat did not seem to be of much importance to the Arabs, as it is not mentioned in their historical accounts. The present veneration of Pelayo as the messianic defender of Christianity may be a shade overblown. However, he is important, as the traditions of the Visigoths were transmitted via Asturias to the Christian kingdoms that emerged. These later became imbued with a crusading spirit of Christianity, so that, more than three centuries after the battle of Covadonga, the conquest of territory began in earnest.

Meanwhile, back in Damascus, in the early part of the eighth century, the Umayyad dynasty was engaged in organising and consolidating its sprawling empire. Arabic was designated as the official language. Arabs began to replace the former Byzantine and Persian administrators. Coinage with Arabic inscriptions was issued. The system of communication across the empire was improved. But all was not well. The level of taxes had been raised by the Caliph, which resulted in much discontent. By the early part of the eighth century the Islamic empire extended from the Pyrenees to Persia, to Central Asia and as far as the Indian sub-continent. It was an empire of extreme distances. From Galicia in the west to the Indus in the east is around 7,000 kilometres. This enormous territory was to prove too big for any polity of that time to hold together, even one with the benefit of the unifying bond of Islam. In addition to the difficulty of ruling from such a distance, weaknesses also arose from social stratification and

Left. Defiant in front of the misty mountains at Covadonga, a statue of Pelayo. A local nobleman, he repelled the Islamic forces here. The event has developed into a major religious and legendary event and is considered by some to denote the start of the Reconquista.

were exacerbated by the human frailties of the caliphs and their supporters. There was an impression abroad that the Caliph was surrounded by a clique of Syrians who were enjoying the fruits of the empire with little benefit to others. As it turned out, the centre, not to mind the extremities, could not hold. Fissures began to appear as events occurred that were to lead to the break-up of the political unity of the empire, never more to be reconstituted.

One such event occurred when the Berbers revolted in some parts of the Maghreb in 739 and the revolt spread to al-Andalus the next year. This revolt was a reaction by the Berbers to an attempt to impose taxes on them as well as to the general treatment of them as second-class citizens by the Arab elite. In Iberia, the Berbers were also perturbed at what they perceived as the unequal allocation of the more marginal land to them and they rose up in the northwest. An army was dispatched from Syria to Ifriqiya to put down the uprising there. The Syrian army was defeated and took refuge in Ceuta. As Berber rebels in the Peninsula marched on Córdoba, the Governor petitioned the Syrians in Ceuta for assistance. These travelled to al-Andalus in 742 and the combined forces defeated the Berbers near Toledo. The agreement had been that the Syrians would depart when the revolt had been suppressed. However, they enter-

Below. Pelayo takes an oath to defend the traditions of the people.

Right. The taking of Lugo by Alfonso I of Asturias. The Asturians expanded westward in the decades after the Berber revolt of 740.

tained other ideas, the fertile lands of al-Andalus being an attraction. The Syrians seized power, sparking a counter-attack by the previously settled Arabs of al-Andalus. In an attempt to restore order there, the Caliph imposed a new Governor in 743. As part of the peace-making activities he settled the Syrian troops across the south of Spain, mainly in districts of present-day Andalucía. One legacy of this was an increase in the Arab presence in these locations. These new settlers were generally from Syria, Palestine and Egypt. The earlier Arab settlers came mainly from the south of the Arabian Peninsula (many of them from Yemen). There was tension among the Arabs as well as with the Berbers. Thus was laid the seed of factionalism which contributed to the turmoil of later years.

A new governor, Yusuf al-Fihri, took power in 747 and began to assert his authority. He was supported by the established Arab settlers and took upon himself a more independent role from the Umayyad dynasty in Damascus, which was in a weakened state and faced many threats along the borders, as well as internal uprisings. There was a groundswell of resentment against the Umayyads and their Syrian adherents from those to the east of Damascus. In 750 the Umayyad Caliph was overthrown by the Abbasid clan, who led this eastern thrust. The Abbasid dynasty proved durable and, despite many vicissitudes, survived as a Caliphate until the thirteenth century. The overthrow was a bloody affair, with members of the Umayyad family and their supporters being rounded up and massacred.

Some Umayyads escaped. Among them was a grandson of the Caliph Hisham who had ruled from 724 to 743. This young man, Abd al-Rahman, spent five years making his way through North Africa. He made contacts with loyalist elements in al-Andalus and in 755 he arrived there. Abd al-Rahman assembled an army comprised of loyalists and other disaffected factions, and advanced on Córdoba in 756. He took the city and defeated the Governor. Shortly afterwards he was declared as Amir (or commander, with civil, but not religious power). The Umayyads did not directly challenge the religious authori-

Left. Abd al-Rahman I. Vigorous and decisive, this Umayyad prince fled from Damascus and established the Iberian branch of the dynasty in 756. Statue at Almuñécar where he first landed.

ty of the Abbasid caliph in the east, until the setting up of the Caliphate in Córdoba nearly two centuries afterwards. Al-Andalus at this time was made up of a myriad of individual fiefdoms. Abd al-Rahman I commenced the task of establishing order. He gained control of the Guadalquivir valley and continued to expand his authority. On two occasions he had to overcome efforts by the Abbasids to topple him. Successful leaders in any arena have to display a steely and ruthless side. Abd al-Rahman I certainly possessed this and was able to demonstrate it in an effective and memorable way. At Carmona he defeated a major revolt fomented by the Abbasids in 763. He ordered that the rebel leaders be executed and that their heads be embalmed with salt and myrrh and shipped to the Abbasids, wrapped in the black flag of that dynasty. The Caliph, on seeing these heads, is said to have exclaimed: 'God be praised who has placed the sea between this devil and me'.

It took Abd al-Rahman I over two decades to establish his rule across the south of al-Andalus. Things were different in the north. The Asturians, successors of Pelayo, had expanded their domain, filling the vacuum left by the Berbers, who had left the marginal lands during their revolt of 740. The expan-

Right. The Umayyad Mosque in Damascus. This was constructed by the Caliph Walid I at the beginning of the eighth century. It has a large rectangular hall, over 136 metres in length and remains one of the finest mosques of Islam.

Below. Mosaic at the Umayyad Mosque in Damascus.

sionary Carolingian Franks had also taken advantage of weaknesses on the northern border. In 752 Pepin took over several towns in Septimania (the old Visigoth province north of the Pyrenees). In 759 the Christians of Narbonne rose up against their Arab rulers and the Franks took the city. In the 770's Abd al-Rahman I made moves towards establishing his authority over the Ebro valley in the north-east. Under this threat, the local independent Muslim rulers in Zaragoza and Barcelona turned for help to the Franks. In 777 these rulers sent envoys to the Frankish King, Charlemagne (Pepin's son) at his court in Saxony. He agreed to assist and mounted an expedition the following year, assigning one army to the east of the Pyrenees, which advanced on Barcelona. He led the other to the west and advanced against Zaragoza. However, his erstwhile Muslim allies had changed their mind. The Frankish armies were repelled at Barcelona and Zaragoza. The armies united near Zaragoza and retreated north to the Pyrenees. This sorry tale continued when the rearguard was ambushed at the pass of

Left. Byzantine influence: mosaics and a Corinthian capital in the courtyard of the Umayyad Mosque of Damascus.

Below. During the construction of the Great Mosque in Córdoba, the problem with the recycled columns being too short was solved by inserting a plinth.

Roncevalles. Centuries later this was remembered in the epic 'Le Chanson de Roland'. The chronicler tells of how the knights valiantly fought what were termed the 'Saracens'. However, in reality the attackers were Basques. Romans, Visigoths, Arabs, and now Franks: to the Basques it did not matter, they continued their fierce independence and resisted all intruders.

The Governors who preceded Abd al-Rahman I in al-Andalus enjoyed only short reigns of a few years. By contrast, his reign lasted for thirty-three years and during this time he extended his rule across most of the Peninsula, thus laying the foundations for the Umayyad dynasty in al-Andalus. During his long reign, Abd al-Rahman I developed a solid administrative structure, which his predecessors had not had the time or perhaps capability to achieve. The original Arab

Right. The two-tiered arches of Roman acqueducts like this one at Mérida may have inspired the structure of the arches employed in the Great Mosque of Córdoba.

Below. The two-tiered arches allow the achievement of a higher space, despite the restriction of the height of the recycled Roman and Visigothic columns. Great Mosque, Córdoba.

35

Left. A forest of columns. The Great Mosque was extended several times, each additional section adding to the feeling of entering a palm forest.

and Berber invading armies had dispersed and settled across al-Andalus. The Amir now changed the basis of military organisation and set up a standing army composed of slaves. A number of these had converted to Islam but others were Christian. He also took the prudent step of setting up an intelligence service, with informers distributed throughout the capital and other cities. The border territories were divided up into what was termed a march or frontier region. The Upper March had its capital at Zaragoza. The Middle March was based in Toledo and the Lower March was governed from Mérida. The central area around Córdoba was divided into districts, with administrators appointed by the Amir. He, in turn, was supported in Córdoba by a group of courtiers and counsellors who reported directly to him.

By the 780's Abd al-Rahman I's two sons were in charge of Toledo and Mérida but the rest of the Muslim entity in the Peninsula was run by local leaders, who gave variable and limited acknowledgement to Córdoba's authority. The Visigoths had exercised general control over the Peninsula, enjoying the support of the Church. However in al-Andalus the Amir did not have the benefit of this arrangement. There was indeed the bond of Islam, but in reality his rule depended on the acquiescence of a multitude of local leaders and factions. Under these, a mix of families and clans maintained primary allegiance to each other.

Empires construct great buildings when they have assembled several ingredients: firstly, the desire for grandeur and reminders for posterity; secondly, the technical skills and resources and finally, the economic means. Abd al-Rahman I certainly possessed a sense of destiny and had the comfort of an increasing flow of taxes from the territory under his control. He had the drive and was fortunate that he had on hand architects and craftsmen with knowledge of techniques, such as those developed in the new mosques in Jerusalem and Damascus. These builders had adopted and improved on the Greco-Roman, Persian and Byzantine traditions in architecture.

In 784 Abd al-Rahman I gave instructions to start construction of the Great Mosque of Córdoba. We are fortunate that this is still intact today and have the

Below. The palms of Elche near Alicante. Was the Great Mosque of Córdoba inspired by nostalgia for the oases of Syria?

Right. Detail of the horseshoe arch of the Puerta de San Sebastián of the Great Mosque in Córdoba. This door in the outer western wall dates from the original construction.

opportunity to savour one of the architectural wonders of the world, a tangible legacy of the greatness of the Umayyad dynasty in al-Andalus. The history of the mosque reflects a relatively tolerant atmosphere between Muslim rulers and the Christians in those days. The original mosque was established in one half of the Visigothic church of St Vincent, which the Amir purchased from the Christians. He bought the rest of the church in 784 so as to erect the new mosque on the site. He allowed the Christians to build churches in other parts of the city. The building of the Great Mosque reflected the increase in population of Muslims in Córdoba, as the Amir consolidated his rule and developed his capital.

Abd al-Rahman I harboured an intense longing for his native Syria to where he could not return. Poetry ascribed to him, referring to a summer palace he had constructed, which he had called al-Rusafa (after an Umayyad palace in Syria), runs:

'In Rusafa I befell upon a palm;
Here in these Western lands a sight so seldom,
I said: you stand alone, like me so far from home,
You miss the children and our loved ones there.'

Nostalgia was reflected in the new Mosque. The tiers of semi-circular arches, springing out of the columns, give an atmosphere of palm fronds rising above a forest of trees in a grove of date palms. This evoked the atmosphere of the oasis and desert to assuage the homesickness of the Arabs of al-Andalus, many thousands of kilometres from their ancestral homeland. The layout of the new mosque was revolutionary for many reasons. The superimposition of two tiers of arch was an innovative solution in achieving an elevated space, despite the restriction posed by the height of the available columns. This may have been inspired by the tiered arches of Roman aqueducts, as found in Hispania. The columns and capitals used in construction were recycled from Visigothic and Roman mansions and buildings in the surrounding region. Another innovation was to break from the more fixed Roman or Byzantine tradition of naves in a line, which had been used in earlier mosques, moving towards the technique of utilising a multitude of columns, which induces a sensation of openness. The initial structure comprised eleven aisles with twelve bays. Part of the Mosque was open for prayer in 785 but was not fully completed by the time of Abd al-Rahman's death in 788. His son Hisham I continued the work and completed a minaret there in 793.

As the eighth century faded, the Iberian Peninsula and its peoples had experienced a traumatic change. The century had started with the low-intensity conflict of the Visigothic succession, followed by the lightning invasion and capture of practically the entire Peninsula and the introduction of a radically different culture. By the mid-century further external events had an impact. The creation of a new dynasty in Damascus was followed by the flight of the ousted Umayyads to the Peninsula. The young fugitive Abd al-Rahman I had the tenacity and courage to arrive in a land many thousands of kilometres from his homeland, seize power and subdue a mass of factions. He set up a centralised administrative and military system which formed the basis of a dynasty that reigned for nearly three hundred years and represented the crowning glory of al-Andalus. In the unstable north the seeds of the Christian legacy had been laid with the inheritors of the Visigoths, now well ensconced in their mountain fastnesses.

Chapter 3
The Turbulent Umayyad Years

It is strange that a superb organiser such as Abd al-Rahman I did not make adequate arrangements in advance for his succession, which ensued in a chaotic fashion. When he died in 788 in Córdoba, two of his three sons were in residence as Governors of their respective marches. Hisham was in Mérida and Sulayman was in Toledo. One account tells how Hisham arrived in Córdoba first. There, the third son, Abd Allah, formally handed Hisham the seal of the Amirate. Sulayman did not accept Hisham's accession and set out with an army for Córdoba. Hisham, the quieter and more pious brother, was to more than pass this test of his abilities. He met the rebel army near Jaén, repelled it and went on to lay siege to Toledo and subjugated the city. Sulayman fled to the south-east where he took shelter among the Berbers of Valencia. Eventually, both Sulayman and Abd Allah went into exile in North Africa, Sulayman's passage made more palatable by the payment to him of a large sum of money.

Over the years the dynasty of the Umayyads in al-Andalus was marked by a series of uprisings and instability. A continuing theme was conflict in the frontier areas along the Duero and the Ebro, from the Atlantic to the Mediterranean. Zaragoza and the associated frontier areas along the Ebro were highly volatile during Hisham I's reign. In 789 there was an uprising in the city by a pretender who declared himself to be Amir. It was put down by one Musa bin Fortun bin Qasi, acting on behalf of the Amir. Musa was a Muwallad, one of the Christians of the Peninsula who had converted to Islam. It is claimed that he was descended from a Visigothic nobleman, Cassius. We will hear more of the Banu Qasi family who became dominant in this frontier area.

Despite the stormy start to his reign, Hisham I inherited a realm which was more stable and under control than in the turbulent years following the Conquest. This period of relative stability allowed him to revive the custom of raiding. He mounted summer raids against the Christian north. Apart from the spreading of Islam, there were many benefits of a raid: there was booty; it provided useful exercise for the troops and taught the upstart Christians a lesson. In addition, it engaged the local rulers on the frontier in a common fight against an external enemy, serving as a useful reminder of where the centre of power lay. During the 790's Hisham I sent out raiding parties to harry the Asturians and the Franks.

Left. The Umayyad Dynasty in al-Andalus.

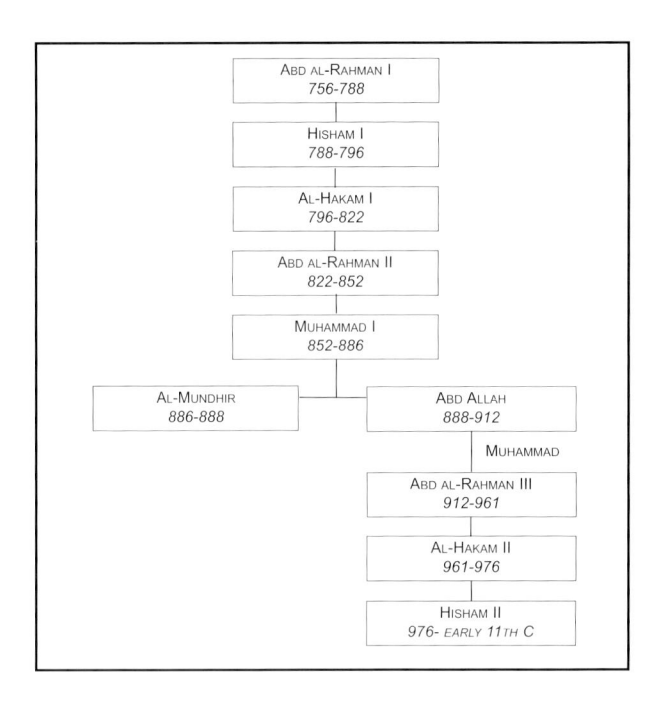

The Abbasid Dynasty had moved from Damascus, further to the east and in 762 set up their new capital of Baghdad. Under the Abbasids this city flowered with great expansion in the arts, literature and sciences. While the Umayyads in Córdoba and the Abbasids were adversaries, there was a continuous amount of religious contact and interchange between east and west. Pilgrims from al-Andalus went to do the *haj* in Mecca. This travel resulted in the transmission of knowledge back to al-Andalus of the eastern developments in Islamic science, arts and religion.

An important development during Hisham I's reign was the introduction of the Maliki interpretation of Islamic law. This orthodox and rigorous form of Islam regulates ordinary life, while discouraging deviation from its doctrine. It took root in al-Andalus and was dominant in the centuries which followed. It was in line with the character of the Amir, a devout and austere Muslim. He carried out acts of piety and completed the first minaret of the Great Mosque in Córdoba, as well as installing an ablution room there for worshippers.

Hisham I reigned for eight years, dying unexpectedly in 796. He was succeeded by his son al-Hakam I, a succession which had been carefully planned by his father. Al-Hakam I was a different character to his father. He was reputed to have enjoyed worldly pleasures. He was energetic and had a ruthless streak, an essential ingredient for keeping the fissiparous al-Andalus under control. This quality proved useful during his reign, a time of significant unrest. When al-Hakam I became Amir, the problems of the previous succession flared up again. His uncle Abd Allah immediately returned from North Africa and laid claim to the Amirate. He tried to start a rebellion in the Upper March but was unsuccessful and moved to the Valencia region where he set up. Eventually he came to terms with his nephew with the result that Umayyad control was established in

Right. The old walls of Córdoba. South of here, across the Guadalquivir river, was the area called al-Ribad which rose up in 818.

that region. Al-Hakam's other uncle, Sulayman, returned to al-Andalus in 797 and revived his claim to the Amirate. After a series of skirmishes, Sulayman was defeated and captured in 800 and executed.

Across al-Andalus dissent bubbled in the cities. Toledo staged a revolt in 797. Al-Hakam I brutally put this down, giving his army a free hand. In the course of this revolt a large number of prominent Toledans were executed. One of the perennial reasons for unrest all across the Islamic world was the imposition of what were perceived as unfair taxes. This was the case in Córdoba where unrest continued over many years. One of the causes was the raising of taxes, to meet, amongst other things, the new costs arising from the creation of a standing army. Al-Hakam had created this army based on mercenaries which included black Africans, Franks and other Christians. There was disaffection among those who had lost power and influence. Added to this, the Cordoban religious leaders disapproved of the new Amir's irreligious ways. In 805, a plot to supplant the Amir with his cousin was defeated and seventy-two of the leading plotters were crucified. The resentment in Córdoba simmered on in al-Ribad ('the suburb'), across the Guadalquivir, south of the Roman Bridge. This was a crowded and lively area where the working class of the city lived. It was a mixed district: Christians lived among the Muslims. It had artisans and small businesses. The tensions were fuelled by the Amir's inflexible manner of dealing with any challenges and there was fear of his network of spies and informers. In the meantime, the Amir purchased arms and built up his private palace guard, which was commanded by a Christian, Rabi, of noble Visigothic antecedents.

Al-Ribad finally erupted in 818. In the course of three days of fierce fighting the Amir's forces put down the revolt. The punishment was severe. He had three hundred of the ringleaders crucified. He ordered the suburb to be razed and ploughed up. He banished the residents of al-Ribad and sent them into exile. These banished Cordobans did not fade from history. What was Córdoba's loss was to be other territories' gain. Most of the refugees fled to Morocco where some settled in the Rif Mountains. Most went to the new city

Left. The city of Fez in Morocco. Thousands of refugees from Córdoba settled here in the early part of the ninth century, establishing in what is still called the Andalusian quarter.

of Fez, which was being expanded by Idris II, following the founding of the city by his father Idris I in 789. The city had also just welcomed settlers who had fled from Kairouan in Tunisia. Idris II equally valued the Andalusi refugees, city dwellers, who brought with them skills such as construction, horticulture and the crafts. Several thousands settled there on the right bank of the Wadi Fas, forming what is still known today as the Andalusian quarter (with the Kairouan quarter on the other side of the river). The influx of these urbanised and highly skilled people gave impetus to Fez becoming the leading force in the arabisation and islamicisation of Morocco.

Not all of the Cordoban exiles went to Morocco – another group sailed east. It is not clear if this group had left due to an earlier upheaval or the al-Ribad expulsion. These Cordobans landed in Alexandria in Egypt. It was a turbulent time in that city and there had been frequent changes of Governor under the Abbasid dynasty. The Cordobans soon dominated the city but in 827 were expelled by the Abbasids. Once more, these exiles set off in their ships. They landed in Crete, occupied it and founded a kingdom. They ruled there until the Byzantines reconquered the island in 961.

During the early years of the Umayyad dynasty, these rulers did not perceive the few Christians ensconced among the mist-laced mountains in the north of the Peninsula as posing any great strategic threat, rather more as a nuisance. However, the continuous upheavals in al-Andalus offered a breathing space for the Christian leaders to enlarge and consolidate their territory. This pattern of the Christians taking advantage of the many troubles that flared up in al-Andalus was to continue over the centuries. The revolt of the Berbers from 740 had given Pelayo's son-in-law Alfonso I (739-757) the chance to expand. As the Berbers withdrew from Galicia, he was able to broaden his area of influence. From his kingdom, centred around the Cantabrian mountains, he also pushed

Right. Alfonso II set up the Asturian court in Oviedo and recreated the Visigothic courtly traditions.

south. However, he was short of manpower and was not able to occupy the Duero valley. He forced the original Hispano-Gothic inhabitants in the valley to move and resettle in the north, thus creating a larger population for his growing kingdom. The mostly barren lands of the Duero valley now became a desolate and uninhabited frontier zone between the Christian north and the Muslim south.

In earlier times the Asturians had resisted the imposition of Roman and Visigothic rule. The Asturian king Alfonso II, who ruled from 791 to 842, now paradoxically recreated the old Visigothic civil and ecclesiastical order, which was based on Hispano-Roman traditions. The Asturian royalty started to use the Visigothic courtly ways, which provided a convenient basis for their expanding kingdom. Alfonso II set up a court in Oviedo and proceeded with the appointment of bishops and the erection of palaces and churches. As the kingdom grew, it also provided a home to those Mozarabs (Iberian Christians who lived under Muslim rule) who fled north from al-Andalus. It was during this reign that the cult of Saint James started. It was claimed that a tomb, which was discovered in Galicia, contained the remains of Saint James the Apostle, martyred in Jerusalem in AD 44. A church was erected on this site, now known as Santiago de Compostela. This developed in later centuries into one of the main centres of Christian pilgrimage in Europe. As this veneration of Saint James took root it developed in Iberia into a symbol of the Christian resistance to the 'Muslim infidel'. The eleventh-century Arab historian, Ibn Hayyan, likened the intensity of worship at the shrine of Saint James to that displayed at the Kaaba in Mecca.

Alfonso II took advantage of the uprisings in al-Andalus and made raids deep into the Muslim south, sacking Lisbon in 798. Frankish chronicles record that Alfonso II used the booty from the raids to send a tribute to Charlemagne. We have seen how, in 778, Charlemagne had led the disastrous expedition against Barcelona and Zaragoza. However, the Franks continued their expansion and occupied Gerona in 785. In the last years of Hisham I's reign the Muslims struck back, mounting raids into Frankish territory. They sacked Gerona in 793, raided the suburbs of Narbonne and vanquished the forces of William, Count of Toulouse. However, the ongoing southerly thrust of the Franks persisted and in 801 they captured Barcelona, under the leadership of King Louis of Aquitaine. Expanding into the areas that now make up Catalonia, they established the Spanish March, split up into counties, including the county of Barcelona. Adjoining this were the Basques who continued to maintain their independence. In line with their historical resistance to all invaders, in the early part of the ninth century they expelled the Franks who had taken Pamplona and set up a kingdom there under their leader Iñigo Arista.

Towards the end of his reign, the rigorous al-Hakam I took steps to ensure that there would not be a repeat of the succession debacles that marked both his and his father's accession. He mandated the members of his court to swear allegiance to his son. In turn, he had members of his family swear allegiance in the Córdoba mosque to this son Abd al-Rahman II. Thus, the heir was nominated a month before his father's death and took some decisive moves, which demonstrated that he was in touch with the popular mood. There had been intense resentment against the palace guard. Abd-al-Rahman II dismissed the brutal Rabi, Christian chief of the guard and ordered him executed. In a move to assuage the *alfaquis*, the Islamic legal experts, he closed down the Córdoba wine market. This showed the pious side of Abd al-Rahman II in that he was more mindful of the perceptions of the Muslim faithful than his father. In time, he was to reinstitute the raids on the Christians to the north. Abd al-Rahman II was invested as Amir in May 822. He received the pledges of loyalty from representatives of all Córdoba as well as from delegates from the provinces. He was to reign for thirty years. Old habits died hard: his grand-uncle Abd Allah, ensconced in Valencia, took advantage of the change and mounted a new uprising in the eastern district of Tudmir. Abd al-Rahman II did not have to take action though, as Abd Allah died soon afterwards. This opened the way for the Amirate to take full control of Valencia.

As well as having had the benefit of a good education, the new Amir had had military experience, He had led armies in the northern zones, as well as participating in the quelling of the Toledo uprising. He was to reap the benefit of his steel-willed father's ruthless suppression of dissent across al-Andalus. A period of relative peace ensued and allowed al-Andalus some space to mature and consolidate.

However, even though the lid was on the kettle of the turbulent kingdom, it boiled over from time to time. In Tudmir there were tensions between the original settlers and the Amir had to send in troops and establish order. Out of this

Above. 'In the name of Allah, the clement, the merciful... this fortress was ordered to be built ... as a place of refuge for those subject to his authority by the Amir Abd al-Rahman'. From an inscription placed over the entrance gate to the Alcazaba in Mérida, where building commenced in 830. Here, the entrance to the double stairway to the aljibe (well) is framed by recycled Visigothic carved stones used as lintels.

adversity came opportunity. He built the new city of Murcia and assigned a governor and garrison to rule the province, thus securing another extension of Umayyad control. Trouble was brewing in Mérida, capital of the Lower March. The Mozarabs there had been encouraged by messages of support from the north: from Alfonso II, also from the Franks. In 828 there was an uprising by the disaffected (both Muslim and Christian) in the city and the Governor was assassinated. Abd al-Rahman II led his forces to put down the rising. They laid siege and unsuccessfully tried to starve the city. In 830 he tried afresh, took the city, imposed a Governor and built the Alcázar there. Nevertheless there was continuing unrest in the Lower March and it took until 835 to suppress it. There was dissension once again in Toledo in the 830's. The new Amir quelled this but with a lighter touch, being less repressive than his father. By the end of the decade, that city was pacified.

On his accession the new Amir extended the raids to beyond the northern frontiers and, in the years to follow, there were repeated raids on the Asturians as well as on the Spanish March. Typically in these raids no land would be seized or occupied but farms were attacked, harvests burnt and lots of booty seized. In 841 a large Muslim force penetrated the Spanish March, crossed the eastern Pyrenees and raided around Narbonne. Reflecting the greater international profile that al-Andalus was gaining, two of its ambassadors were received in the

Frankish court in Reims in 847. As a result a treaty was negotiated between Abd al-Rahman II and Charles the Bald.

The Banu Qasi of the Upper March played a significant and colourful part during the early centuries of al-Andalus. At one point these mercurial Muwallads were on the side of the Amir. At another, they would be his enemy. So it was during the reign of Abd al-Rahman II. Musa bin Musa Banu Qasi, a son of Musa bin Fortun, took full advantage of the instability of the frontier zone and expanded his control. He was Governor of Tudela, then a Banu Qasi stronghold. During a joint raid against Álava in 842 he was insulted by the Amir's general and on return to Tudela, declared war against the Amir. The Amir duly sent a force that put down the rebellion. Musa fled to the Basque territories. The Amir sent several expeditions and in 843 he defeated Musa and his Basque allies. Musa yielded to the Amir and was reinstated as Governor of Tudela. One year later he rallied to the colours by coming to aid the Amir in the defeat of the Vikings.

The Viking enemy had emerged over the Atlantic horizon, to threaten al-Andalus. They had perfected the art of maritime raiding and were now extending their theatre of operations to the south. In 844 they attacked the coast of Christian Asturias and then sailed south to sack Islamic Lisbon. After three bloody days of pillage, they departed. The Governor of Lisbon hastened to send a warning to the Amir. The Vikings reached the mouth of the Guadalquivir. They proceeded upriver and set up their base on a large marshy island, down river from Seville, the Isla Mayor. They then sailed to the city, landed and proceeded to sack it. By now most inhabitants had fled. Of the remaining inhabitants, the Vikings massacred the old and the sick and took the women and children as slaves. After seven days of rampage they retreated to their island base, laden with booty. As the river was not navigable further on, the Vikings set off on horseback (their island base had been a horse breeding area) to raid along the wide river valley. In the meantime, the Amir had mobilised his troops and gathered reinforcements from all over al-Andalus, including, as we have seen, a contingent from Musa bin Musa Banu Qasi. The Amir's forces defeated the Vikings decisively, at Tablada, to the south of Seville, killing a large number. The captured prisoners were executed by the Muslims in full sight of the fleeing Vikings. As the Vikings sailed home to Aquitaine, en route they raided Niebla, the Algarve coast and, once again, Lisbon. The few remnants of the Viking forces in the region surrounding Seville were rounded up. These, sensibly, submitted, were spared and then converted to Islam. They settled down and became farmers, raising cattle. They developed a dairy industry producing a cheese that was in great demand in Seville and Córdoba.

Following this attack the Amir ordered that defensive walls be erected around Seville. He also ordered that naval shipyards be developed there, in which were built the ships of a new Andalusi navy. A sentinel system was set up along the Atlantic coast. The Vikings made some later attempts on al-Andalus but, due to the initiatives taken to put in place better defences and a naval fleet, they were more readily repelled.

Right. The Vikings attacked al-Andalus in 844 but were repulsed. Replica of a Viking warship originally built in the Viking settlement of Dublin. Thirty metres long, it had a crew of around seventy. National Museum of Ireland, Collins Barracks, Dublin.

    The Muslim population of al-Andalus continued to grow. The early invading armies consisted of Arabs and predominantly Berbers. Then came an influx of Syrians who had migrated before and during the establishment of the Umayyad dynasty in the Iberian Peninsula. Added to that was a steady influx of Berbers from nearby North Africa. Most of these married local Christian women and the children of the union were brought up as Muslim. In turn there was a steady conversion of the existing Christian Hispano-Roman population, who, when

Left. The Reales Ataranzas in Seville. This naval arsenal has been much modified since King Alfonso X in 1252 ordered its construction outside the Almohad city walls. In the times of al-Andalus a shipyard was originally built in Seville in reaction to the attack by the Vikings in 844.

converted, were known as Muwallads. We have seen the emergence of strong Muwallad families like the Banu Qasi. There were many motives for this conversion to Islam. In addition to general social pressures the opportunities for Muslims were greater in society. While some Christians were employed in the administrative offices of al-Andalus, prospects to rise in the ranks were better for Muslims. An important advantage was that the poll tax applied to a Christian would cease on conversion. By the end of Abd al Rahman II's reign in 852, one estimate puts the general Muslim population as around twenty-five percent. Population estimates interpolated back into antiquity are notoriously difficult and unreliable. Another study suggests that it was a much higher proportion. Whatever figure it may have been, the proportion of Muslims continued to rise during the time of Islamic Iberia. By the mid-thirteenth century, on the eve of

Right. The castle at Alcalá la Real. This area was an important settlement in al-Andalus from the time of the initial invasion. The stronghold was finally captured by Alfonso XI in 1341. The la Mota fortress was begun in 727 and was reconstructed in the twelfth and thirteenth centuries by the Almohads and Nasrids, respectively. It underwent more renovations in later centuries.

the seizure of most of al-Andalus by the Christian kingdoms, Muslims were in an overwhelming majority.

As al-Andalus moved into a more settled and established phase, the taxes gathered by the Amirate grew. It has been estimated that Abd al-Rahman II's Amirate gathered nearly double that collected during his father's reign. This new wealth allowed greater spending by the State. There was adequate money to pay for the administration, palace guard and army. The court existed in a state of sumptuous luxury. In times of drought the State could afford to distribute grain to the subjects and did this several times during Abd al-Rahman II's reign. Public works were not neglected. We have already seen the rebuilding of city walls and creation of naval arsenals in Seville and the creation of the new city of Murcia. Mosques were built in Jaén and Seville. The bridge in Córdoba was strengthened. A system of aqueducts brought water to the city from the nearby Sierra de Córdoba. Córdoba was growing with a rising Muslim population. To accommodate this, Abd al Rahman II made an extension to the Great Mosque, which had been built by his grandfather. It also gave an opportunity to manifest and reflect the splendour of the Amirate. The Mosque was extended to the south by eight new aisles. Like the original section, Roman and Visigoth capitals and columns were used. They were not sufficient and seventeen new capitals were sculpted in local workshops.

In the early days of the Umayyad dynasty in Damascus, the caliphs had introduced the ways of an imperial court, which were a far cry from the simple life style of Muhammed and his early followers. This pomp and ceremony was heavily influenced by the style of the Byzantine emperors. In turn, when the Abbasids moved to Baghdad the influences of the Sassanian Empire were used as a basis to develop the formality and stylised court practices to an even higher level. Far-away al-Andalus was not immune from this. The Umayyad exiles in the Peninsula brought with them the practices of their former court in Damascus. The continuous stream of pilgrims and other travellers from the East brought Abbasid influences to Córdoba. As his State expanded in wealth and power, Abd al-Rahman II embraced the Abbasid court practices and implemented his own interpretation of these. The court and administration were organised in a formal and stratified manner. In the hierarchy there was a prime minister (*hachib*) who organised a court, the *majilis*, at the entrance to the palace. Amongst other officials were the secretaries (*khatib*) and a vizier or senior administrator. There was a treasury which minted silver and gold coins, as well as a workshop devoted to producing the royal textiles. This was a state monopoly. In addition to the Amir's personal palace guard, there was a central standing army as well as regional levies.

Abd al-Rahman II lived a life of some seclusion. One recreation consisted of his occasional forays to the mountains nearby to go hunting. He had a harem and was reputed to have had a large number of children. Eunuch slaves, all the better to operate near the harem, became trusted servants in the inner court and gradually gained influence. The Amir and his court enjoyed a luxurious environment. To cater for the affluent tastes of the ruling elite, there grew up a market in luxury goods, including jewels and spices, brought from the east. We have previously seen how there had been contacts between al-Andalus and the Franks. There were also contacts with the Byzantine Empire. This was a manifestation that al-Andalus had arrived and had become a player on the early medieval stage. In the case of the Byzantine Empire, its contact with Córdoba was driven by necessity. It had lost its North African possessions and was under pressure. We saw how a band of exiled Cordobans had seized Crete in 827. As well as problems in the Adriatic and Aegean, the Empire's domains in Sicily were being

Above. The second extension of the Great Mosque of Córdoba, commenced by Abd al-Rahman II in 833. He created eight new aisles. Half of these are now subsumed by the Christian Cathedral, parts of which can be seen to the left and right of the photograph. Works on the Christian chapel, transept and choir were commenced in 1523.

attacked by the Muslims of the Maghreb. In a sign of desperation, the Byzantines sent a delegation to Córdoba to see if they would use their influence. Nothing concrete came of this but it opened the way for further links that were to bear fruit during the next century.

Abd al-Rahman was an educated and learned man and took a great interest in literature and the arts and sciences. He maintained a lively coterie of writers and poets at the court. Emissaries were sent to Iraq to bring back books. As it developed in the east, the Abbasid dynasty had encouraged the translation of the old Greek learning and science into Arabic. This covered many disciplines including medicine, science, pure and applied mathematics, and literature. Thus al-Andalus was to benefit from this unlocking of ancient wisdom and learning. This influx of knowledge was to lay the foundations for Córdoba's flowering in later years as the most advanced city in Western Europe. The Amir was interested in science and encouraged scientists and their work. One of these included an intrepid pioneer, interested in the concept of flight, who put on wings and tried to fly by jumping off high points. Abd al-Rahman II did not neglect religion; he tried to establish directions in the application of religion for the community of believers, based on Maliki thought. While he was genuinely pious, he also managed to protect his literary group from the disapproval of the *alfaquis*.

The Abbasid Empire with its capital in Baghdad (and briefly in Samarra) was at the height of its prosperity. There was a ferment of new social mores, fashion and popular culture and it set the scene across the Islamic world. The arrival in Córdoba in 822 of the Iraqi singer Ziryab, who originally came from Baghdad, was to have a big impact on the emerging society of al-Andalus. Welcomed by the Amir, he seems to have been an extraordinarily influential figure in ninth-century Córdoba. Ziryab set up a school of singing and developed the five-stringed lute. He introduced the latest Baghdadi practices in many spheres: music, furniture, dress, etiquette and cuisine. These were embraced by the nouveau riche of Córdoba, the elite of the Amirate that was growing in power and wealth. This was part of the process whereby al-Andalus was developing from being a mere provincial outpost to a leading independent state. In time, as we shall see, al-Andalus was to become one of the most sophisticated societies in the medieval world, not to mind the Islamic one.

During Visigothic times the Church and State had combined to persecute the sizeable Jewish population of the peninsula. The arrival of the Arabs resulted in a reversal of fortune for the Jews. Now, as 'people of the book', they were treated fairly and on the same basis as Christians. It was natural that, as their situation radically improved, they would cooperate enthusiastically with the invaders. Over the centuries they blended into society and prospered under the Islamic rulers. They gained influence and featured prominently in many fields including commerce, diplomacy, medicine and philosophy, during the Umayyad era and beyond.

A curious episode occurred during Abd al-Rahman II's reign: the affair of the Christian martyrs. During this time, the Mozarabs (Christians living under Muslim rule) had been accorded a level of tolerance. Just like the Jews, they had

Below. In the Great Mosque, a Roman capital with a fluted and translucent white marble column. In the extension of 833 old columns were again reused but seventeen new capitals had to be crafted.

Left. The castle at Trujillo in Extremadura. It has four gates and is thought to date from around the end of the ninth century. The square towers are typical of the Islamic military style.

a special status in al-Andalus. The Mozarabs had to pay taxes, but apart from that they were able to maintain their churches, monasteries and bishoprics and hold ecclesiastical councils. Christians were free to worship within their churches (but not hold public processions). Christians engaged in business and trade, they were members of the state administration and the palace guard. A Muslim man could marry a Christian woman but she had to convert to Islam. In spite of the appearance of normality, there was an undercurrent of dissatisfaction among the Mozarab community and Church. In Córdoba, Eulogius, a priest, supported by his friend Paulus Alvarus, was to act as a focus and channel this dissatisfaction. Some in the clergy did not like that the laity were using Arabic rather than the romance language for everyday use, as well as their gradual adoption of Islamic ways and culture. In 851 the issue came to a head in a dispute which arose between a Mozarab monk and Muslims on the merits of the respective religions. It led to the monk insulting the Prophet. He was denounced, brought before a *qadi* (judge), sentenced and executed. Eulogius and his followers encouraged the dissatisfaction, it took hold and there arose a wave of Mozarab 'martyrs', imbued with the mystical sense of giving one's life for one's faith. Over the next few weeks ten others followed and were executed, as were a further thirteen some months later. The broad mass of Mozarabs, including their clergy, as well as the Amir, were dismayed at this suicidal outbreak. Abd al-Rahman II arranged for the convocation of a church council, where the Metropolitan of Seville, Recaredo prohibited his flock from behaving like this. The ringleaders of the movement, including Eulogius, were arrested. He was later released and travelled to Pamplona, then returned to Córdoba. He restarted the agitation in concert with Alvarus. In the middle of this Abd al-Rahman II died in 852. The new Amir did not feel the need for the restraint of his father and razed the monastery of Tábanos, a centre of the agitation. When the Mozarabs of Toledo chose Eulogius to be the Metropolitan there the Amir did not approve this. In the years after 853 there was a further wave of martyrs. In 859 Eulogius was

Below. Oviedo cathedral. The relics of Eulogius are preserved in the Cámara Santa of the cathedral.

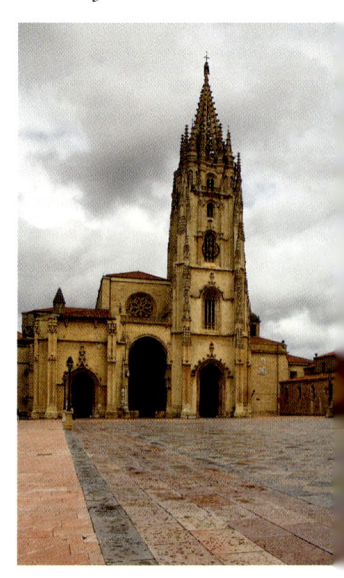

Above. Prominent and commanding: the castle at Belmez. This was a defensive position dominating the route northwest from Córdoba. There are remains of typical Andalusi defences but the present castle was constructed by the Christians centuries after they captured the position in the thirteenth century.

arrested again and eventually executed. The unrest fizzled out thereafter. In later years Eulogius and Alvarus were venerated as Christian martyrs in the Christian north. In 883 the Asturian king Alfonso III, as part of truce negotiations with Córdoba, arranged for the transfer of the remains to Oviedo.

When Abd al-Rahman II died suddenly in September 852 he was succeeded by his son Muhammad I. The new Amir is reported to have been learned, devout and sharp, with a keen mathematical mind. He had inherited the Umayyad ruthlessness, namely, the willingness to shed blood if necessary. This was a useful trait in those turbulent times, as the al-Andalus State was now moving into a period of intense instability. The pattern up to now was that crises flared up on the accession of an Amir and there was no exception for Muhammad I. The background to these current crises was the underlying feeling of disaffection by the Muwallads. These converts to Islam felt that they were treated unequally in an al-Andalus where they did not enjoy equality or influence. They saw the Arab elite as a privileged group who treated the Muwallads as second-class citizens. The Berbers, also treated as inferiors, shared the discontent. As the new Amir came to power, the Muwallads of Toledo took advantage, led a revolt and seized the city's Governor. In response Muhammad I sent a column of troops to garrison Calatrava to the south, with the intention of dominating the region around the rebel city. The tactic did not succeed, as in the summer of 853 the Toledans made raids across the Sierra Morena. They also made contact with Ordoño I of Asturias who sent troops to assist. A Toledan and Asturian force, led by Gaston, Count of Bierzo, met a strong army led by the

Left. Perched on the hilltop, the castle of Alange, in Extremadura. The rebel Ibn Marwan, 'the Gallician', set up in this town in 875. After a siege by the Amir's forces, Ibn Marwan surrendered. Later, in the thirteenth century, the victory at Alange by the Christian forces was an important advance during the Reconquista.

Amir at Guazalete in 855. In a deft series of manoeuvres, Muhammad I defeated the enemy force, killing many thousands of the enemy. The Cordoban forces mounted a siege on Toledo in 856; it was unsuccessful, but two years later in a redoubled assault they captured the city. Toledo was calm for the next ten years but this was followed by more upheaval. The city was subdued once more, with a surrender involving the handing over of hostages and indemnifications.

Mérida, capital of the Lower March, was another city with a history of upheaval. On the death of Abd al-Rahman II in 852, it seized the opportunity to revolt but this was soon put down by the new Amir. The instigator of the revolt was a Muwallad named Ibn Marwan al-Jilliqi, 'the Galician'. His family came from northern Portugal and, on conversion to Islam, had become part of the ruling establishment. Ibn Marwan was no stranger to strife – his father had been the Amir's Governor in Mérida and had been assassinated during the previous uprising in 828. Ibn Marwan fled but reappeared years later and in 868 led another revolt in Mérida. Muhammad I once again set out for the city and put down the revolt. One of the surrender terms was that the leaders of the revolt had to transfer to Córdoba. Ibn Marwan went there under this arrangement. It transpired that while in Córdoba, he was insulted in 875 by the Vizier and General Hashim Abd al-Aziz (who, we will see, features in subsequent important campaigns). In high dudgeon, Ibn Marwan headed west again, where he and his followers set themselves up in the castle of Alange, less than twenty kilometres to the south of Mérida. The Amir's forces set out, laid siege and Ibn Marwan surrendered once again. The terms this time allowed him to set up in Badajoz, then little more than a hamlet. He installed fortifications there and shortly afterwards this perpetual rebel rose up again. This time he enlisted the help of the Asturians, now under Alfonso III. The Amir's army (including General Hashim) set out to defeat the combined force of Asturians and the Badajoz rebels. The Amir's forces were defeated and the captured General Hashim was sent by Ibn Marwan to Alfonso III as a gift. This was a major humiliation for the Amirate. Hashim spent two years in Oviedo, before being ransomed. Aware that this insult was likely to be avenged, Ibn Marwan decamped to Asturias and remained there for eight years. He fell out with Alfonso III and returned to Badajoz in 884. The Amir's son, al-Mundhir, led a force that promptly expelled him. Ibn Marwan fled along the valley of the

Right. The horseshoe arch in granite stone of the Puerta del Alpendiz in Badajoz, which dates from the Almohad times. Under the terms of his surrender at Alange, Ibn Marwan was allowed to set up in Badajoz, at the time little more than a hamlet. Ibn Marwan expanded Badajoz, built fortifications and recommenced his rebellion.

Below. Some of the underground brick chambers of the Alcazaba in Badajoz, near the Puerta del Alpendiz.

Guadiana. His forces made guerrilla attacks in the area from the north of the Algarve across to the Seville region. Muhammad I, now near the end of his reign, allowed Ibn Marwan to return to Badajoz. The new Amir, al-Mundhir, had other more pressing problems and tolerated the old rebel as an independent ruler in that region.

In the midst of the internal turmoil, a different enemy returned to the Iberian Peninsula. In 859 the Vikings raided the Asturian coast. They sailed south and were attacked en route by an Andalusi naval squadron. The Vikings diverted to Algeciras, attacked it and burnt the principal mosque. They were soon decisively beaten off. Later, a commemorative mosque was built in the town, with the doors made from the wood of the captured longboats. Some Vikings went on to attack the Atlantic coast of Morocco, while others headed up into the Mediterranean and made raids along the Levante coast. Most were inconclusive and the Vikings suffered more losses en route. There was one notably successful incursion, however; the Vikings made a foray along the upper reaches of the Ebro and reached Pamplona, where the Navarese king was captured and subsequently ransomed.

Left. The tower of San Juan de los Caballeros church in Córdoba was once the minaret of a mosque constructed around the end of the ninth century or the beginning of the tenth century.

    We have seen the high degree of dissatisfaction in the Amirate among the Muwallads. Of all the rebels to plague al-Andalus, the most persistent, colourful and potentially dangerous to the Amirate was a Muwallad, one Umar bin Hafsun. He emerged in the south and was to become an inspiration for disaffected Muwallads all across al-Andalus. Many of the other rebellions against the Umayyads had occurred on the periphery, along the frontiers. By contrast, the rebellion of Ibn Hafsun was firmly set in the heartland of al-Andalus, lasted a long time and at one stage threatened the very survival of the Amirate.

    Ibn Hafsun came from a well-to-do Muwallad family, which had a *cortijo* (country estate) near Torrecilla, in the Ronda region. The story runs that in his early youth he was involved in the murder of a neighbour. He became an outlaw and then fled to North Africa where he worked as a tailor. He soon returned to al-Andalus and, with a small band of like-minded outlaws, set up in the rugged mountainous district around the Guadalhorce valley, thirty-five kilometres north-west of Málaga. From his base there at Bobastro he made attacks around the region. Other rebellions were also underway in the territory and it became a time of general disorder. In 883, an army of the Amir, led by the redoubtable General Hashim, made an offensive against these rebellions and ranged through the mountains of Málaga. Ibn Hafsun was flushed from his fortress and he surrendered. He was brought to Córdoba where he was inscripted into the Umayyad army and served in a raid against the Christian north. Ibn Hafsun did not take to Cordoban life, not least to the attitude of the Arabs to Muwallads. He returned to Bobastro and reconstituted his band of rebels. Once again, he raided the countryside and expanded the territory under his control. In 886 an army led by Muhammad I's son, al-Mundhir, was sent out to prosecute the rebel. However the Amir died in August 886 and the prince had to return to Córdoba to assume the throne. Al-Mundhir was regarded as a brave, enterprising and effective leader. He was experienced, having fought in many campaigns. However, his reign was a short one and he never had a chance to fully demonstrate his talents.

One casualty during al-Mundhir's reign was the ubiquitous General Hashim who was not viewed with favour by the new Amir. Whatever infraction was involved, it must have been serious, for al-Mundhir promptly ordered him executed, his sons imprisoned and his lands seized. The change of regime provided a respite for Ibn Hafsun, who continued spreading his incendiary message of liberation from the unfair Arab yoke across (present-day) Andalucía. In 887 the new Amir sent out expeditions to put down the rebellion. Dissatisfied with their progress, the Amir himself set out in the spring of the following year with a large army. An associate of Ibn Hafsun, the rebel leader of Archidona, was captured on the way. He was executed, nailed to a cross between a dog and a pig. From Archidona, the army headed to Bobastro and laid siege to Ibn Hafsun. There were negotiations, the rebel indicated surrender but reneged on this. The siege resumed. Once more, fortune (that of an Amir's death) was to favour Ibn Hafsun. Al-Mundhir fell ill and died during the siege. The Umayyad forces retreated to Córdoba and the rebels began to harry them. Al-Mundhir's brother, Abd Allah, who had arrived earlier from Córdoba, had to endure the indignity of sending a messenger to the rebel to ask for the funeral cortege to be allowed proceed peacefully back to the capital.

So it was that Abd Allah was duly invested as Amir in 888. The sons of Muhammad I had different mothers who were concubine slaves. Reflecting his mother's European origins, the new Amir had blue eyes and reddish hair. He was reclusive, secretive and very religious - a characteristic which endeared him to the *alfaquis* of Córdoba, who continued to support him through all the vicissitudes of his reign. He presided over an al-Andalus that was to be buffeted by dissent and upheaval and which, by the end of his twenty four years of rule, had sunk into a parlous state.

The new Amir was of a murderous disposition, which soon proved dangerous for his family. He became irritated by his oldest son Muhammad (who had been designated heir and, as it transpired, was father of the future Abd al-Rahman III). He induced another son, al-Mutarrif, to stab Muhammad, his brother. Al-Mutarrif later fell foul of his father. In 895, persuaded that al-Mutarrif was disloyal, he ordered him to be beheaded. Two of the Amir's brothers were also killed on his orders.

The lands of al-Andalus, where disaffection had been brewing, now exploded in open revolt. There were many uprisings, some inspired by Ibn Hafsun. One historian counted thirty uprisings, both major and minor, which sprang up towards the end of the ninth century. Against this upheaval, local rulers across the Amirate asserted more independence from central control and the taxation system broke down. The coffers of the Amirate began to empty. A serious revolt had broken out in the lands of Tudmir (Murcia) where a rebel had established himself, with a large cavalry force. Over in the south-west, adherents of Ibn

Left. Poley (now Aguilar de la Frontera): Ibn Hafsun suffered a decisive defeat here in 891. Little remains today of the castle which was destroyed and rebuilt several times in later centuries. Built on the highest point of the town, the Peñón del Moro, the fortification dominated the surrounding plain.

Marwan (the 'Galician') had set up statelets in Faro, Beja and Mértola. In Elvira, to the north of Granada, conflict broke out between the local Muwallads and Arabs. The Muwallads looked on the Amir in Córdoba as an honest broker and requested his help but, following a series of encounters and defeats, later threw in their lot with Ibn Hafsun who sent troops to Elvira. Repulsed by the Arabs, he turned back to Bobastro, vowing revenge.

Ibn Hafsun was a curious character: mercurial, given to periods of inactivity and marked by sudden impetuous bursts of activity. He was brave and at times, chivalrous (as seen by the decision to let Abd Allah proceed peacefully to Córdoba with his brother's funeral cortege). He accepted offers of peace but just as quickly rejected them. The ambitious Ibn Hafsun even made contacts with Ibrahim II, the Aglabid prince of Kairouan in North Africa, suggesting collaboration in attacking the common Umayyad enemy. Ibn Hafsun continued his campaign, capturing more territory and strongholds, while the Amir reacted

Above. Alcaudete. The tower of the castle rises above the town, surrounded by fertile valleys and hills. The Alcaudete pass separates the Guadalquivir valley from the plains of Granada. The first fortification was built here after the Islamic conquest. The location was involved in the Ibn Hafsun rebellion and the castle was destroyed and rebuilt several times.

ineffectually. Ibn Hafsun set himself up in the castle of Poley (now Aguilar de la Frontera), which was scarcely more than forty kilometres to the south of Córdoba and commenced to fortify it. Well ensconced, Ibn Hafsun was increasingly able to threaten Córdoba and sent nightly raids into the surrounding countryside.

The capital began to suffer food shortages. With morale low, the Amir was forced to end his vacillation and deal meaningfully with the rebellion, now literally at the gates of Córdoba. Abd Allah assembled a great force which set out from the capital in May 891. On arrival at Poley, the Amir's troops attacked and managed to overcome the rebel forces who fell back to the castle. Things began to fall apart for Ibn Hafsun, as his men deserted him the next night, escaping through a breach in the castle walls. He sensibly fled and took refuge at Archidona. The Amir, meanwhile, occupied the castle at Poley and a slaughter of prisoners ensued. The Amir's army then advanced through rebel territory, capturing strongholds. Ibn Hafsun requested peace and was granted it by the Amir, subject to the submission of a son as a hostage. The wily Ibn Hafsun tried subterfuge and sent an adopted son. This was soon found out but the episode had earned the rebel a breathing space. Once more he broke off relations with Córdoba and, over the next few years, proceeded to retake some of the cities that he had lost. Characteristically, the Amir only responded in a desultory manner to the renewed rebel activity.

Ibn Hafsun now took a step which seriously damaged him. The story runs that, in 899, he decided to convert to Christianity and was baptised along with his family, taking the name of Samuel. There was an almost universally negative reaction against this by his Muwallad supporters, who took their Islamic religion seriously. Two prominent lieutenants of Ibn Hafsun now defected and treated

Left. The castle of Calatañazor (Qalat al-Nasur), near Soria. This location was originally fortified by the Muslims. Most of the extensive system of defensive walls was constructed at the beginning of the twelfth century, during the era of Alfonso I 'el Batallador'. The castle, now in a dilapidated state, was built during the fourteenth century.

him as an enemy. This apostasy even galvanised a prince in Nakur on the Maghreb coast to assemble a troop and set out to attack the now Christian rebel. Ibn Hafsun swatted this impudent expedition but in reality he was now severely weakened in the rebel territories of southern al-Andalus.

This unstable character asked for help from all directions. He made contact with the many opponents of the Amir, whether in the Iberian Peninsula or in North Africa. We have seen how he contacted the Aglabids in Kairouan. He also wrote to the ruler of the Idrisid statelet in the north-west of Morocco, Ibrahim bin Idris, and undertook to have his name read out in the Friday prayers in the mosques in the rebel territory. He wrote to Alfonso III and established ties with the independent ruler of Seville, Ibrahim bin Hajjuj. In Ibn Hafsun's ever-changing world, once more reconciliation came to the fore and he and the Amir agreed peace. As usual, the conditions required that hostages be handed over. In 902, yet again, the peace collapsed, skirmishes occurred and, this time, the Amir ordered the execution of hostages. However, although severely weakened, Ibn Hafsun continued to be a power in the land and he maintained his rebellion for the rest of Abd Allah's reign and as we shall see, continued it into the next reign, that of Abd al-Rahman III.

By the second half of the ninth century, Seville had become the second city of al-Andalus in terms of wealth and population. It had recovered from the savage sacking of the city by the Vikings in 844. In the middle of fertile countryside, and with a thriving port, it was a prosperous place. Rich aristocratic Arab families had established their houses in the city, along with substantial estates set along the Guadalquivir valley. The city was home to many Muwallads and Mozarabs. Tensions had built up between these and the Arab elite. This was manifest in 889 when a prominent Arab fomented attacks on Muwallads. Disorder broke out in the city. After initial inactivity Abd Allah sent expeditions to establish order. These proved to be inept; the uproar increased and

Above, Clash of civilisations: the Cross versus Islam. The eastern end of the great fortress of Gormaz, situated on a commanding ridge looking over the Duero valley. This Islamic stronghold was a strategic location on the northern frontier during the conflict with the Christian kingdoms.

many Muwallads and Mozarabs were killed. In the midst of the disturbances and given the vacuum of central power, a local Arab leader, Ibrahim bin Hajjuj, came to the fore. He seized control over Seville and Carmona and the Amir had no choice but to tolerate his independence. The ruler of Seville proved to be an able administrator and established a miniature Amirate with all the trappings of power. He appointed a *qadi* and a head of police for Seville. He established his court and had a workshop for luxury textiles. He even imported a singer from Baghdad (mimicking the Cordoban practice). The court attracted a coterie of poets and writers from Córdoba who decamped to Seville. Over the years, the relations between Seville and Córdoba were tense and uneasy, stoked by the Amir's holding of Ibrahim's son as a hostage. Eventually the son was released in 902, whereupon Ibrahim accepted vassalage to Córdoba. He continued to rule Seville until his death in 911.

How were the Christians in the northern regions surviving under the pressures of their Islamic opponents to the south? The Asturians and the Basques were frontier peoples. Those communities, which live near frontiers marking the edges of empires or cultures, possess unique qualities. In recent times this was evident with the Afrikaners, the Northern Irish Unionists and currently the Israelis. Under continuous threat, these people are on the front-line in defence of a perceived culture, religion or concept of nation. They are usually a tough breed and can be obstinate with a reluctance to compromise. The principal adversaries

Left. A section of the walls of Daroca, which extend for nearly four kilometres. Founded in the eighth century, this was a stronghold of Muwallad local rulers, who guarded the northern frontier in uneasy alliance with the Amir in Córdoba.

on both sides of the northern frontier in the Iberian Peninsula were certainly that. On the Muslim side, the parvenu Muwallads of the Upper March, such as the Banu Qasi, maintained the frontier in their own interests, which may or may not have coincided with those of the Amir in far away Córdoba. From a small and modest beginning, the Asturian kingdom proved to be resilient against the continuing pressure from al-Andalus. The Basques continued their fierce history of independence.

The pattern of conflict was usually one of raids and forays into each other's territories. There was an inverse mechanism at work on the northern frontier: the fortunes of one side rose as that of the other declined. As one side was in the ascendant, or perceived weakness on the other side, they mounted raids. The motives were many, including booty, promoting their prestige and authority as well as teaching the upstart enemy a lesson. For the Christians, in the early years from the eighth to the eleventh centuries, the essential motivation was self-preservation against their substantially more powerful Islamic enemy. However, as we are to see, Christian tactics changed from the ninth century; as part of their attacks they began to retain territory. From now on they were to maintain a creeping advance southwards, gradually nibbling away at the frontiers of al-Andalus. By the eleventh and early twelfth centuries, the Christians had become more powerful and, after the fall of the Caliphate in 1030, the Islamic side was much weaker. The ideology moved with the times and the Christian idea of Reconquista, always in play, then came to the fore. This was the concept of expelling Islamic invaders who had captured territory that 'by right' belonged to Christians. One might question whether the mixed bunch of northern kings were quite the same as the Visigothic Christians (who earlier had seized Roman Hispania) and had thus inherited 'rights'. In any case, by the twelfth century, the

Above. The castle at la Guardia de Jaén. During the early years of al-Andalus this was originally the capital of the Cora, or administrative district of the region. In the ninth century, Abd al-Rahman II moved the capital to nearby Jaén.

Reconquista concept, always attractive and in play, was then seen as realistic and achievable and it became a true driving force for the Christians.

Alfonso III, who came to the Asturian throne in 866, was a vigorous and capable ruler. He launched several successful raids deep into Muslim territory. After the death of Muhammad I in 886, the turmoil in al-Andalus gave Alfonso III twenty-five years of breathing space and facilitated the continued expansion of Asturian territory. He settled the depopulated lands of the Meseta around the Duero with incomers from the northern mountains as well as Mozarab migrants who had left al-Andalus. The region of Castile began to take shape in the area south of the Cantabrian mountains reaching across to the upper Ebro valley. The nobility of this frontier area began to operate in a manner increasingly independent of the King in Oviedo. This was to lay the basis for the territory of Castile, which eventually developed into the powerful Christian kingdom many centuries later. Not surprisingly, being a vulnerable border region experiencing much conflict, many castles and fortifications were built there, hence the eponymous title.

The Upper March was ruled by volatile and independent minded Muwallad clans. Foremost among these were the Banu Qasi. Musa bin Musa Banu Qasi of that clan, as we have seen, had been assigned as Governor of Tudela by Muhammad I. Musa continued in power there until he was killed in a battle in 862 with Berbers from the Guadalajara region. This opened the way for

Muhammad I to assign his own Governors in the Ebro valley. However, in 871 Musa's sons rose up and took over Huesca, Tudela and Zaragoza. Muhammad I's forces attacked these areas on several occasions. On other occasions, members of the family allied with Córdoba. Later, the Amir used the Tuchibi clan in Zaragoza to counteract the power of the Banu Qasi. However, despite their unreliable and troublesome nature, these clans were mainly useful for Córdoba, forming a tough cordon against the Christian enemy to the north.

A curious example of religious exuberance occurred in the peninsula during the last part of the ninth century. An Islamic mystic travelled around al-Andalus and dramatically preached salvation. In Córdoba, he was joined by a man of Umayyad ancestry, an astrologist known as Ibn al-Qitt. They moved to the north of Mérida, spreading their message among the faithful and gained adherents among Berber settlers in the mountainous regions. Ibn al-Qitt was pronounced as the Mahdi (the expected Messiah of Islam) and declared holy war against the Christians in the north. Zamora, which had been recently re-fortified by Alfonso III, fell in their sights. In 901 an army with a reported size of 60,000 was assembled, and they set out for the city. The Mahdi announced that he would make the walls of Zamora crumble. He also made the mistake of sending a highly disrespectful letter to Alfonso III, threatening his destruction unless he and his family converted to Islam. Alfonso III immediately set out with his troops to meet the Mahdi's forces which put the Christian army to flight. The Mahdi then moved to Zamora and laid siege, but then his luck ran out. The

Above. Church at Almonaster la Real, to the north-west of Seville. It was originally a mosque which was built in the early tenth century and incorporates earlier Visigothic and Roman remains.

Right. Patio of the ablutions, at the entrance to the former mosque, now a church, at Almonaster la Real.

Right. Interior of the former mosque at Almonaster la Real. The mihrab can be seen in the central background.

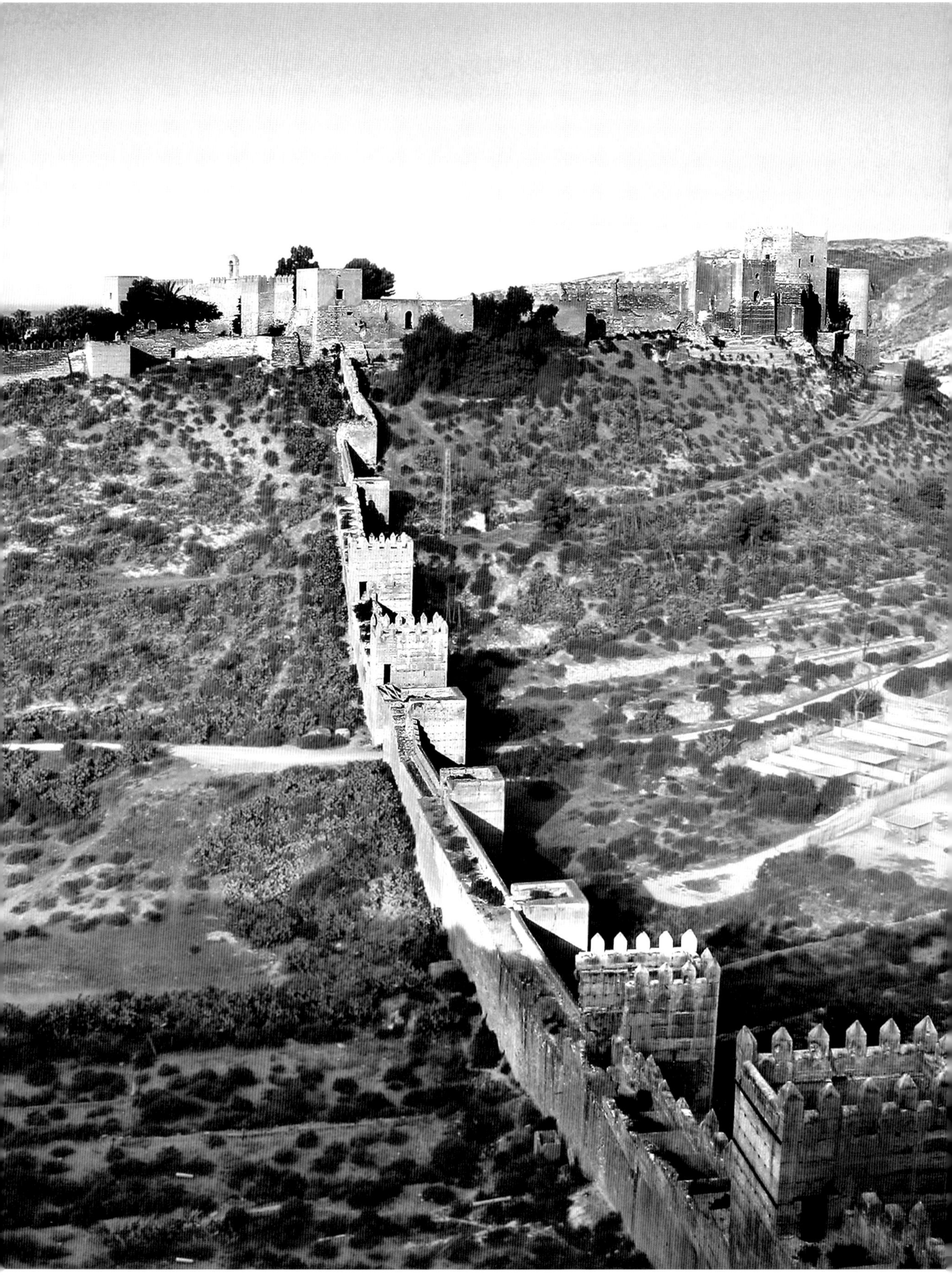

Right. The parapets of the Alcazaba in Almería, which dominates the city whose name comes from 'al-Mariya' or watchtower. The port of Almería grew from the nearby town of Pechina which became a flourishing entrepot during the times of the Umayyad Emirate.

Left. At Almería: the fortified curtain wall as it traverses a valley, with the Alcazaba in the background. Abd al-Rahman III ordered the construction of the Alcazaba here in 955.

Berbers began to desert en masse. The Mahdi continued the attack and was killed shortly afterwards. This farcical and dramatic episode ended with the display of the Mahdi's head on the gates of Zamora.

Amongst all the unrest and bloodshed that characterised Abd Allah's reign, by contrast, there was a satisfying example of progress and prosperity. Sailors, mainly of Andalusi origin, plying the Mediterranean trade, had set up a trading base in Pechina on the south-east coast of the peninsula. This was located on the river Andarax, ten kilometres inland from a sheltered bay, which was overlooked by a watchtower. This bay now forms the port of Almería (*al-Mariya* or watchtower). These mariners (most of whom were Muwallads and Mozarabs) had reached agreement with the local Arabs and set up a small maritime republic there but recognised Córdoba's overall sovereignty. Over time it prospered and grew. Within the walls, a mosque was built as well as a church for the Mozarabs. A silk industry was established and crafts flourished. The Arabs of the nearby

Left. Entrance to the Alcazaba at Almería.

stronghold of Elvira looked covetously at this plump and thriving statelet and in time sent a raiding expedition. As luck would have it, other eyes had sized up this appetising morsel. Fifteen ships of the Frankish Count of Ampurias had just anchored in the bay and these sent a force to sack Pechina. The defenders in the town soon put the Franks to flight. However, in the meantime, the Elviran forces, on seeing the anchored ships in the bay, decided these were reinforcements that had come to Pechina's assistance and promptly retreated. By 922, Pechina had become an integral part of the Amirate and the port of Almería grew. Over the years Pechina fell into decline and faded out of history. Abd al-Rahman III made Almería the capital of the province and expanded and developed the city.

    Abd Allah barely managed to keep the al-Andalus State intact during his twenty-four year reign. He died in October 912, aged sixty-eight, leaving the Amirate to his grandson, Abd al-Rahman III. It was the end of a turbulent and perilous era for the Umayyad dynasty in Córdoba and was the dawn of its greatest age.

Chapter 4
The Caliphate

Abd al-Rahman III came to power in 912. He had been nominated as successor by his grandfather, the Amir Abd Allah, who had previously murdered his own son, Abd al-Rahman III's father. Abd Allah had been much taken by the young Abd al-Rahman and paid great attention to his upbringing. In the end, he favoured his grandson over his sons. Like his grandfather, the new Amir inherited a mix of European and Arab blood: he is reported to have had blue eyes and fair hair. His mother was a European concubine slave and his grandmother a Basque princess. Following Abd Allah's death, the investiture of his successor went smoothly, with due pomp but mixed with mourning for the death of the Amir. It was attended by the princes of the blood, the new Amir's uncles and grand uncles. The foremost of these made a solemn address, proffering on the princes' behalf, their obedience to the new Amir.

The chroniclers of the time praise Abd-al-Rahman III's qualities: he was generous, intelligent, methodical, and tenacious. Apparently, he had a facility to think laterally, outside the confines of the accepted viewpoints of his court. He was a pious Muslim but under his rule Christians and Jews were able to prosper. Indeed, all the qualities listed for Abd al-Rahman III are not mere hyperbole, because during his reign he was to demonstrate these abilities and was to prove an extraordinarily effective ruler. When he took office, the State left by his grandfather was in a ramshackle condition, near to collapse. It took twenty years of inspired and methodical exertion to restore equilibrium.

The new Amir proceeded to gather submissions of obeisance from the vassal lords all over al-Andalus. Asserting his own authority, he began a wave of renewal throughout the administration, appointing new governors and other high officials. All through his reign, he continued this practice of periodic replacement and did not allow office holders to get too comfortable in their positions.

The new ruler had problems on three principal fronts: an external threat to the south - the emergence of the Fatimids of North Africa (of whom more later); the perennial threat of the Christians to the north; and, within al-Andalus, the most pressing threat - the festering sore that was the revolt emanating from the rebel of Bobastro, Ibn Hafsun. Abd al-Rahman III immediately embarked on a clever campaign to deal with this latter revolt. He did not immediately begin a frontal assault on Ibn Hafsun but sent out his forces to attack the edges of the rebel's sphere of influence. His troops began to attack and seize the

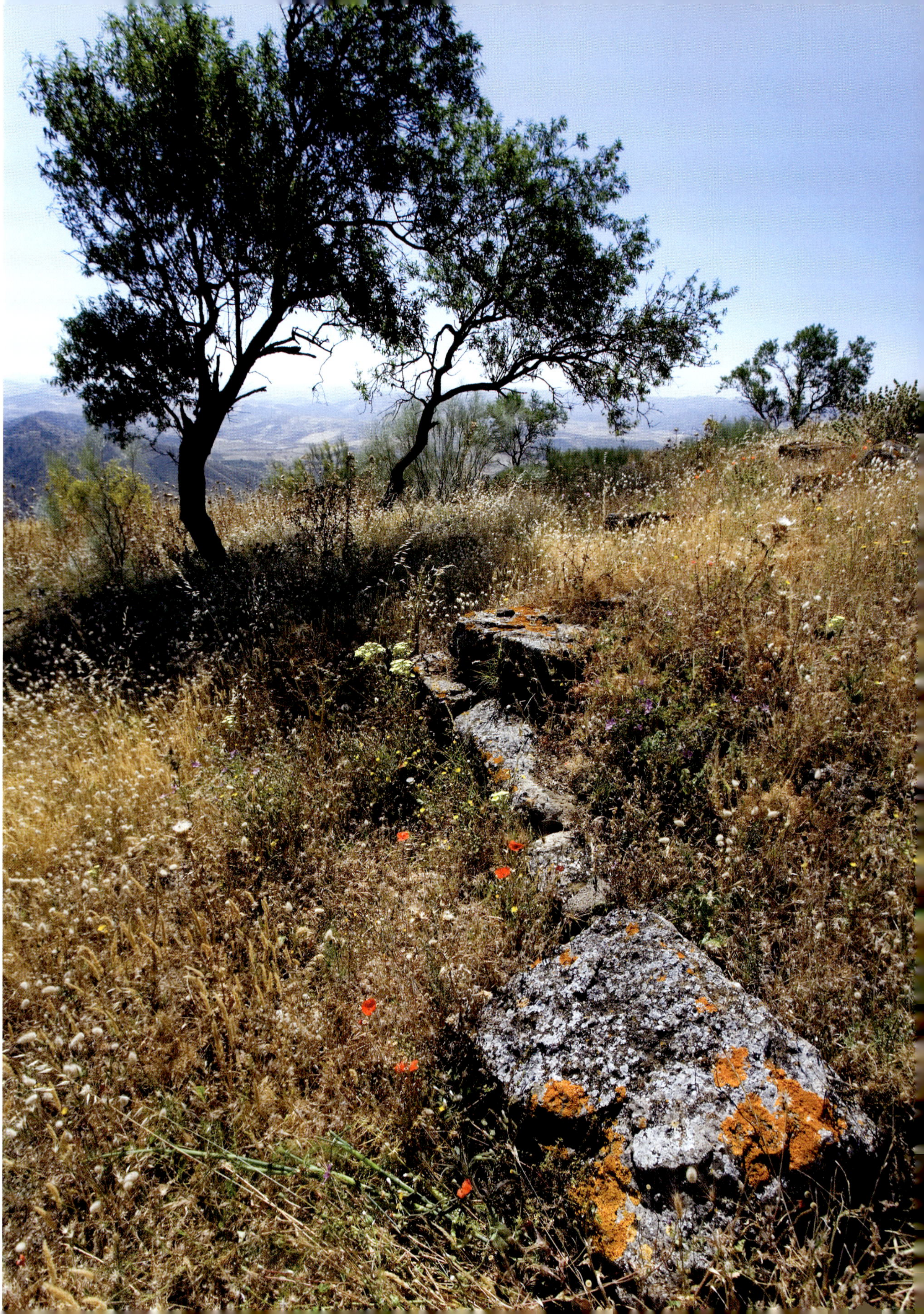

Left. The highest point at Bobastro, by the rugged and remote Guadalhorce valley. Little more than rubble remains of Ibn Hafsun's fortifications.

strongholds of supporters of Ibn Hafsun all across the territory of present-day Andalucía. This new and successful campaign caused a domino effect as many of the petty rebel lords, gauging the new and enhanced power of the Amirate, submitted en masse. Later the Cordoban troops kept up the pressure and made a foray through the area immediately surrounding the rebel stronghold at Bobastro and ranged through the Serranía de Ronda.

Another problem for the Amir was Seville. This city was a jewel in the land of al-Andalus, being the second city, rich and prosperous. However, as we previously have seen, Seville had long maintained its independence from Cordoban rule. That was soon to change. It happened that Muhammad bin Hajjuj, lord of Carmona, following the recent death of his father Ibrahim bin Hajjuj, the ruler of Seville, was embroiled in a struggle for power with another family member who had taken over in the city. Muhammad submitted to the new Amir, who assigned troops that laid siege to Seville. The defenders called for help from Ibn Hafsun. He set out with his forces but was repulsed and had to return to Bobastro. The Sevillans decided to negotiate and surrendered the city in December 913. The reintegration of Seville into the Cordoban fold was a great coup for the new Amir.

Drought and epidemics spread through Andalucía in 914, making it difficult for Abd al-Rahman III to launch expeditions and continue the momentum against Ibn Hafsun. However, the old rebel was sick, isolated and by now did not pose much of a threat. He remained in Bobastro, praying piously in the Mozarab church he had had built there. He died there in 917 and was given a Christian burial. News of his death caused a sensation across al-Andalus; the Muslims celebrated at the death of this apostate; the Mozarabs were devastated. Ibn Hafsun's sons took up their father's mantle and it took the Amir ten hard years to extinguish the last flames of resistance in the region. It was not until 928 that Bobastro was finally besieged and taken by the Cordoban forces. This was an exceptional victory for the Amir: Ibn Hafsun had posed a severe threat to him and his predecessors, challenging the very existence of the Umayyad State. On hearing the news, Abd al-Rahman III set out from Córdoba and made a triumphal procession through the region to Bobastro. The vengeance of the Umayyads was manifested in the Amir's orders: the body of Ibn Hafsun was exhumed and sent back to Córdoba where it was put on display. The fortress complex at Bobastro was razed, leaving it as described by an Arab chronicler, like a 'bare mountain'. In the meantime Abd al-Rahman III continued south through the Málaga region, destroying castles that had belonged to the rebels and exiling those Mozarabs who had been reported disloyal. This defeat of the famous rebel caused Abd al-Rahman III's prestige to grow immeasurably, not only in al-Andalus, but also across North Africa and the rest of the Muslim world. This victory over such a major threat and the resulting enhancement of his power and prestige were among factors that allowed him to consider declaring himself Caliph.

Abd al-Rahman III had to keep an eye on the external threat from the Maghreb. At the end of the ninth century a preacher set up in the Ifriqiya region

Left. Carved into the rock, the remains of the Mozarab church at Bobastro. Ibn Hafsun's rebellion lost momentum when he converted to Christianity in 899.

(present-day Tunisia and eastern Algeria). He was part of the Ismaili sect of the Shia branch of Islam, a sect that was active in many parts of the Islamic world. The Ismaili message took root and in 903 the Aglabi rulers in Ifriqiya were overpowered. The insurgents called for their Immam who, in 910, was proclaimed Caliph, with the title the Mahdi (the expected Messiah of Islam) in Kairouan. Their name, the Fatimids, arose from their claim to be descendants of the Prophet through his daughter Fatima and her husband Ali. They were opposed

Right. View of the remains of the Mozarab church at Bobastro. One historian speculates that the cavity to the right was Ibn Hafsun's grave. After Bobastro was captured by Abd al-Rahman III's forces, the rebel's body was disinterred and put on display in Córdoba.

to those of the Sunni persuasion: the Abbasid caliphs in Baghdad and, similarly, the Umayyad rulers of Córdoba, all of whom they regarded as impostors. Around the same time as Abd al-Rahman III ascended the throne, the Fatimids were beginning to expand energetically. While their main target was the eastern Islamic world, they also expanded to the west. Córdoba had long had ties of trade and had built up generally friendly relations with several of the rulers in the western Maghreb. When these rulers were attacked Córdoba was in danger of being drawn into conflict. In 917 the Fatimids made an attack that was dangerously close to the shores of al-Andalus. This was on the small western city-state of Nakur (west of present-day Melilla) whose rulers were vassals of Córdoba. In 921 the Fatimids built a new caliphal capital called Mahdya, located on the coast of (present-day) Tunisia. They built a large naval shipyard there which allowed a rapid expansion of their fleet. Abd al-Rahman III reacted to this by ordering the building up the Andalus fleet. Coastal defences were improved by setting up a series of watchtowers along the Mediterranean coast.

A form of cold war ensued, which occasionally got hot at the edges. Just as in the twentieth-century version, there were opposing ideologies and each had its own followers. The Fatimids utilised the services of the Sanhaja Berbers; Córdoba had the Zanata Berbers. In 927, Abd al-Rahman III took a more direct approach and ordered the occupation of Melilla, a strategic harbour on the Rif coast. He followed this in 931 with the taking of Ceuta, another strategic and easily-defended harbour convenient to the port of Algeciras. Abd al-Rahman III consolidated his grip on North Africa by occupying Tangier in 951.

Left. The Spanish flag flies over the defensive walls known as the 'Monumental Group of the Royal Walls' at Ceuta. This port is now a Spanish enclave surrounded by Morocco. Around the middle of the tenth century, fearful of the threat from the Fatimids, Abd al-Rahman III ordered that Ceuta's fortifications be improved. New defensive lines were built over subsequent centuries.

The two sides mainly used their adherents to maintain their interests and direct conflict was rare. However, in 955, a clash brought the Fatimid threat close to home. An Andalusi ship captured a Fatimid ship en route to North Africa from Sicily. The Fatimids reacted by attacking Almería. Abd al-Rahman retaliated by sending a fleet, under General Ghalib (a freed slave of whom we will hear more later), to raid the Fatimid coast. The Andalus fleet was increased again and the defences of Ceuta were strengthened. Matters changed in 959 when a new Fatimid leader took power and demonstrated a new belligerence. A Fatimid army now ranged over present-day Morocco, taking Fez in 959 and reached the Atlantic. Córdoba was left with only the enclaves of Ceuta and Tangier. This was the scene as Abd al-Rahman III's reign ended. His son, al-Hakam II, on inheriting the throne, continued the struggle against the Fatimids and their Berber allies.

Below. Historic street sign in Ceuta.

Right. Puente de Alcántara at Toledo, spanning the Tagus River. This was originally built by the Romans but reconstructed several times during the era of al-Andalus. Toledo sits on a hill and is surrounded on three sides by the river, which made it easily defensible in medieval times.

Below. Horseshoe arch on the eastern abutment of the bridge.

We now return to Abd al Rahman III's continuing elimination of resistance in the Peninsula. By the fall of Bobastro in 928, most of the centres of opposition in the west and east had submitted to the Amir. However, he still had to deal with the two last principal outposts of dissidence: Badajoz and Toledo. Badajoz had continued as an independent statelet and was still ruled by a descendant of the old rebel, Ibn Marwan 'the Galician', whom we have previously encountered. In 929 Abd al-Rahman III led his troops to the city. After a long siege the city surrendered and its ruler was allowed to live in Córdoba. Next on the list was Toledo, the former Visigothic capital, with a long history of independence and revolt. On a height above a bend in the river Tagus, the city enjoyed an easily defensible position. It was also well provisioned and the Toledans refused peace overtures from Abd al-Rahman III. A siege was mounted in 930. The Christian Kingdom of León sent an expedition to assist the city but

Left. Experienced veteran of conflict with the Muslims, Ordoño II ascended to the Asturian throne in 914, whose capital had been transferred south to León. He continued raiding the territory of al-Andalus but the newly-installed Abd al-Rahman III soon proved to be a formidable opponent

this was repulsed. After much hardship and famine Toledo eventually surrendered in 932. Abd al-Rahman III stationed garrisons in the city and in strongholds in the surrounding region. He returned to Córdoba, where he rewarded his troops and organised a sumptuous celebration of his victory.

The Amir had not neglected to pay attention to the north: the Muslim frontier districts of uncertain loyalty and the Christian enemies beyond. He took a pragmatic view of the turbulent political life of the Upper March. While the local lords could continue to exercise power, he wanted merely to have them declare as vassals to him in order to achieve a sometimes nominal obedience and collect taxes. He maintained relations with the Tuchibi and the Banu Dhu l'Nun who were based in the mountains of Santaver (near Cuenca). The Tuchibis ruled Zaragoza and, on the accession of Abd al-Rahman III, their ruler sent his message of submission. The family continued to rule the city up to the period when their reluctance to assist Abd al-Rahman III in a campaign in 934 was followed several years later by their joining forces with the Leonese and their loss of Zaragoza (as we shall see later). Other branches of the Tuchibis ruled Daroca and Calatuyud. The once powerful Banu Qasi were in charge of Tudela. The incumbent ruler submitted to the Amir who allowed him remain as Governor of Tudela. After this the Banu Qasi recede from al-Andalus history.

During the early years of Abd al-Rahman III's reign, the struggles between al-Andalus and the Christians to the north continued as before. These hardy Christian states were able to give a good account of themselves in the struggle with the Muslim south. However, by the end of his reign, Abd al-Rahman III

Above. Rising above the Duero valley in the morning sun, the great northern fortress of Gormaz. It sits on a ridge and is around 380 metres long.

established a position of dominance, so that the Christian rulers, undermined by internal struggles, finished up recognising his suzerainty. By the time Ordoño II ascended to the throne of the Asturian kingdom in 914, the capital had been moved south to León (reflecting the increasing southerly extent of its domains) and it later became known as the Kingdom of León. A veteran of successful raids against al-Andalus, Ordoño continued with his assaults, on the assumption that the new Amir, like his grandfather, would be preoccupied with the internal rebellions occurring across the Amirate. However, Abd al-Rahman III promptly went on the offensive and, in 916, sent out a force that made a successful (and profitable) raid against Ordoño's territory. The next year another large expedition was launched and they laid siege to the Leonese stronghold of San Esteban de Gormaz (not to be confused with the nearby fortress of Gormaz). This was part of the new line of Christian fortifications recently put in place along the right bank of the Duero. The Christians made a strong attack, the Cordoban army was badly defeated and its general killed. His head was later put on display in León alongside the head of a boar. However, the Leonese were soon to discover that this Amir was of a different character to his predecessor. Abd al-Rahman III determined to avenge this humiliation. He built up his armies and, in the following two years, new expeditions were sent out to punish the Christians. Still mindful of the San Esteban defeat, in 920 he led a major campaign called the 'Muez'. His column started off in a north-easterly direction but made a sudden turn towards Osma and, after a forced march, took the Christians by surprise. He took, sacked and demolished places in the Duero

Left. Gormaz: double-arch entrance gate.

region including Osma and San Esteban de Gormaz. The army now swung towards Navarra, with the intention of teaching King Sancho García of Pamplona (who had been raiding the Muslim frontier) a lesson. The Banu Qasi governor of Tudela joined the Cordoban army in the attack on Navarra. The Muslim forces met the combined Navarese and Leonese forces (Ordoño had come to Sancho's help) in the valley of Junquera to the west of Pamplona. The Cordoban army decisively defeated the Christians there in a bloody battle. Abd al-Rahman followed this by sacking the nearby castle of Muez, went on to ravage lower Navarra and then returned to Córdoba. He arrived, three months after he had set out, having greatly enhanced the prestige and power of his Amirate with this famous victory. However, the doughty Christians still continued their raids. In 924, Abd al Rahman III once more headed north with a strong force. He crossed the Ebro and advanced towards Navarra, sacking Pamplona and burning its cathedral. Having devastated the surrounding region, he returned to Córdoba.

Ordoño II's death in 924 was followed by squabbles over the succession. As a result the frontier conflicts with al-Andalus diminished. In 932 a strong Leonese king, Ramiro II, took power. An energetic leader, he had previously led the expedition to support the Toledans during the siege by Cordoban forces. And so, the

Right. The Iberian Peninsula at the beginning of the Caliphate, during the first half of the tenth century.

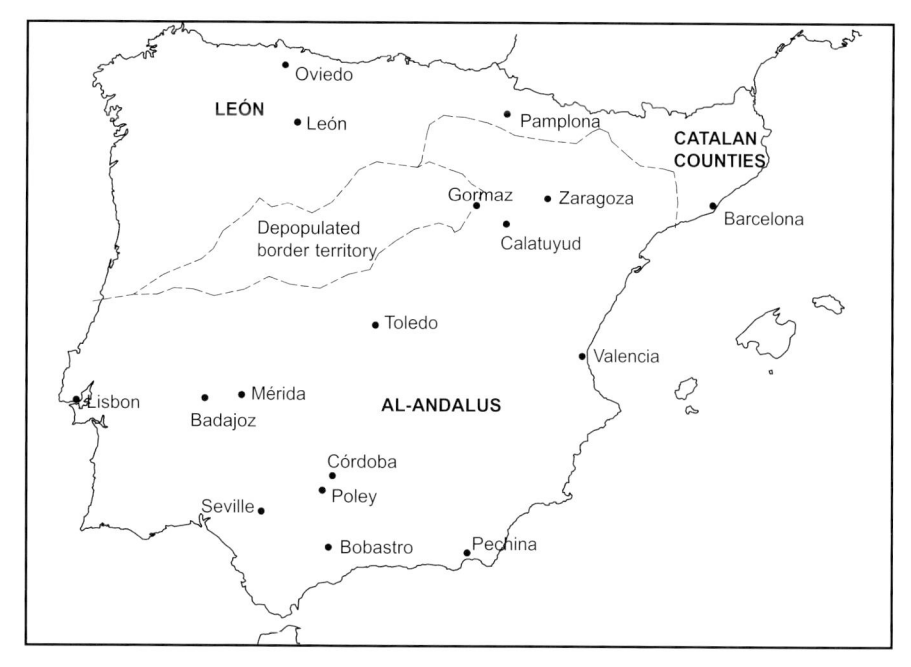

frontier incursions by the Leonese recommenced. In response, Abd al Rahman III (by now Caliph, as we shall see later) set out in 934 to mount a siege on Ramiro who was at Osma in the Duero region. The Christians did not emerge to fight and, leaving the siege in place, Abd al- Rahman III went on to demolish Burgos and nearby strongholds. The Tuchibi ruler of Zaragoza had only reluctantly joined with the Cordoban forces during the attack on Osma. Three years later, in an example of the dizzying, shifting loyalties on the frontier, the Tuchibis decided to openly join forces with the Christians. The Caliph set out north and laid siege to the Tuchibi garrison at Calatuyud, which was reinforced by Ramiro's troops. The garrison surrendered and the Cordoban troops ravaged the region. They then sieged and captured Zaragoza. In the summer of 939 the Caliph decided to deliver a decisive blow to the Christians. He gathered a great expedition (unwisely announcing it as the 'campaign of omnipotence') and set out on the well-travelled road to the north and the Duero valley. The Muslim army met the combined armies of León, Castile and Navarra at Simancas. The struggle lasted for several days. Adroitly led by Ramiro II, the Christians routed the Muslims and harried them over a long distance, causing great casualties. During the rout, the Caliph had to flee, abandoning his tent and leaving behind his golden coat of mail and personal Koran, which were recovered by the Christians. He and the remains of his army beat a hasty retreat back to Córdoba. Clearly smarting at this humiliating blow to his prestige, the Caliph promptly had 300 officers of his cavalry crucified for cowardice on the banks of the Guadalquivir. Following this disaster, he never returned to personally lead an army to the north again. The news of the defeat resounded through Christian Europe. It increased the prestige of Ramiro, as well as giving the (over-optimistic) impression that Islamic al-Andalus was weakened and could now be easi-

80

Right. The arched portico leading to the palace-city at Madinat al-Zahra.

Left. Ivory casket with the same type of decoration as in the reception hall in Madinat al-Zahra. The inscription tells that it was made for a daughter of Abd al-Rahman III. Victoria and Albert Museum, London.

Right. Capital at Madinat al-Zahra. The honeycomb pattern is characteristic of the style during the Córdoba Caliphate.

Left. Remains of the mosque at Madinat al-Zahra. The palace-city was destroyed during the civil war that broke out at the beginning of the eleventh century. Reconstruction continues at the site and much of the complex still has to be excavated.

Left. Carved marble basin at Madinat al-Zahra.

ly defeated. Following this victory, Ramiro took advantage and set in train a vigorous repopulation of the area around Salamanca.

Over the years the region of Castile had begun to assert its independence from León. Conflict now broke out between the Count of Castile Fernán Gonzaléz and Ramiro II. The Caliph, eager for revenge, took early advantage of this. In 940 he sent an expedition to the north. With the Leonese lacking the support of Castilian troops, this was successful. Abd al-Rahman III kept up the pressure. In the following years regular raids were mounted and ranged all over the Christian north. In support of this offensive the Caliph had the fortress of Medinaceli rebuilt and garrisoned. This proved to be an important advance base in support of the offensive against the north. When Ramiro II died in 951, chaos ensued as competing factions struggled to take over. When the dust had settled, Ordoño III, son of Ramiro, was in power. The Muslims harried the Leonese who sued for peace and obtained a truce. Ordoño III died in 956, and another succession dispute ensued, ending with the flight of another son of Ramiro, Sancho I '*el Gordo*' (or 'fat one'), to Pamplona, to be sheltered there by his grandmother, the Navarese Queen Regent, Toda. It is recorded that Toda turned for help to Córdoba to sort out two pressing problems: one to cure her grandson's obesity and, secondly, to help him recover the throne of León. This provided an opportunity for the Caliph and he acted decisively. The story runs that he sent his trusted physician, linguist and diplomat, the Jewish Ibn Shaprut, to cure the obesity, which apparently this gifted man achieved with great dexterity. He also obtained the agreement that, if Sancho regained the throne of León, he would hand over ten frontier fortresses. The negotiations were sealed by a visit to Córdoba to see the Caliph. The Queen Regent, her son the king of Navarra, and her grandson Sancho I (presumably no longer '*el Gordo*'), travelled to Córdoba where they were received with great ceremony in Madinat al-Zahra by the Caliph. Matters proceeded satisfactorily for Sancho I. Shortly after the visit, in line with the agreement, the Cordoban forces attacked those of the Leonese ruler Ordoño IV. The Navarese forces, in turn, made a diversionary attack against Count Fernán Gonzaléz in eastern Castile. The Muslims took

Zamora and, a short time later, in 960, Ordoño IV was deposed by Sancho I, who occupied León.

It was one year after he had decisively dealt with the Ibn Hafsun rebellion that Abd al-Rahman III decided to take the title of Caliph. This is the supreme position in Islam, claiming both temporal and spiritual leadership of believers. There were several reasons for this. His rule was now well established throughout al-Andalus. The Christian threat on the frontier marches had been significantly reduced. The growing peace across the State was in tandem with a new era of prosperity and the organisation and administration of the State had reached a new level of sophistication. In Umayyad eyes, the Abbasids in the east had usurped the Caliphate and, in addition, they had now grown weak and decadent. The concept of 'Caliph' had fragmented, by virtue of the disunity in the Islamic world. However, the nearby proclamation of a Caliphate by the 'heretical' Fatimids presented an affront as well as a direct threat. For Abd al-Rahman III, well-consolidated and firmly in control, it was time to restore the Umayyad caliphal line. The title of Caliph held in al-Andalus may well have been of academic importance to the by now far-flung Muslim lands to the east. Nevertheless, it reflected the rise in importance, power and respect that Abd al-Rahman III and his State of al-Andalus had achieved. Thus, in a solemn ceremony in the Great Mosque in Córdoba, he took the title in early 929. He also took the honorific designation of *al-Nasir* (the Victorious). His name as Caliph, the Commander of the Faithful, was proclaimed from the minarets of mosques all over al-Andalus.

Abd al-Rahman III had inherited existing royal palaces and buildings in Córdoba. The principal one was the Alcázar, which accommodated the court and administration, the royal quarters and the great gardens. There were also many palaces dotted around the outskirts of Córdoba, which were used as summer palaces for the ruler or as residences for visiting dignitaries. However, as the pace of state affairs increased, he felt the need for new accommodation. Mindful of his new status as Caliph and supported by the increased taxes that were flooding in to the state coffers, Abd al-Rahman decided that he would build a new palace to the north-west of the city. In 936 the construction commenced on one of the great monuments to Islamic architecture in Iberia, the caliphal palace that is located some five kilometres from the centre of Córdoba. The site chosen for the new palace was magnificent, set on the slopes of the Sierra de Córdoba and overlooking the verdant Vega of Córdoba, through which runs the Guadalquivir. It was named '*Madinat al-Zahra*', or 'city of Zahra'. Accounts are not quite clear who Zahra was, perhaps a favourite concubine, but one can assume that she had been a significant woman in his life.

It has been said that a third of the tax revenues of the State was diverted for the new palace complex. 10,000 workers toiled in its construction. The palace proper was set on three stepped terraces cut into the slope of the hill: on the topmost level were the exquisite palaces for the Caliph and his dependants; the next level was made up of office and court buildings, magnificent gardens and orchards; and, on the lower level, there was a mosque and the quarters of the palace servants. There were military quarters, with stabling for the cavalry. Reflecting the wealth of the Caliphate, the best and most sumptuous materials were sourced from afar. Pink and green marble columns came from Ifriqiya in the Maghreb. Onyx came from the Málaga region, while white marble was sourced from Almería province. As had long been the custom in al-Andalus, remains of Roman buildings were re-used. The Caliph also received gifts of building materials and fitments from wealthy individuals. The great enterprise was directed by the heir to the throne, al-Hakam, in conjunction with the Caliph's chief architect, Maslama bin Abd Allah. Construction of Madinat al-Zahra continued over many years but the Caliph used it from an early stage - there is a record of a state reception there in 945.

The royal reception hall was exquisitely decorated with precious jewels, gold and silver, the walls clad in sheets of translucent jasper, multicoloured marbles and arches of ebony and ivory. In the middle of the hall was a shallow bowl of mercury. High windows were angled so that sunbeams shone on it. By command of the Caliph, the bowl was rocked, causing the mercury to reflect a dazzling array of sunlight around the room. Following the custom of other rulers across the Islamic world, this was no mere palace, it was a full city. It had its own administration with a *qadi* and police chief. There were fountains, baths and a market for the large number of people who came to live there.

Work continued on the palace. In 949 the Mozarab bishop Rabi bin Zayad, who had been on a diplomatic mission in Constantinople, procured treasures, including an elaborately sculpted basin from the Orient, for the new palace. During the early part of al-Hakam II's reign more buildings were added. However, the glory of Madinat al-Zahra was short-lived. It was sacked and

Above. The restored Salón Rico of the palace-city of Madinat al-Zahra near Córdoba. No expense was spared in the construction of the complex, which Abd al-Rahman III ordered to begin in 936. Receptions for visiting dignatories were glittering affairs. Delegations came from the Emperor of Byzantium and the Saxon King Otto I, reflecting the importance of the Córdoba Caliphate as a pre-eminent Mediterranean power.

Right. Madinat al-Zahra is one of the great monuments of Islamic architecture in the Iberian Peninsula. It fittingly reflected Abd al-Rahman III's new exalted status as Caliph.

destroyed by Berber troops in 1010 at the beginning of the civil war that racked al-Andalus and caused the fall of the Caliphate. During Abd al-Rahman III's rule he built elsewhere in al-Andalus. He developed the courtyard, arcades and façade of the Great Mosque in Córdoba. He built a new minaret there, just under fifty metres high, no longer visible, as it was built over and enclosed by the Christian bell tower that is in place today. There were improvements to the city gates and various constructions as well in cities around al-Andalus. Nevertheless, the main architectural monument to Abd al-Rahman III that we have today are the remains to be found at Madinat al-Zahra, being painstakingly restored to vestiges of their former glory.

In the medieval world of the time slaves were part of everyday life. Al-Andalus was no exception and a large number of slaves were imported. Many were European; they came from north of the Pyrenees, the Mediterranean coast and from as far as the Slavic lands on the Black Sea. During Abd al-Rahman's III reign there was a large increase in the number of slaves. The name 'slave' (in Arabic *saqalibah*) came from 'Slav'. In Madinat al-Zahra a significant proportion of the servants, administrators and military were slaves (or former slaves). It has been estimated that, by the end of the Caliph's reign, there were 3,750 there. Quite a number of the court servants were eunuchs, a need driven by the requirement for servants and functionaries to pass easily through the private quarters where the Caliph's concubines were situated. As time progressed, the status of the slaves improved. Some were manumitted or freed. Many former slaves rose to the highest military and administrative positions, with great wealth, large houses and in turn, their own slaves.

The elevated position of Caliph that Abd al-Rahman III now occupied and the magnificent palace just constructed went hand in hand with the development of a grand court protocol. The Umayyad dynasty in Iberia had, over the years, established complicated court protocol, usually with an eye to that devel-

Above. The Valdepuentes Aqueduct near Madinat al-Zahra. The Romans originally constructed a water network from the Sierra de Córdoba to supply the city. This system was reconstructed and diverted to serve Madinat al-Zahra, where there was a supply of potable water throughout the palace-city.

Right. Patio de los Naranjos of the Great Mosque of Córdoba. This, and a 47.5 metre-high minaret, was constructed by Abd al-Rahman III. In 1593 a second storey was added to the minaret to accomodate a bell tower whose outer walls conceal the original structure.

oped by the old enemy, the Abbasid court in Baghdad. However, with his new stage set at Madinat al-Zahra (and on occasion at the Alcázar in Córdoba) the Caliph was now able to hold sumptuous receptions on important occasions, at a level reflecting his caliphal status. There were formal receptions for foreign embassies and great affairs of state as well as important festivals of the Muslim calendar. There were also smaller events of a more intimate nature for his circle, for high officials, generals and for scientific and literary luminaries. These were more relaxed: they also had musicians, dancers and others to entertain the attendance. However, the ordinary subjects had no easy access to the ruler. He surrounded himself with favourites and, increasingly, with the slaves, who ran the royal household. This distance between the ruler and the ruled of al-Andalus is likely to have contributed to the later disintegration of the Caliphate.

By now al-Andalus had grown into one of the important states of the Mediterranean world: it had come of age. Indeed Córdoba, in wealth and power, was approaching the great eastern cities of Constantinople and Baghdad. The city had grown. As well as many mosques, it had markets and shops. There were hundreds of public baths as well as libraries and gardens. The upper levels of society lived a life of opulence. There was a large industry producing beautiful books, richly decorated textiles, intricately carved ivory and wood, precious jewellery and metal wares, glazed ceramics and furniture to cater for the needs of the rich. There was public order and the city was well-administered. The streets were paved and lit. By comparison, the cities of Christian Europe to the north were poor, small, unhygienic and unsophisticated.

In the Islamic society of the time great importance was attached to learning and knowledge and this was manifest throughout the history of al-Andalus. The level of education on offer was sophisticated, where students spent lengthy periods under the tutelage of scholars. Many travelled to gain further knowledge to study with learned men in the east and North Africa. The rulers were well educated and were patrons of literature and science. Many were poets. The whole environment was one of encouragement of learning and knowledge, with a rich cultural and intellectual tradition. In the time of the Córdoba Caliphate, coinciding with the rise in economic prosperity, there was a corresponding surge in culture and science. Poets, scholars and scientists flocked to the court of Madinat al-Zahra. A multitude of poets wrote poetry, with learned men producing other works such as books on grammar, history, geography and genealogy. In science, al-Andalus was particularly advanced in the fields of mathematics, which of course assisted the development of astronomy. One Maslama, a native of Madrid (then a small town) came to live in Córdoba and came to the fore in the later years of the Caliphate. As well as a producing a book on mathematics, he became the leading proponent of astronomy. He translated Greek astronomical tables and developed advanced techniques on the construction of astrolabes. In other scientific areas there were works on zoology and mineralogy. We have already encountered one of the leading medical experts of Córdoba, the distinguished Jewish physician Ibn Shaprut. Medicine was highly developed in the Caliphate. Books were produced on obstetrics as well as one on surgical techniques and tools. A medical encyclopaedia was produced which was later translated into Latin and was important in the development of medieval medicine in Europe. A book written in the first century by the Greek physician Dioscorides, *De Materia Medica*, was given as a gift to Abd al-Rahman III by the Byzantine Emperor. This, a treatise on the medicinal qualities of plants, was translated into Arabic and updated, becoming a fundamental pharmaceutical text. In art, architecture, literature, science, medicine and technology, al-Andalus had clearly reached new levels of brilliance. Such was the aura projected by the city that a tenth-century Saxon writer, in the course of a critical poem denouncing the martyrdom of a Christian there, nevertheless described Córdoba as 'the ornament of the world'.

Marking this new prestige, rulers in other states sent embassies to the Cordoban court. There was the visit, as we have seen, by Sancho *'el Gordo'* and his grandmother. Other Christian rulers from the north of Iberia also visited. The splendour of Madinat al-Zahra must have been highly impressive to these visitors from their simple castles and domains. The distribution of lavish gifts to the visiting ruler and his entourage must have impressed also. The minnows also

Right. Bronze deer from Madinat al-Zahra. Archivo Fotográfico, Museo Arqueológico Nacional, Madrid.

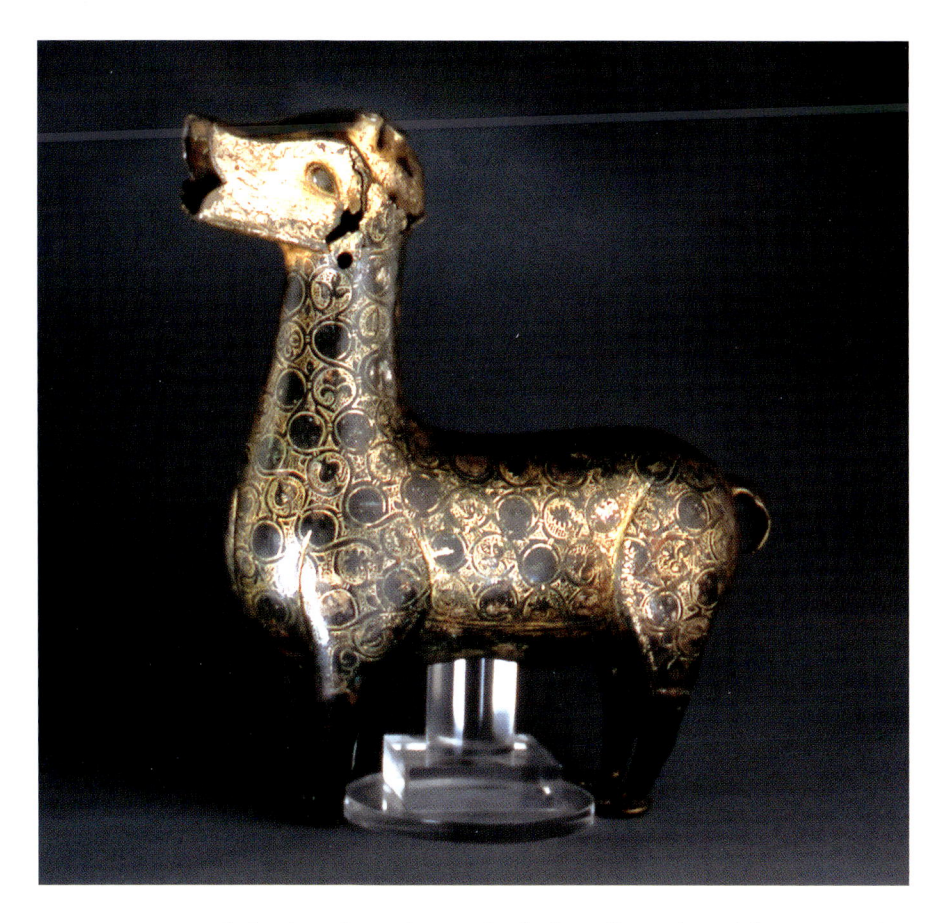

came; various tribal rulers, from the Maghreb, friendly to al-Andalus, were welcomed. Ambassadors were sent from the large Christian states of Western Europe. One ambassador went there to remonstrate about the conduct of a notorious band of Muslim pirates, of Andalusi Muwallad extraction, that had been ravaging the Mediterranean coast. Pirates, Christian or Muslim, were a constant danger to shipping and coastal communities in those times but this particular group was singularly daring. During the 890's they seized the area of Fraxinctum (near present day St. Tropez) and proceeded to lay waste all around. During the early tenth century they extended their sphere of operations, attacking Italy and went on to harass pilgrims proceeding to Rome. It took the local rulers a surprising amount of time to respond to this menace. The Saxon King, Otto I, had come to the conclusion that Abd al-Rahman III was to some extent behind this. He sent an Abbot, John of Gorze, to Córdoba around 950, with a letter that spelt out this in a blunt manner. The Caliph, on establishing the contents of the letter, refused to receive it. While John of Gorze was put up in a palace in Cordoba, an envoy (the Mozarab bishop Rabi bin Zayad) was sent in 955 to the Saxon court. Rabi returned to Córdoba a year later, accompanied by another emissary of Otto I, bringing a new friendlier message. The Caliph now deigned to receive John of Gorze in Madinat al-Zahra with full honours. As it happened, the pirates of Fraxinctum were only finally expelled in 972.

A very significant connection was established between al-Andalus and Byzantium. We have already seen that inconclusive contact had been made in 848 during the reign of Abd al-Rahman II. Most contacts made with al-Andalus by foreign rulers meant that these rulers wanted something and this was no exception. The Byzantines had long wanted to recapture Crete, which as we have seen, had been seized in the early ninth century by Cordobans who had been expelled from al-Andalus. As there were cultural and trade relations between Córdoba and the Cretan Muslims, the Byzantines estimated that Córdoba might be able to exercise some influence in their favour. It transpired in the end that the Byzantines recaptured the island in 961, the year of Abd al-Rahman III's death. In turn, Abd al-Rahman was interested in Byzantium: with its Greek inheritance, it was a fount of civilisation and a leader in the art, architecture, science and philosophy of the time. Contact with the Byzantines offered a chance to diversify from influence of the Abbasid culture in Baghdad. There were several exchanges between the rulers. One was around 947 when ambassadors arrived bearing gifts for the Caliph. Another ambassador from Byzantium, some two years later, came, as we have seen, with the gift of the precious Greek manuscript by Dioscorides. There was a request to Constantinople for help in establishing a group of Greek translators for al-Andalus. The Caliph attributed high importance to relations with Byzantium and the highest ceremonial welcome was proffered to another ambassador some months afterwards, from the time he landed in Pechina all the way to a lavish reception at Madinat al-Zahra. We have seen how a diplomatic visit in 949 to Byzantium by the peripatetic Rabi bin Zayad was used to procure fine pieces for Madinat al-Zahra. The Byzantine influence was also taken to a further level later on, during the extension to the Great Mosque in Córdoba, executed under al-Hakam II, when magnificent polychromatic mosaics were used, using materials and craftsmen sent from Byzantium.

History tells that the Caliph had eleven sons. As befits their status, they did not want for any material thing. As they reached adulthood, each was given as a residence, a minor palace, as well as lands and large incomes. The first born, al-Hakam, was nominated heir early on. He did not succeed to the throne until middle age. His father had a long time to groom him for succession, arranging a good education and assigning him posts of responsibility in the administration. Another son, Abd Allah, was not so fortunate. He was accused of being linked with a conspiracy against his father. Despite the fact that his own father had been similarly killed by his grandfather, the Amir, Abd al-Rahman III likewise gave orders for his son to be executed and had his throat cut in his presence. In the cold light of the Iberian Umayyad world, what mattered was security of the throne, not filial ties.

Abd al-Rahman III died in October 961. What were his lifetime achievements? They were many. He had inherited a State that was barely functioning. There was in-fighting and insurrection all around, the most dangerous threat being that of Ibn Hafsun, close to Córdoba and the heartland of al-Andalus. The State was barely managing to collect taxes and was in dire circumstances.

Right. Caliph al-Hakam II. Accounts tell of a protruding lower jaw but this statue in Córdoba depicts a more handsome figure. He was middle-aged when he succeeded to the throne in 961. He presided over the third extension to the Great Mosque, an exquisite example of the architecture of the Córdoba Caliphate. A man of great culture, he is reputed to have possessed a library of 400,000 books.

This highly competent ruler, in his deliberate and methodical way, managed to change all this. Forty-nine years later, on his death, al-Andalus had been transformed into one of the most advanced states of the medieval world - prosperous and a beacon for the Muslim world, equalling, if not excelling, the Islamic states to the east. Al-Andalus put the lumpen Christian states in northern Europe to shame. The Caliph's territory was now pacified; the troublesome Christian statelets on his northern frontiers were under a form of tutelage, at least for the time being. However, he did not capture any significant Christian lands; he was satisfied with the booty from raids. He set up a highly organised, cultured state, albeit governed by a ruler, who was remote from his subjects, solely dependent on his will. Abd al-Rahman III created the magnificent palace-city at Madinat al-Zahra to match his elevation to the exalted title of Caliph, which position, he hoped, was in tune with the destiny and glory of his Umayyad ancestors.

Al-Hakam II was into middle age, at forty-six years old, when he assumed the reins of power on his father's death. He was well prepared: his father had

Left. The Mihrab, which forms part of al-Hakam II's extension to the Great Mosque in Córdoba.

Below. In the Great Mosque, plaque with inscription, dating from the time of al-Hakam II's extension.

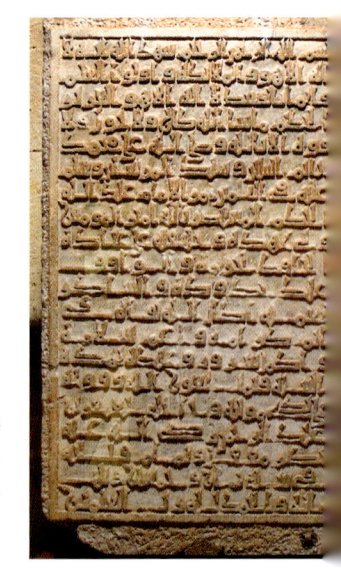

named him heir quite early on; he had had a good education; he had participated in affairs of state and had been consulted on key decisions. As we have seen, he had directed the construction of the palace-city complex of Madinat al-Zahra. Chroniclers tell that, while he had the fair hair that the Iberian Umayyads inherited from their European maternal lineage, he was stocky (like his father) and possessed a protruding lower jaw. He was pious, interested in literature, the arts and architecture but was not of robust health. He inherited an al-Andalus that was at peace, vastly rich, well organised and recognised around the medieval world as a major power. Despite being in the shadow of his illustrious father, he was to bring the Caliphate to a new level of achievement and sophistication, a time of great learning and development. His lasting legacy is the outstanding and exquisite extension that he made to the Córdoba Great Mosque.

How were relations with the Christian north during the reign of the new Caliph? Abd al-Rahman III had subdued the Christians, establishing the dominance of Córdoba. He had even helped the King of León, Sancho I, to regain his throne. Part of the agreement was that the Leonese would hand over ten frontier fortresses to the Muslims in return for this aid. Once installed in power, and perceiving that the new Caliph had a pacific nature, Sancho declined to keep his

Right. The Maqsura of the Great Mosque is the area outside the Mihrab, reserved for the Caliph. This was constructed using multi-lobular arches, a technique borrowed from the Abbasids in the east.

side of the bargain. In addition, the Castilian Count Fernán Gonzaléz had reverted to his old ways of harassing the Muslim frontier. However, the visit of Sancho's rival, the deposed Ordoño IV, to Córdoba, caused momentary panic in Sancho. He in turn sent an emissary to Córdoba, promising to abide by the accord. When Ordoño appeared to have disappeared from the stage, the fickle Sancho regained his courage and formed a coalition of the (Christian) willing, namely, the Count of Castile, King of Navarra and the Counts of Barcelona. And so, from the summer of 963, the familiar dance began once again. The Muslim armies, led by al-Hakam II, set out for the north and captured San Esteban de Gormaz (on the Duero), then marched on Atienza. The stronghold of Gormaz, further up the Duero from San Esteban, was strengthened, a key part of the frontier defences. The brave and effective General Ghalib (who we have seen on an earlier expedition to the Maghreb) took part in this campaign, seizing the stronghold of Calahorra. He was commander of the Middle March, with his base at Medinaceli and the Caliph relied on him to mount important military expeditions. The raid to the north demonstrated once again the might and superiority of the caliphal armies. Once again internal disputes broke out among the northern Christian statelets. This contributed to a period of peace and stability, from the Cordoban viewpoint, along the frontiers. Recognising Córdoba's predominance, the Christians (Kings, Counts and local lords) sent emissaries to the caliphal court declaring vassalage.

The news from North Africa was not so benign. As we have seen, at the time of Abd al-Rahman III's death, al-Andalus was involved in the politics of the Maghreb. It had a foothold in the two enclaves of Ceuta and Tangier. The

Left. A view of the Maqsura, looking out from the Mihrab. Great Mosque of Córdoba.

Fatimid enemy had previously seized most of the rest of the surrounding Maghreb. Fortunately for Córdoba, Fatimid attention now turned to the east. In 969 the Fatimids chose a location in Egypt called Fustat, where they immediately began to build a new capital, called *al-Qahira* (Cairo) or 'the triumphant'. As the Fatimid court moved to Cairo, control of the western Maghreb was assigned to a Sanhaja Berber chief, Ziri bin Manad. In 971 the Sanhaja attacked their deadly rivals, the Zanata tribe (vassals of Córdoba) and badly defeated them. However, in a later encounter that year, the Sanhaja were defeated and Ziri was killed. His head was sent as a victory trophy to the Caliph in Córdoba. Ziri's son Buluggin entered the fray and ranged through the western Maghreb, capturing territory and pushing back the Zanata. However, Buluggin was ordered back to the east by his Fatimid masters. The turmoil continued. The people of Tangier, discontented by high taxes, ejected the Umayyad garrison. The Idrisids, having switched sides, were now enemies of Córdoba and occupied the north-west of Morocco. Al-Hakam II sent army reinforcements to Ceuta and a squadron of the fleet to the North African coast. In 972 the fleet retook Tangier. The battle against the Idrisids proved to be difficult. In 973 the Caliph called the best of his generals, Ghalib, from Medinaceli and sent him to the Maghreb. Ghalib succeeded in pushing back the Idrisids, taking their mountain fortress after a siege. The Idrisid lord capitulated in March 974 and he and Ghalib appeared together at Friday prayer in the grand mosque of the Idrisid stronghold, where the sermon was announced in the name of al-Hakam II. The Idrisid leaders went to Córdoba where they paid homage to the Caliph. Command in the Maghreb was passed onto one of the Tuchibis of Zaragoza, who had brought reinforcements from Zaragoza for the campaign. Ghalib was

Above. A vertical view of the exquisite dome of the Mihrab. In the form of a scallop shell, this was carved out of a block of white marble. The shell symbolises the word of the Koran.

awarded the highest military accolade of 'holder of the two swords'. However, his services were soon required again. The conflict with the Christians on the northern frontier had restarted.

In 974 the newly succeeded Count of Castile, Garci Fernández, taking advantage of the absence of Ghalib and the Caliph's forces, engaged in the Maghreb. He attacked the fortress of Deza, about fifty kilometres north-west of Medinaceli. The Castilians then formed a coalition with the Leonese and the Navarese. A large Christian force then set out to lay siege to the strategic fortress of Gormaz. Ghalib was sent to Medinaceli and immediately set out to break the siege, aided by troops from Zaragoza and Lérida. Having taken some nearby Christian strongholds, the Muslim armies arrived at besieged Gormaz and put the Christians to flight. Ghalib continued on to raid through the lands of Castile, while the Zaragozan troops pursued the fleeing Basques. Once again peace broke out in the north for a short period. It was the calm before the storm that was to be Almanzor.

Al-Hakam II was a man of culture, a patron of the arts and literature. It is said that he built up a great library in Córdoba with over 400,000 volumes, gathering many of these from the Islamic east. The city also provided a welcome

Left. Corner detail. The inscriptions around the enclosure include the names of the craftsmen who decorated the Mihrab. Great Mosque of Córdoba.

haven for learned exponents of science and medicine. However, it is for architecture that al-Hakam II is principally remembered - for his magnificent extension to the Great Mosque in Córdoba. As we have seen, he had relevant experience, having directed the construction of the palace-city at Madina al-Zahra. Mindful of the growth in population of the city and the lack of space for the faithful, on taking power, he immediately set about extending the Mosque. The southern wall was demolished and a new wall was built as near to the banks of the Guadalquivir as possible, allowing twelve aisles to be added. The *mihrab* (niche indicating the direction of Mecca) that was built is exquisitely decorated. A screen forming a *maqsura* (a sanctuary reserved for the Caliph) was built in front of the *mihrab*. This was framed by a series of multi-lobal arches of great delicacy. These, in turn, supported three ribbed vaults. The architecture of early Islam had drawn from other influences including those of Byzantium. Now, again in al-Andalus, it drew on the same source. Using the links with the Byzantine Emperor, re-established by his father, al-Hakam II acquired from the Emperor fifteen tonnes of materials, including glass mosaic cubes for his new construction. A mosaicist was also despatched who instructed local craftsmen in the art of Byzantine mosaics. The results can be seen today in the sumptuous and glittering gold mosaic decoration of the *mihrab* arch and the cupolas above. The Caliph's devotion to extending the Mosque reflected his deep piety. This aspect of his character may have been spurred on by the state of his health which was not good. He suffered a stroke in 974 and had to devolve more of the state business to his Vizier, Ja'far bin Uthman al-Mushafi. Al-Mushafi was the son of al-Hakam's tutor and proved to be a competent administrator, prudent with the state budget. He became the Caliph's trusted confidant.

Above. The main cupola soars over al-Hakam II's Maqsura. With gold predominating, the multi-coloured mosaics crown this airy and luminous space.

On ascending the throne, the new Caliph, al-Hakam II, had a problem, a major one in the context of the Umayyad succession: he had no children. Thus, there was joy when a Basque concubine called Subh presented the Caliph with a son; however the child died a few years afterwards. Subh subsequently gave birth to a new son in 965, the future Hisham II. Care was lavished on the young heir that, in turn, as we shall see, left the way open for a malign presence in the palace, which came to the fore after the death of al-Hakam II. This presence was that of one Muhammad bin Abi Amir (later to be known as Almanzor). He had been born in 940 to a good family of the Arab aristocracy, with lands on the Rio Guadiaro near Algeciras. The family had a learned and pious reputation and was descended from an Arab warrior who accompanied Tariq bin Ziyad, during the invasion of 711. The young Ibn Abi Amir set out for Córdoba where he

97

studied law under eminent tutors. In due course, the bright and ambitious young man secured a position in the Cordoban administration. Being talented and personable, he came to the notice of the Vizier, al-Mushafi. It so happened that, some time later, the mother of the new heir to the throne, Subh, made a request for an able and educated assistant, to help manage her estate and finances. Ibn Abi Amir was assigned by al-Mushafi and this proved to be his great opportunity, being the first step in his rise to power. This young official had the capacity to switch on an immense charm and thus capitalised on his new position: he bought presents for the ladies of the harem and flattered them. There is a certain reserve in Arab historians' accounts of the time. There are hints that he was the lover of Subh, perhaps during al-Hakam II's reign but it is suggested that it was most likely after the Caliph's death. With his eye for the main chance, underpinned by his efficiency and competence, Ibn Abi Amir rose higher in the ranks and gradually gathered appointments to various positions. He took it upon himself to ingratiate himself with the important people of the

Above. Detail to the side of the Mihrab in the Córdoba Mosque. The shimmering mosaics used in al-Hakam II's extension were crafted using around fifteen tonnes of brightly coloured mosaic cubes sent from Byzantium.

Right. Pyxis (casket) carved in ivory. The Córdoba Caliphate represented the apogee of al-Andalus. Luxury products were produced to cater for the needs of the ruling circle. This was made for the prefect of police in Córdoba during the reign of Caliph al-Hakam II. Victoria and Albert Museum, London.

court and leaders of Cordoban society. In time, he was assigned an important post of supervision of funds of an expeditionary army being dispatched to Morocco to fight the Idrisids, which was to afford him important contacts for the future. Ibn Abi Amir carried out his assignment well, flattered the military and established good relations with them, including General Ghalib who commanded the expedition. Back in Córdoba, he was appointed in mid 976 as Inspector General of the mercenary troops based in the city.

A few months later, in October, 976, al-Hakam II died. Two senior court officials (both slaves) attended the death. Mindful of maintaining their privileges, they made an attempt to have a younger brother of al-Hakam, al-Mughira, appointed to the throne, instead of succession by the Caliph's eleven-year old son, Hisham. Ibn Abi Amir joined with al-Mushafi to deny this usurpation and maintain the succession of the Caliph's son. This outcome became a certainty when Ibn Abi Amir's troops surrounded al-Mughira's residence. Ibn Abi Amir initially believed the terrified prince's denial of interest in the succession but al-Mushafi insisted and the unfortunate prince was strangled. The following day, the young heir Hisham II was formally enthroned in Cordoba, as the third Caliph. With al-Mushafi presiding, Ibn Abi Amir read out the act of investiture. The high dignitaries of the State attended, with no one daring to mention the assassination of al-Mughira.

And so, the direction of the State moved forward under al-Mushafi as Prime Minister and Ibn Abi Amir as Vizier. Of the two slave usurpers, one was executed and the other was banished to the Balearic Islands. Gradually the power of the palace slaves who held high positions was reduced under the new duumvirate. This was warmly received by the Cordobans who felt the slaves had become arrogant arrivistes. Soon a challenge came from the north: the Christians, seeking to capitalise on the advent of the child Caliph, began raiding the Muslim frontier in the area between the Tagus and the Duero. A hastily convened council of war in Córdoba offered expeditionary command to Ibn Abi Amir, who accepted. He chose the best soldiers and, fully equipped with arms and provisions, he led them to the north in 977. The expedition duly besieged a Christian castle, took it and arrived back in Córdoba some time later with the requisite prisoners and booty. This success increased his prestige and popularity, not only with the soldiers but also with the Cordoban citizenry.

Can Ibn Abi Amir be compared to Machiavelli or Stalin? Perhaps he shared some characteristics. Machiavelli admired resolution and cunning, qualities the aspiring new leader had in abundance. During his rise to power, nearly a millennium later, Stalin proceeded to eliminate those who had allied with him. A similar experience occurred in Córdoba. Al-Mushafi, the Prime Minister and ally,

Above. Baños de la Encina, one of the best-preserved of the castles of al-Andalus. With a panoramic view over the surrounding countryside, it has fifteen square towers. Constructed in 968, this was a fortification on the route from Córdoba to the Meseta Central and onwards to Toledo.

Right. Interior view of the castle at Baños de la Encina.

Below. A memorial tablet at the entrance to the castle of Baños de la Encina. It commences with: 'In the name of Merciful God, the Forgiving, al-Hakam II... ordered that this tower be built...'

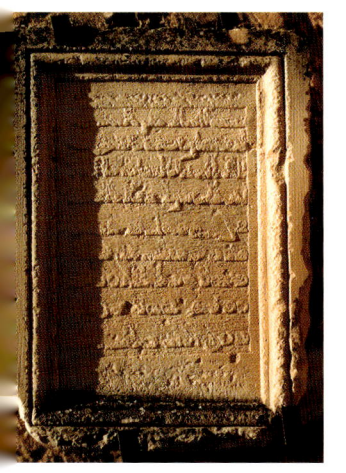

now became an obstacle. He fell into the sights of Ibn Abi Amir who now proceeded to establish his ground. He consolidated his close relations with the strong man of al-Andalus, General Ghalib. A low-level campaign was started against al-Mushafi, which suggested nepotism, highlighting that his sons had been appointed to many high positions. In a further step, Ibn Abi Amir took over the title of Prefect of Córdoba, deposing al-Mushafi's son from the post. The situation then took on an element of farce. Al-Mushafi, feeling threatened and desperate for the protection of Ghalib, requested the hand in marriage of Ghalib's daughter Asma for one of his sons. Ibn Abi Amir quickly intervened and, in 978, he himself married the fair Asma, with great ceremony. The ill-fated al-Mushafi was deposed some months later and, together with his sons, was imprisoned on charges of financial irregularity. He died five years later in prison.

We now pass to the next phase in the inexorable rise of Ibn Abi Amir. Over the years, as the young Caliph moved towards his majority, Ibn Abi Amir ensured that he stayed within the confines of the Alcázar, remote from the reality of state business. He ensured that he was plied with luxury and had no serious matters to deal with. This was initially supported by the princess-mother Subh, but eventually she saw Ibn Abi Amir's true motives and in time she began to harbour an implacable enmity towards him. A defining moment came in 979 when Ibn Abi Amir ordered the construction of a new palace-headquarters. These were located upriver on the banks of the Guadalquivir on the outskirts of Córdoba. Completed in two years, he named this *al-Madina al-Zahira* 'the city of brilliance'. Not to be confused with Abd al-Rahman III's '*Madinat al-Zahra*', it had similar features: there was a magnificent palace as well as spacious quarters for the administration of the State. It was well fortified, had a guard and stores

Left. Carved ivory plaque inlaid with quartz and pigment, dating from the reign of al-Hakam II. Metropolitan Museum of Art, New York.

of arms and provisions. The seat of power has its own magnetism and soon people started to live close by; the population grew and a market was established.

Ibn Abi Amir's move to al-Madina al-Zahira finally made clear the reality: he was in absolute charge of al-Andalus. From now on Ibn Abi Amir did not bother to consult the young Caliph on matters of state. However, he never made claim to the title of Caliph. This master strategist and manipulator realised that he would not have had the credibility to openly usurp the Umayyad credentials. Instead, he concentrated on maintaining his control and left the nominal Caliph in place. All state administration was moved out of the Alcázar to al-Madina al-Zahira. Ibn Abi Amir did not neglect to station troops to 'guard' the young occupant of the Alcázar. Entry to the palace was only by special permission and close note was taken of those who entered or left the palace. Within this gilded cage, Caliph Hisham II lived a life of mindless indulgence.

While the Cordoban citizenry most likely knew what was really going on, they did not dare or even feel inclined to object. The State was well administered, it was richer than ever and there was internal peace. In addition to a generally contented citizenry, Ibn Abi Amir knew how to maintain support from other elements of Cordoban life: he exuded piety to curry favour with the *alfaquis*. In accordance with their absolutist interpretation of Islam, he organised the culling of al-Hakam II's magnificent library of any books not in line with orthodox thought. As we shall see, he also maintained continuous raids against the Christian enemy to the north.

However, there was one grandee of the State, who was affronted by the de-facto usurpation of the Caliphate. This was the veteran General Ghalib, by now in his eighties. Even though he was a father-in-law of Ibn Abi Amir, this honourable man was loyal to the Umayyad Caliphate. Ibn Abi Amir, however, was mindful of this disaffection. As it happened, he had greatly increased the numbers of Berber tribesmen recruited from North Africa in the army, and these-formed a force loyal to himself. Matters came to a head in 981, the same year as the move to al-Madina al-Zahira. There appears to have been an altercation between Ghalib and his powerful son-in-law. Ghalib fled to Castile and asked for help from the Count of Castile. Ibn Abi Amir gathered his army, made up of Berbers, garrison troops from Córdoba and contingents from the Tuchibis of

Right. Carved ivory box. This was commissioned in 964 by al-Hakam II for Subh, his favourite wife. Victoria and Albert Museum, London.

Zaragoza and set out northwards to stamp out this threat. In July 981 they met Ghalib, leading his own loyal troops, plus Castilian and Basque forces, in front of the Castle of San Vicente, near Atienza. In this, his last battle, Ghalib fought bravely, but was thrown from his horse and killed. The Christian forces were routed and the Cordoban army went on to sack Castile. Thus, later in 981, in line with his new pre-eminence, with no rival in sight, as well as being installed in his splendid new palace, Ibn Abi Amir decided to award himself a grander title than a mere *Hachib*. This was the honorific *Al-Mansur bi-Allah* or 'made victorious for God' – popularly known as Almanzor.

Regrettably, there is no trace of al-Madina al-Zahira to be found today. It lasted a mere thirty years and was razed, as we shall see, early in the civil war at the beginning of the eleventh century. Notable public works carried out under Almanzor included revamping the great bridge of Córdoba and we still have today the very tangible evidence of his large extension to the Great Mosque at Córdoba, which was commenced in 987. Reflecting once again the need for more space for the faithful, the expansion of the Great Mosque also pandered to his constituency among the *alfaquis* and was one more public manifestation of his piety. Al-Hakam II had extended the Mosque to the south up to the boundary formed by the Guadalquivir, so this extension had to be on the eastern side. Eight new naves were added. While this was an efficient creator of the desired large new area, there was no particular architectural innovation: double tiered arches were once again utilised but, this time, the multicoloured effect on the arches was achieved by painting the stone red. In summary, Almanzor's extension is what could be called a reproduction in great quantity of that previously constructed, but lacking the sublime inspiration of al-Hakam II's southern extension, twenty years before.

By the time Almanzor had taken power, the interests of al-Andalus in North Africa were represented by its well-fortified enclave in Ceuta and its local clients in the western Maghreb. The Fatimids had moved to their new capital of Cairo, while their pro-consul still ruled on their behalf in Ifriqiya. The main threat to

Left. Resolute, strong, calculating, Ibn Abi Amir (Almanzor) climbed the ranks, accumulating power. He intrigued to become the de facto ruler of the Córdoba Caliphate after the death of al-Hakam II. The young Caliph was confined to the Alcázar, surrounded by mindless luxury. Statue at Calatañazor.

the Umayyad zone of influence in the Maghreb was now from the local tribes, sometimes allying themselves with Córdoba, sometimes moving into opposition and fighting with their neighbours. During his reign, Almanzor had to send several military expeditions to deal with the challenges that arose, either from Ifriqiya or from the agglomeration of leaders and tribes in the region. However, despite these fluctuations, by the end of his reign, Almanzor, either directly or indirectly, kept the western Maghreb under Córdoba's control. These vassals, the local tribal leaders, were well received with suitably impressive ceremonies on the occasions they visited Córdoba. Almanzor was very interested in North Africa as a source of military manpower and over the course of his reign, as we have seen, readily recruited Berber tribesmen from there into his army. Large numbers of Berbers (allies, or very frequently, former enemies), in cohesive tribal units, were inducted into the armies of al-Andalus. This policy led partly to the disintegration of the Caliphate some decades later. The battlefields of North Africa have always presented military experience and career opportunities for the sons of Iberia, even up to the early twentieth century We saw how Almanzor established his credentials with the military during an earlier expedition there. Almanzor's son Abd al-Malik (later to rule as al-Muzaffar) also led forces there. He captured Fez and served as Governor there for a time.

A prosperous land with its interior generally at peace, a reorganised army, reinforced by troops from the Maghreb and a strong and ruthless ruler: these were the ingredients that were to spell trouble for the Christian states on the frontiers of al-Andalus. Over the last twenty years of the eleventh century, Almanzor instigated around fifty offensives against the lands and peoples of

Right. The extension by Almanzor to the east increased the size of the Mosque by around forty percent. Unlike the earlier arches with brick insets, the multi-coloured effect is achieved by painting the arches in red.

105

Left. The eastern wall of the Great Mosque of Córdoba. The fourth extension was begun by Almanzor in 987.

León, Castile, Navarra and the Spanish March. Unlike the previous pattern of an occasional summer offensive, now several onslaughts were mounted regularly every year. Farms were ransacked, harvests burnt, cities pillaged and monasteries and churches destroyed. There was a continuous flow of booty and captives to Córdoba. Indeed, there were so many Christian slaves available that their market price fell sharply.

It is not entirely clear why Almanzor (nor, in similar circumstances, Abd al-Rahman III, for that matter), with his overwhelming force, did not attempt to finally end the danger and nuisance of the Christian statelets to the north of the Peninsula. Was it an ingrained habit of making raids, with rewards of easy and immediate booty, as opposed to the inconvenience of colonisation of conquered lands? Was it simply that some of the lands in question included mountainous, damp territory, which was not attractive to the prevailing culture and psyche? Nevertheless, with the exception of an attempt to repopulate Zamora, the victorious armies never occupied these lands for the long term and always returned to base.

A notable raid was the great expedition made against Barcelona in 985. A large force, supported by an Andalusi naval squadron, laid siege to that city, which was taken, sacked and burnt. The sack of Santiago de Compostela was the most notorious of Almanzor's raids and one that resounds through history. He set out in July 987 with a strong army and made for Porto on the Atlantic. There

Right. In Almanzor's extension to the Great Mosque simpler capitals were employed, using a stylised acanthus leaf form.

he received provisions, which were transported by a naval squadron. Almanzor was also joined by several Christian lords who had sworn vassalage and, obviously, were not averse to the benefits of rapine and booty, from whatever source. The army headed north, travelling along the Gallician coast, reaching parts where Islamic forces had never reached before.

Santiago de Compostela, where the remains of Saint James the Apostle were buried after reputedly having been miraculously found, had developed into one of the main places of pilgrimage of Christian Europe. In August 987, Almanzor arrived at the city, sacked and burnt it. The main basilica was destroyed. However, not the tomb of the saint, which was spared, according to one account, by order of Almanzor. And so, the Muslim army went home and the Christian lords went their separate ways, with their share of booty, as well as gifts from Almanzor. Many captives were brought back to Córdoba. The bells of the basilica were carried off by the captives, to be used in the Córdoba Great Mosque. The doors of the city gates were also taken and were used in constructing the roof of Almanzor's extension of the Mosque.

Events did not go smoothly when Almanzor set out on another raid in 1000. The Christians had formed a coalition. A large Christian force, led by the Castilians, met Almanzor at Cervera (near Clunia). It was a hard battle, and the Cordoban forces won, but at great cost, with major loss of life. In the summer of 1002, another raid was mounted by Almanzor against the Rioja region. After the usual sack and pillage, the army returned to the south. On the way back, Almanzor, now in his sixties, fell gravely ill. He had to be placed on a litter and was brought to the frontier fortress of Medinaceli. A few days later, in August 1002, he died and was buried in that city. There had been a legend that Almanzor suffered a defeat at Calatañazor and the shock and remorse caused him to expire, but this does not seem to be borne out by the facts.

As Almanzor lay dying, he gave advice to his son and heir, Abd al-Malik, which can be summarised as to be careful and to continue on the same path as his father. And, in effect, that is what Abd al-Malik did. He did not make any radical changes to the arrangements and manner of governing of his father. Abd al-Malik, on return to Córdoba, went to see Caliph Hisham II. A decree of investiture of the new successor was duly read out from the minaret of the Great Mosque. The smooth changeover of power reflected the Cordoban population's respect for and acceptance of the new leader, as well as the good rapport he had established with Hisham II. The Caliph was still the nominal ruler of al-Andalus and was still living within the gilded confines of the Alcázar and Madinat al-Zahra. Abd al-Malik offered him more respect than his father had and, later on, on ceremonial occasions, Hisham II was invited to al-Madina al-Zahira.

Above. Detail from an ivory casket from the early eleventh century, possibly from Córdoba or Cuenca. Its iconography is considered similar to that of a casket now in the Museo de Navarra in Pamplona, dating from 1005, which was made for a son of Almanzor. Victoria and Albert Museum, London.

Right. Aljibe (well) at the castle of Calatuyud. This was one of the important fortifications in the northern frontier lands.

The new ruler, although only twenty-seven years old, had had an impressive career up to this point; he had proven himself in leading military campaigns and had acted as Governor in North Africa. He was to have a short reign, only six years, cut short by his premature death. In what was to prove the calm before the storm, al-Andalus continued in its prosperity, good administration and peace. Perhaps characteristic of societies at their zenith, it was a period of ostentatious consumption, with the rich avidly pursuing jewellery, fine clothes, and luxury, in which pursuit Abd al-Malik participated, displaying a taste for high living. For all that, the young man did not neglect literature or good works. He was popular, not least for having reduced taxes for his subjects. However, he did not reign for long and, beneath the prosperous veneer of the State, there were many problems seething below the surface. These were to erupt into chaos in the years to come.

The relations with the Christians to the north continued as before, a shifting mass of alliances and reversals, with punitive expeditions sent out from Córdoba on a regular basis. Towards the end of his reign, after a victorious expedition to the north, and, having secured Caliph Hisham II's assent, Abd al-Malik took the honorific title of *al-Muzaffar*, 'the triumphant'. In October 1008 he set out once more on a raiding expedition, but he died of a mysterious chest illness within a day's ride of Córdoba. He was succeeded by his younger brother, Abd al-

Left. The former mosque, now the church of Cristo de la Luz in Toledo. This small building was constructed around 1000.

Rahman, who was quickly sworn in. He was known as Sanchuelo, as his mother was a granddaughter of a Navarese King, Sancho Garcés II. Only in his middle twenties, he was immature and, as events were to prove, totally unsuited for the reins of power. His advent was to result in a wild period of civil war and the rapid disintegration of the al-Andalus that had been painstakingly created by the Umayyads. At the start of his reign, in thrall to the Berber military influences that had grown, he made it a requirement that court functionaries wear a Berber-style turban. This did not endear him to the Arab aristocracy of Córdoba. Within months of accession, he made a fatal mistake: he induced Caliph Hisham II (who had no children) to sign a decree designating himself, Sanchuelo, to be his successor. This was a step too far that his father or brother had never dared take. It was highly unpopular among the citizens of Córdoba. The extensive Umayyad royal family was outraged at the usurpation of the dynasty and immediately started planning a coup. A young member of the Umayyad family, Muhammad bin Hisham, a great-grandson of Abd al-Rahman III and popular among the masses, was chosen to lead the conspirators.

The Christian kingdoms to the north were well informed of the events in Córdoba. As ever, they knew when their Muslim adversary was weak. Sancho García, Count of Castile, began attacking the frontiers of al-Andalus. Sanchuelo duly gathered an expeditionary force and set out for the north in January 1009. A few weeks later, when confirmation came that Sanchuelo and army were far away, the conspirators struck. The people of the market and the lower classes stormed the Alcázar and Muhammad bin Hisham set up headquarters there. The weak and ineffective Caliph Hisham II did not require much pressure to abdicate and invest, as Caliph, his Umayyad relation, who took the honorific title of *al-Mahdi*. The new Caliph let the mob release their pent-up tension. They headed for Almanzor's great palace of al-Madina al-Zahira where the garrison promptly surrendered. The mob proceeded to loot, pillaging the fittings and rich possessions. Al-Mahdi then gave orders for the demolition of what was by now a shell. The marble and column stonework and the elaborate timber carvings were all taken away, leaving simply a pile of rubble.

Sanchuelo heard the catastrophic news of the uprising and the loss of his palace when he was in Toledo. He set out immediately for the capital. However, the army was not impressed by Sanchuelo's character and began to desert in droves. By the time he was close to Córdoba, all the Berbers had deserted and gone over to the other side. Now, with scarcely more than a handful of his guard, he reached one of his summer palaces, about a day's ride from Córdoba. Sanchuelo obviously believed in military expeditions with full logistic support and he had with him on his campaign seventy women of his harem. He had to leave these in the care of a nearby Mozarab monastery. Sanchuelo's end was swift: a detachment of troops sent from Córdoba seized him; he was killed on the way back to the city and his body nailed up for public display. Thus, in one fell swoop, the Amirid power over al-Andalus was eliminated. However, as we will see, one last vestige survived in the Taifa of Valencia.

The new Caliph, al-Madhi, soon proved to be an incompetent and unpopular ruler. The provinces had not submitted to his rule and he antagonised the various factions of al-Andalus. The slave administrative class had once again risen to high levels. Reflecting his base among the Arab aristocracy and their dislike of the slaves, al-Mahdi sent important slave functionaries into exile. We shall see later that they gathered power in the Levante and became players in the turmoil. The Berber mercenary soldiers were also antagonised by the new Caliph. They were not allowed bear arms in Córdoba. A prominent Berber leader, the Sanhaja Zawi bin Ziri (of whom more later), was prevented from entering the Alcázar. In addition, the mob pillaged the quarters of some of the Berber troops. In mid-1009, incensed at this treatment, the Berbers sourced another Umayyad, Sulayman bin al-Hakam, as a figurehead. They formed a coalition against the current regime, also enlisting the support of the Castilian Count Sancho García. In November 1009 they captured Córdoba and Sulayman was pronounced

Caliph. There now followed over two decades a time of extreme instability and descent into chaos. The Caliphate became a revolving door. New claimants to this office, who reigned for short times, were supported variously by the Cordoban mob, the Berbers, the slaves, the Arab aristocracy. Some caliphs, like al-Mahdi, managed to achieve a second reign. Most ended up losing their lives. The Umayyad lineage still had cachet and most of the caliphs came from a seemingly inexhaustible supply of Abd al-Rahman III's descendants. In a new development, on several occasions Hammudids from North Africa, possessing the prestige of Idrisid ancestry, with a lineage traced back to the Prophet and supported by their tough Berber troops, seized power and appointed themselves caliphs. In the middle of this maelstrom, the assistance of the Christian states was requested on occasion, by one faction or the other. The Catalans were enticed into the fray on one occasion by being promised a large payment for their services. The Castilians were promised a string of frontier fortresses, including San Esteban de Gormaz, Osma and Gormaz in return for their aid. The Berbers besieged and pillaged Córdoba in the period 1010 to 1013, during which time they looted Madinat al-Zahra. The true Caliph, Hisham II, fades out of direct history around 1013, most likely assassinated (but there was to be a later sighting of an impostor). And so it went on, one caliph after another, mostly mediocre, each worse than the last. Finally in 1031 a group of the great and the good of the city decided to end the farce that the Caliphate had become. They induced a coup against the sitting Caliph, who promptly fled. Now the Caliphate was abolished and Córdoba was run by a committee comprised of these notables.

And thus, in scarcely more than twenty years, fell the great Caliphate of Córdoba. It had been one of the richest and most prosperous states of medieval Europe. It had been well administered, with many talented figures in senior positions in administration and in the military. It had reduced the Christian states to the north to the condition of being mere vassals. The Fatimid threat had receded in North Africa and al-Andalus had a strategic grip on that territory. It had grand cities, great scholars and artists, being probably amongst the most cultured places in Europe at that time.

So why did it fall? The immediate blame can be attributed to the fallibility of the incompetent Sanchuelo and the useless Hisham II. But the underlying causes were many; the resentment of the Arab aristocracy at losing its influence; the slaves who lost power and dispersed to the regions; the large number of Berbers inscribed in the army. All these centrifugal forces grew and the great Andalusi State flew apart and fragmented into a myriad of small states: the taifas.

Chapter 5
The Taifas

The Umayyads were directly descended from the original dynasty based in Damascus, a family that had been part of the Prophet's Quraysh tribe. This gave them the legitimacy to exercise central power, a legitimacy which was fully accepted by the citizens of al-Andalus in the days of the Caliphate. This concept of the Umayyad dynasty was the glue that had held the State together. A hereditary monarchy works when there is a succession of strong and capable heirs. This model faltered when the new Caliph Hisham II, a child, was overwhelmed by Almanzor. In the eyes of the populace of al-Andalus, Almanzor's usurpation of power was acceptable in that he maintained what was in effect a fiction, the legitimacy of the reigning Umayyad Caliph. The strong hand of power coupled with efficient administration and resulting general peace and prosperity, plus the Umayyad aura, kept al-Andalus under control. Almanzor's son Sanchuelo, politically maladroit, undid the concept of legitimacy when he tried to undermine the Umayyad dynasty and get the Caliph to name him as successor. This was one of the main triggers that unleashed the civil war.

When the great and the good of Córdoba decided, with justification, in 1031, to abolish the Caliphate, they were just confirming the reality that the Umayyad dynasty had collapsed. The glue evaporated and al-Andalus fell apart. By now the political landscape of al-Andalus had changed. Over thirty taifas (or 'party') states had been formed all across the State. Some were large, others were small and the smallest ones were scarcely more than a castle and its immediate surroundings. The taifas had been set up by notables from the locality (or in some cases by those who had been invited in) who were in a position of power and influence at the time. These stepped, with agility, into the vacuum caused by the rapid fall away of central power and control. They fell into three main categories: the Andalusis (those with established roots in al-Andalus) and two types of outsiders, the 'new' (recently arrived) Berbers and the Slaves. These then were the new rulers of al-Andalus until the Alomoravids emerged from the Maghreb to sweep the taifas away towards the end of the eleventh century.

The Andalusis came from those Muslim peoples established on the Peninsula since the time of the conquest. This was a diverse mix: the pre-eminent Arabs; the Berbers who arrived with the conquest and the Muwallads (the original inhabitants of the Peninsula who, increasingly over the years, had converted to Islam). The history of al-Andalus over the nearly 300 years of Umayyad rule

Above. The Puente Romano over the Guadalquivir at Córdoba. Originally constructed by the Romans (and still resting on Roman foundations), it was much rebuilt during the times of al-Andalus.

includes conflict among these groups but, by the time of the Caliphate and that of Almanzor, they had merged to some degree to form a more homogeneous group, referred to here as Andalusis. They may have maintained their diverse social structures but they could identify with the Caliphate and the land of al-Andalus, with its common Arab language, Islamic religion and culture.

We begin this part of our story with the taifas set up by the Andalusis and first look at Córdoba, the once illustrious centre of Umayyad al-Andalus. The decision to abolish the Caliphate was taken by local prominent citizens, part of the Arab aristocracy, most of whose ancestors had been early arrivals in Muslim Iberia. These now controlled the small territory that remained. During the around twenty years of the civil war Córdoba's power over the rest of al-Andalus had disintegrated and its glory days were gone forever. By 1031 its area of control extended only to the city and the surrounding region. It was now hemmed in by other taifas, principally the substantial ones of Seville to the west, Toledo to the north and Granada to the east.

The group that emerged to run what had become the Taifa of Córdoba was initially a triumvirate. Of these, Ibn Yahwar, whose ancestors were clients of the original Umayyad caliphs of Damascus, became pre-eminent. He faced a difficult task. During the civil war the great city had been besieged, brought to starvation, sacked, the treasury emptied and the citizenry brutalised. By all accounts, the city was fortunate in this new leader: Yahwar proved himself capable and soon brought order to the city. He set up a citizens' militia, thus reducing the need for reliance on the Berber troops. As a new-found peace emerged, he brought the economy into shape and normalised taxes. He had a reputation for modesty and piety: apparently, he refused to take on the trappings of power and lived in his own home, declining to live in the Alcázar. On the peninsular stage he also appears to have had a calming influence among the frequently squabbling taifas. He gave shelter to various other rulers displaced by the inter-taifa wars, as well as mediating in these and giving wise counsel. This exceptional man died

Right. Niebla, a taifa which was soon taken over by Seville. One of the gates of the city, set among the well-preserved urban defensive walls, which extend for around two kilometres.

in 1043 and was succeeded by an equally capable son who reigned for another twenty years. Yahwar's grandson, who became the new ruler in 1063, was of different character, being corrupt and tyrannical. However, Córdoba's days as an independent taifa were numbered. The large neighbouring taifas were looking at Córdoba with predatory eyes: Toledo launched a siege of the city. The Cordobans called for help from Seville, which duly obliged and then took over the city in 1070, exiling the ruler and his family. Toledo captured it in 1075 and it reverted to Seville around 1077.

The Taifa of Seville was ruled by Andalusis and turned out to be the most predatory of all the taifas, eventually ending up with a large swathe of territory ranging from the Atlantic coast of present-day southern Portugal, all across to

Left. The Puente Arabe in Ronda, a taifa formed by 'new' Berbers. Captured by the Taifa of Seville, Ronda was shaped during the taifa era, with the construction of important buildings and reinforcement of the city walls and defences.

the Mediterranean coast near Murcia. It was formed during the latter years of the civil war as the central power declined; a triumvirate of local Arab notables came forward to rule the city. From amongst these a strong man emerged, Muhammad bin Ismail bin Abbad, *qadi* of the city, who set himself up as sole leader. Among all the new taifa rulers there was a desire for legitimacy and this propelled Muhammad in 1036 to set up a pretender who claimed to be the true Umayyad Caliph Hisham II. He had disappeared in 1013, most likely murdered. This pretender maintained that he was indeed the real Hisham, having returned to al-Andalus after escaping from Córdoba and spending the intervening years in the east. The aura of the Umayyad dynasty still had currency in al-Andalus and Muhammad seized the opportunity. As an exercise in proving identity, he

Right. Seen seen through a gap in the city walls, the Puente Nuevo, which spans the Tajo de Ronda, through which runs the Guadalevín river. Much of the city walls date from the time of the Taifa of Ronda.

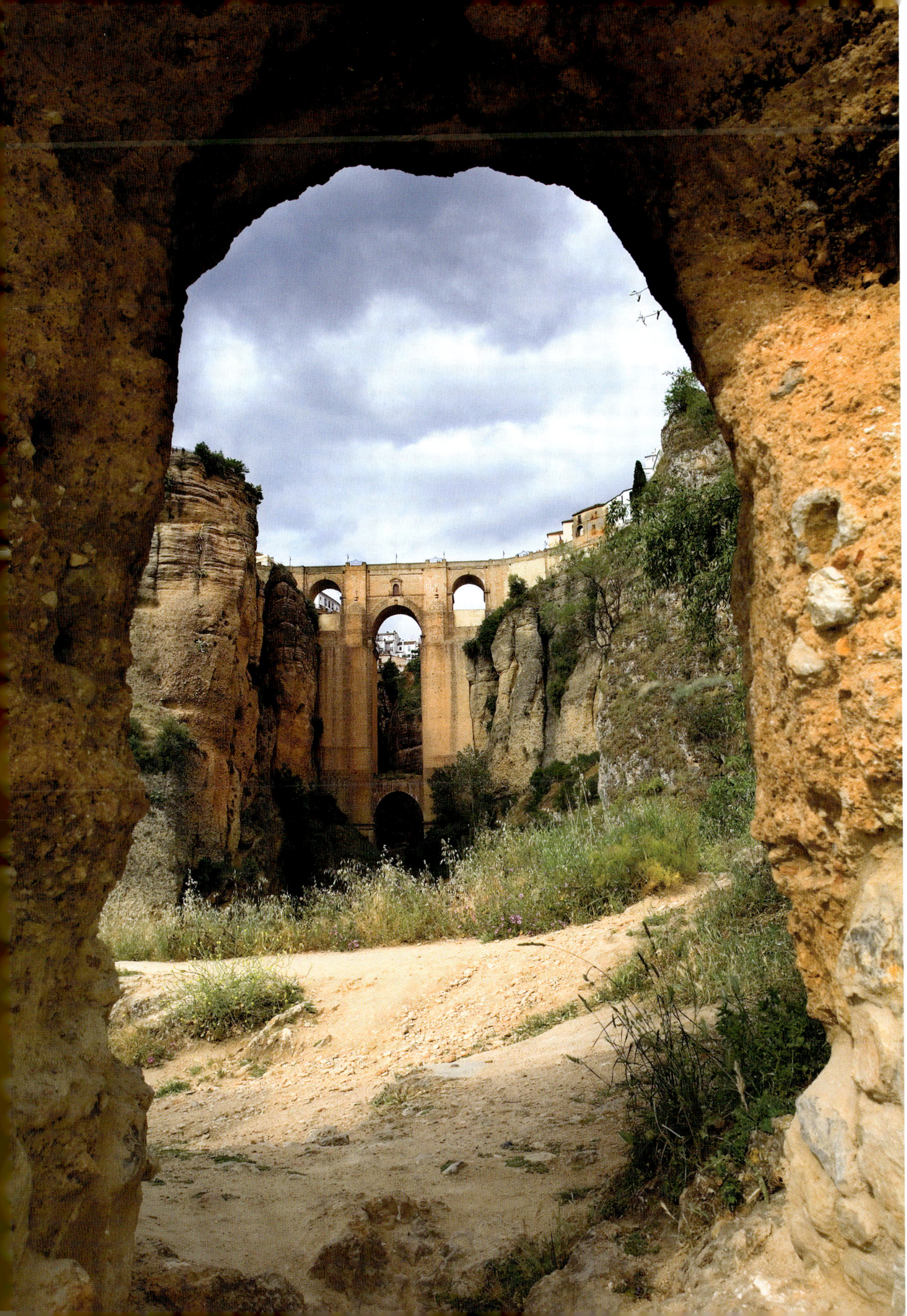

Left. The horseshoe arches of the Puerta de Sevilla in Carmona. The Taifa of Carmona was founded by 'new' Berbers, but was eventually consumed by Seville.

called the surviving women of the former harem of the Cordoban Alcázar to confirm the self-styled Caliph and most of these recognised him as Hisham II. Muhammad now had a caliph in residence and he appointed himself as *Hachib*, with a higher status and with the supposed Umayyad stamp of authority, all the better to expand his territory. His relations with various taifas of the 'new' Berbers were bad, he had conflicts with them, and made expansive moves against Granada and Badajoz. On his death in 1042 he was succeeded by his son, al-Mutadid, who gave serious impetus to the expansion of Seville. The small taifas to the west like Mértola, Huelva, Silves and Niebla were taken over. So too, in the period 1055 to 1069, were the taifas to the south: Ronda, Algeciras and Morón, and Carmona to the east. By the time most of these had been captured,

Right. Arcos de la Frontera. This was another taifa run by 'new' Berbers which was taken over by the expansionary Taifa of Seville.

the artifice of the 'Caliph' was not necessary and al-Mutadid then announced that the 'Caliph' Hisham II had died, years before, in 1044.

We now see a new phenomenon: the payment of tribute to the Christians by the taifas. In al-Mutadid's case he paid this tribute to Fernando I, the ruler of Castile and León. This reflected a complete reversal of fortune for the Christian states to the north. From the end of Abd al-Rahman III's reign all the way through to that of Almanzor, the Christians had been reduced by the powerful al-Andalus state to mere vassalage and had to undergo payment of tribute, interspersed with regular raids through their territory. With the disintegration of the Umayyad state, the Christian states were able to flex their muscles and raid deep into Muslim territory. They soon established the practice of offering protection or non-aggression on the basis of the payment of *parias* or annual tribute. In time this became institutionalised and the amount of exorbitant tribute the taifas had to pay to their more powerful northern neighbours threatened to reduce some to a near-penniless state. The populace of the taifas were in high outrage at the level of taxes they had to pay, which in turn weakened the authority of the taifa rulers.

On al-Mutadid's death in 1069 he was succeeded by his son, who took the honorific title of al-Mutamid. As we have seen, he soon took over Córdoba. Seville briefly lost Córdoba to Toledo in 1075, but regained it soon afterwards. Seville ruled Córdoba until the takeover there by the Alomoravids in 1091, in whose invasion al-Mutamid was to play a key role, as we shall see later. In the era of the taifas, Seville emerged to take a pre-eminent role across the Peninsula, eclipsing the caliphal dominance of the former capital of Córdoba.

Another important Andalusi taifa was that of Zaragoza. The city and the Upper March along the Ebro had long been dominated by the Tuchibi family.

Left. The taifa rulers of Zaragoza left the wonderful legacy of the Aljafería palace. Archways in the north portico.

By the time of the dissolution of the Córdoba Caliphate, a relatively minor branch of the Tuchibis from Daroca had set up in the city. The rulers of Zaragoza intermittently fought with their Christian neighbours in Castile and León, Navarra and Barcelona. Around 1039, Sulayman bin Hud, the ruler of Tudela and Lérida and a member of the Arab Banu Hud family, took advantage of internal Tuchibi disputes in Zaragoza and took it over. He assumed the honorific title of al-Mustain and assigned his sons as governors across the taifa. When a dispute erupted between Toledo and Zaragoza, there now took place what was to be another common feature of the taifa era – that of forming alliances with the Christians. Toledo enlisted the aid of Navarra and Zaragoza that of Castile, a situation that proved to be very profitable for the Christian kingdoms. Al-Mustain was succeeded on his death in the mid-eleventh century by his son who took the honorific al-Muqtadir. This new ruler had expansive tendencies and succeeded in taking over Tortosa and Dénia. Despite his expansionary profile in Muslim lands, he had to yield to superior power and on occasion paid *parias* to the Christian kings. He was a cultured ruler who supported

Right. Pictorial inscriptions and kufic characters in a room of the Aljafería.

Below. Intricately carved capitals in the Aljafería, Zaragoza.

the arts and it is due to him that we have today the remains of his palace in Zaragoza, the Aljafería. As we will see later, his son and successor, al-Mutamin was a notable mathematician.

Many of the 'old' Berbers had settled in mountainous areas. Two taifas situated in a line from the Levante to Zaragoza were in such terrain: Alpuente and Albarracín. Both were led by Andalusi rulers of 'old' Berber lineage, the Banu Razin giving their name to Albarracín. Perhaps due to their remoteness and the astuteness of their rulers, these taifas were able to survive until 1104 when they were absorbed by the Almoravids.

Badajoz was also ruled by 'old' Berbers, the Aftasids, who had taken over the taifa that had originally been set up by a senior slave called Sabur, a *hachib* who died in 1022. This taifa was large, with territory extending from Mérida all the way to Lisbon, bordering the Taifa of Seville to the south, (with which there were intermittent disputes). Originally, the taifa extended to Coimbra and onwards to the southern bank of the Duero, with the Christian kingdom of León as its northern neighbour. As we have seen, the Christians took full advantage of the fragmentation of al-Andalus and, in the case of Badajoz, gradually encroached on its territory. Coimbra was lost in 1064 and in 1079 Coria was taken by Alfonso VI, who also extracted *parias* from Badajoz. The Aftasids were leading protagonists in the group that invited the Almoravids to 'save' al-Andalus and even encouraged their takeover of Granada and Seville. Eventually, Badajoz's turn came and the Almoravids took it over in 1094.

In al-Andalus the practice of using slaves in the army had become established during the rule of the early Amirs. Slaves were increasingly being placed in the royal court and its administration during the reign of Abd al-Rahman III. These began to rise to leading posts in the palace and upper levels of administration. Unlike the other groups that made up the al-Andalus population, the slaves were

Left. A street in Albarracín. This taifa was named after the Banu Razin, of 'old' Berber lineage. It survived until the Almoravids took it over in 1104.

a separate group of disparate origins (many from the Balkans, others from the Mediterranean and northern Iberian areas). They did not have roots in al-Andalus and did not manage to establish any of significance. Their emergence into positions of great power and influence was greatly resented by the 'old' Andalusis. Some of the slaves had been assigned to provincial administrations by Almanzor and thus were in place during the break up of the Caliphate. One of the initial effects of the anarchic overthrow of Almanzor's son Sanchuelo in 1009, by forces representing the old Andalusis of Córdoba, was the flight into exile of influential slaves to the Levante (the provinces of Castelleon, Alicante, Murcia and Valencia in today's Spain). These capable men, skilled in administration and the manipulation of power, eased into taking control in these areas, most likely taking advantage of a local power vacuum. As the civil war proceeded slaves formed taifas across the Levante, including Valencia, Dénia (which ruled the Balearic islands), Játiva, Tortosa, Almería and Murcia.

    These slave taifas were to prove transient. As the eleventh century progressed, they were taken over by their generally larger neighbours. The slaves were a small, generally disliked, group without the bonds and support of the

Above. Fortifications ascend the hill, dominating the town of Albarracín, once a taifa.

Arab and Berber clan system. They were rulers who had superimposed themselves on the local region with scarcely any links to it. With one exception (that of Dénia), they did not establish dynasties like those of the other classes of taifa rulers. Part of the reason for this may have been a purely physical one – as seen in the previous chapter, some slaves were eunuchs (all the better to be able to function as a palace official in the royal court, with its caliphal harem).

Valencia had a chequered history during the taifa era. It started off under slave rule, which did not last long. At an early stage during the civil war, two slave administrators of the highly important Valencian irrigation system, Mubarak and Muzaffar, emerged to take control. During their short rule the local citizens became unhappy, burdened by high taxes and called in the ruler of Tortosa, another slave, who continued the high tax regime. In 1021, this slave rule came to an end when Abd al-Aziz, son of Abd al-Rahman Sanchuelo (grandson of Almanzor, thereby bearing the perceived prestige of his Amiri heritage), was proclaimed leader by the Valencians. He ruled in an effective manner until his death in 1061, despite the attacks and pressures of neighbouring taifas. His son and successor Abd al-Malik, under pressure from Fernando I of Castile, turned to his father-in-law, the ruler of Toledo, for aid. He in turn took it over and ruled it from 1065 to 1075. Valencia then separated from Toledo and was ruled by a local ruler. Alfonso VI (as we see later) occupied Toledo in 1085 and, as part of the deal, contrived to place as ruler in Valencia (by power of intimida-

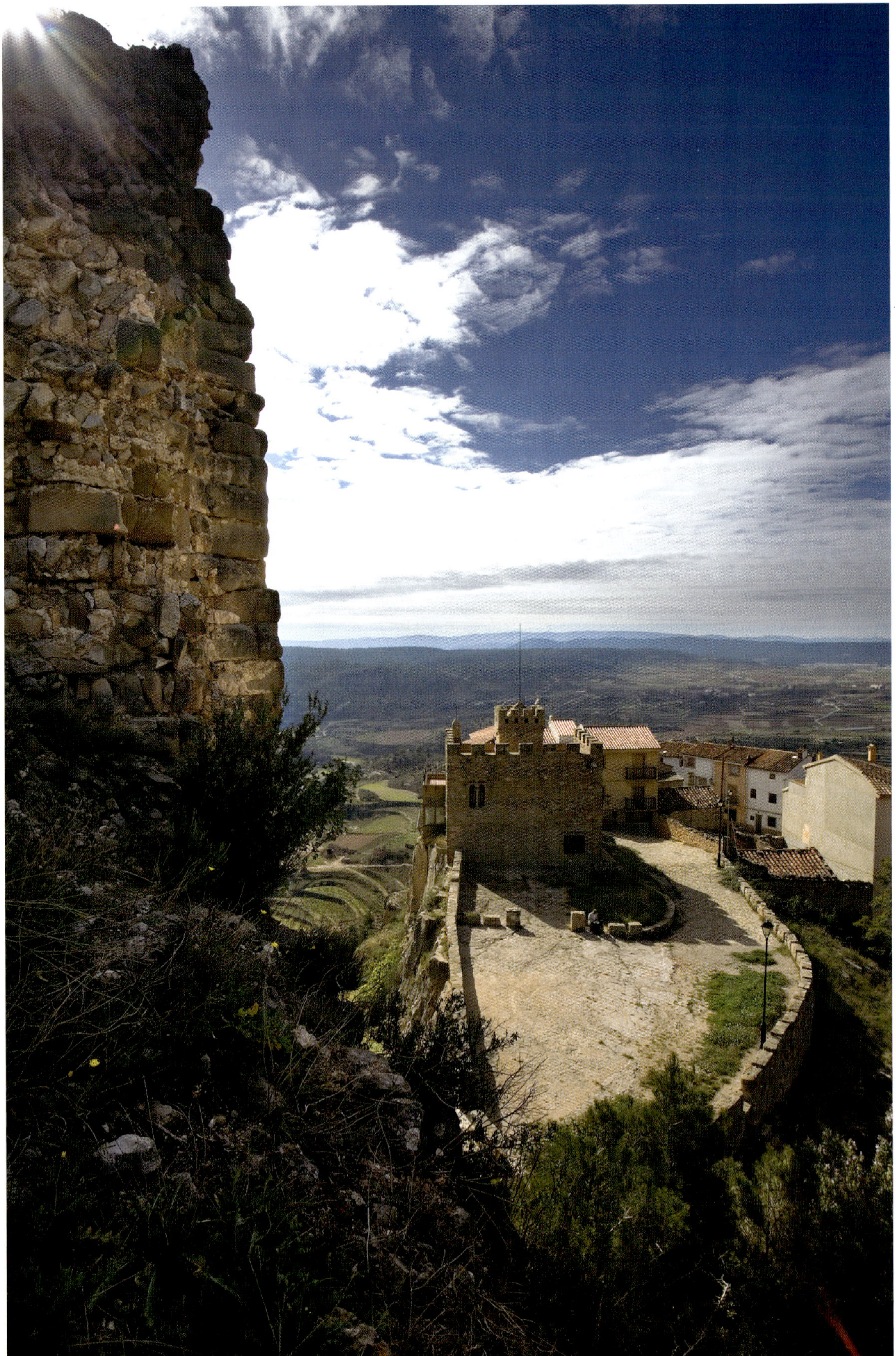

Left. Alpuente was another taifa that lasted until 1104. The castle, which looms over the town and the surrounding plain, is now in ruins.

Right. The Puerta del Capitel of the Alcazaba at Badajoz. This was the main entrance to the Alcazaba, with the busy souks of the city clustered outside.

Right. The Taifa of Badajoz was initially founded by a slave, Sabur. It was soon taken over by 'new' Berbers. The funeral stone of Sabur, who died in 1022. Museo Arqueológico Provincial de Badajoz.

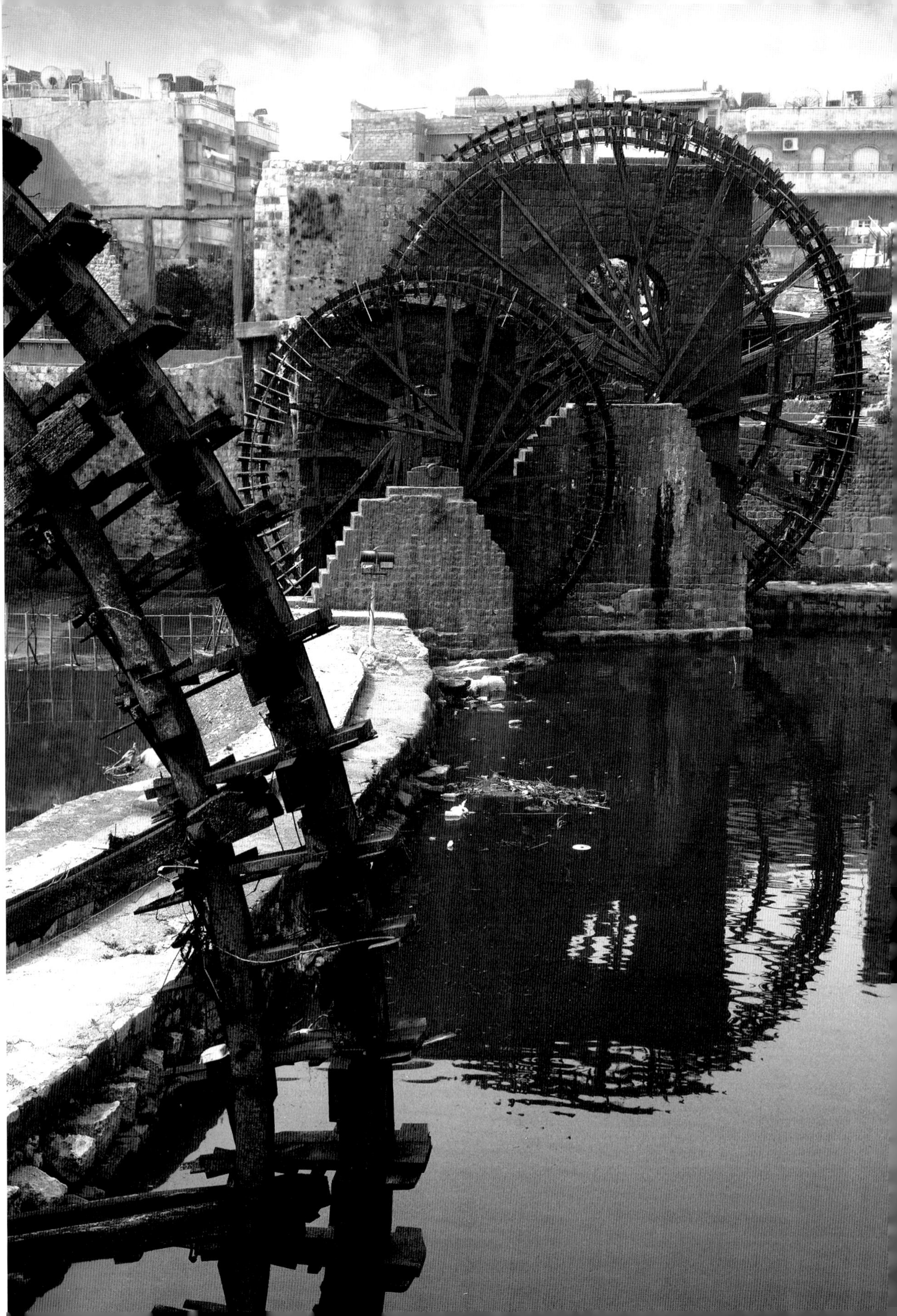

The Muslims brought new plants and techniques from the east to al-Andalus. Agricultural output greatly increased.

Left. The great norias (waterwheels) on the river Orontes in Hama, Syria. Driven by the river current, these raised water to aqueducts for irrigation and drinking. There are still sixteen of these giant wooden waterwheels in Hama.

Right. Noria at Córdoba, known as the Albolafia, on the Guadalquivir. Legend has it that Queen Isabel requested that it be stopped, as the noise disturbed her sleep at the nearby royal Alcázar.

Right. The centre spindle of the noria of la Nora, near Murcia. On the site of a medieval noria, the present example was reconstructed in 1936.

Left. Agricultural activities in al-Andalus. Detail from a plaque in Archez in the Axarquia, to the east of Málaga.

tion) the displaced Toledan ruler al-Qadir. Against a background of Alfonso's intimidation, the Valencians in turn deposed their local ruler and handed power to al-Qadir. His rule was not a success and discontent built up amongst the citizens. They were burdened by high taxes - one cause of which, it has been suggested, was due to the cost of employing mercenary Christian troops. Al-Qadir continued to curry favour with Alfonso VI, sending him a steady stream of delegations bearing gifts.

We pause here to look at the figure of El Cid (from the Arabic, *sayyid* or lord), also known as Rodrigo Díaz de Vivar, whose exploits still resonate through history. He has garnered the mantle of hero in Spain. There are various views of this remarkable man: mercenary and opportunist, or a towering military genius, fighter in the cause of Christian Spain against the Muslims. As is usual in these cases there is no simple answer. He did have extraordinary military success, reputedly never losing a battle. However he did switch sides on occasion, fighting on the Muslim as well as the Christian side. El Cid, who was of noble origin, established his career fighting in the succession battles of Castile and León as well as the usual excursions against the Muslim taifas. When Alfonso VI gained power, El Cid came to hold an important, though insecure, position in his court. He fell into disfavour with Alfonso and was forced into exile around 1081. This capable soldier soon found employment with the Muslim ruler of Zaragoza and led the defence against the attacks of the surrounding enemies, both Christian and Muslim. El Cid began to focus on the zone around Valencia, making raids there and around 1090 was extracting tribute from local rulers. In time, he exercised power over Valencia, dominating the hapless ruler al-Qadir. Later we shall see how El Cid managed to capture the city in 1094

The Berber heritage ran deep in al-Andalus. They had formed a major part of the Muslim army during the conquest of 711. Soon afterwards, in 740, a Berber revolt occurred, driven by the reality that the Berbers were assigned a lower position than the Arabs in the social order and were relegated to the more marginal lands of the Peninsula. Throughout the years of the Amirate and the Caliphate, there had always been a flow of Berbers from the Maghreb to the Peninsula and they eventually melded into the Andalusi population. However, it

Right. Horseshoe arches in the palace of the Alcazaba in Málaga. The taifa here was ruled by the Hammudids, of Idrisid origin from the Maghreb.

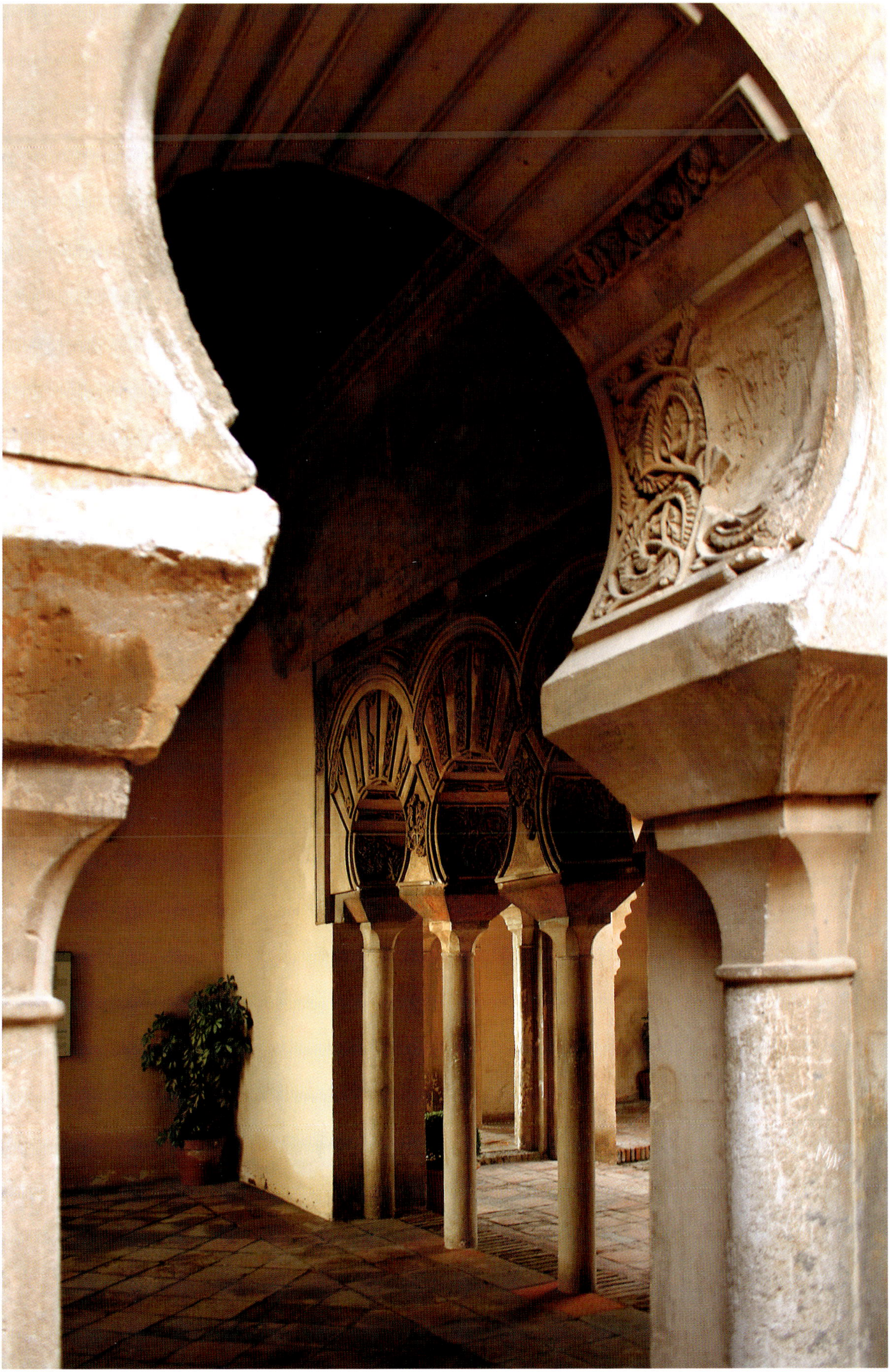

Above. The walls of the Alcazaba of Málaga.

was during the reign of al-Hakam II (961 to 976), in tandem with the Umayyad intervention in the Maghreb, that a new and large influx of Berber mercenaries came to the Peninsula. This reflected the fact that, as al-Andalus grew more prosperous, the citizens of the State lost their appetite for military service, forcing more dependency on the buying-in of those who were able and willing to do military service. During Almanzor's rule (again, against the background of continuing engagement in the Maghreb), there was an acceleration in the recruitment of Berbers from the principal tribes in the al-Andalus zone of influence in the Maghreb. These were dispersed across the State and dislike of them built up amongst the 'old' Andalusis. One of the events that triggered the civil war occurred when the incompetent Sanchuelo (second son of Almanzor), in a possible attempt to flatter the Berbers, issued a decree that court officials had to wear Berber style turbans. This caused intense resentment. The Berbers were to play a leading role during the civil war, with their faction laying siege to and capturing Córdoba. As the Caliphate began to disintegrate, several of these 'new' Berbers took power in various districts of southern al-Andalus and formed taifas. Amongst these were the smaller taifas of Carmona, Ronda, Arcos and Morón. Other Berbers took charge of the region around Elvira which was to develop into the significant and leading Taifa of Granada, as we will see later. The taifas of Algeciras and Málaga may be classified as part of the 'new' Berber category. They were led by the Hammudids from North Africa. Although of princely Arab antecedents (descended from the Idrisids of Fez, of the family of

Right. Játiva, once a taifa. A view of the castle in the evening sun. From the twelfth century onwards, Játiva was a pioneer on the European continent in paper manufacture. This catered for the highly literate and cultured society of al-Andalus.

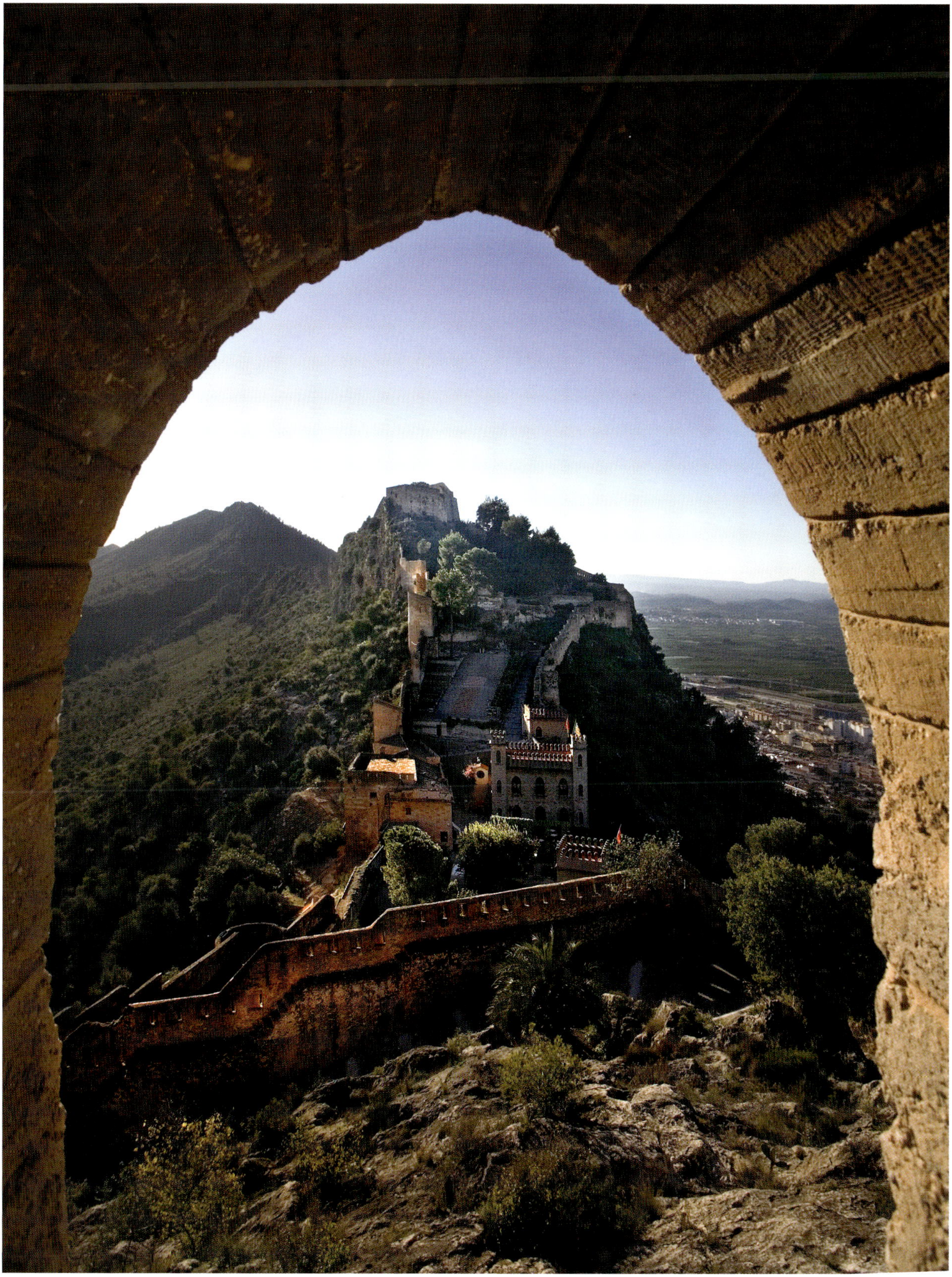

Left. Multi-lobular arches in the Aljafería at Zaragoza.

Left. Plaster decoration from the Aljafería.

Right. Shifting sands: during the latter half of the eleventh century the taifa frontiers were ever-changing. Toledo is shown here as it stood after its capture by the Christians in 1085.

Ali, son-in-law of the Prophet Muhammad), in reality they were 'berberised', even down to their leaders reportedly speaking poor Arabic. The Hammudids played a leading role during the civil war, laying claim to the Caliphate, on the basis of their ancestry back to the Prophet. They had succeeded in imposing their Caliph in Córdoba in the period 1016 and 1023, followed by a brief interlude around 1026. By the end of the civil war, Málaga and Algeciras were ruled by separate members of the family who still retained caliphal ambitions. Each of these taifas had a turbulent history, riven by inter-family feuds. They came to an end when, in 1055, Seville took control of Algeciras and, in 1058, when Málaga was occupied by Granada. In general, the rationale for 'new' Berber taifas rested on the military power of the Berbers rather than having any great roots or prestige in the community: the local people paid the Berbers in return for protection and defence. Most were small taifas and did not have great lasting power and with the exception of the large Taifa of Granada, were absorbed by the expansive Seville by 1069.

Granada had been a settlement from ancient times but its ascent to prominence can be traced to the arrival of Zawi bin Ziri and his Sanhaja Berber tribesmen in the Peninsula during the beginning of the eleventh century. Zawi had previously played a prominent part in the conflicts in the al-Andalus zone of influence in North Africa. Zawi continued his activities and was a principal leader of the Berber faction during the civil war. In 1010-13 he led the siege of Córdoba, which commenced with the occupation and looting of Madinat al-Zahra. In the period following the defeat and sack of Córdoba by the Berbers, Zawi is reported to have been assigned the province and town of Elvira by the Caliph Sulayman (who had been installed by the Berber faction). Zawi and his Sanhaja made it their base while they continued to make further interventions

Left. Ramparts of the Alcázar located by the Puerta de Sevilla gate at Carmona.

Left. Astrolabe made during the taifa era. Archivo Fotográfico, Museo Arqueológico Nacional, Madrid.

Right. A textile from the eleventh century, the Estandarte de Colls. Museo de Huesca.

Below. Stucco work, with the shape of a bird, at the Aljafería in Zaragoza.

in the civil war. They set up a taifa in this area which extended north to Jaén and south to the Mediterranean coast, reportedly by agreement with the local inhabitants, who sought protection in return for paying taxes. Seeing a need to move to a better, more defensive location, they abandoned Elvira, which was located on a plain. They moved to Granada, situated nearby in the foothills of the Sierra Nevada and developed the city. Zawi returned to North Africa around 1020 and was succeeded by his nephew. The Zirid dynasty that thus came into being proved to be able administrators. Granada grew to be a powerful taifa and expanded its borders. It took Málaga as we have seen, in a pre-emptive move arising from Seville's takeover of Algeciras. In 1073 the Zirid Abd Allah came to power in Granada. A well educated man, he left behind his memoirs which give an illuminating description of the history of the time. He ruled until 1090 when he was dethroned by the Almoravids and ended his days in exile in the Maghreb.

We finish with the taifa of Toledo, ruled by 'old' Berbers. Its eventual seizure by the Christians was to provide the principal impetus for the end of the taifa era in al-Andalus. By the end of the Caliphate, Toledo was under the control of an assimilated clan of Berbers who had been dominant in the region of Santaver, near Cuenca, to the northeast of Toledo. This was the Dhu l-Nun, who had come to Iberia at the time of the conquest. They had been invited by the Toledans to rule the city and proved to be good administrators. Their endeavours included the construction of important public buildings. In what was a usual feature of taifa politics, these Toledan rulers had intermittent disputes with their neighbours. In a conflict with Zaragoza around the middle of the eleventh century, the ruler of Toledo turned to Navarra for help. Zaragoza requested the aid of Castile. This proved to be a lucrative business for the Christian states, which demanded and got large, even exorbitant *parias* (annual tributes). Toledo also played the expansionist game. In 1065 it took over Valencia (which it lost to Seville in 1078). Toledo tried to take over Córdoba, lost it to Seville in 1070, regained it five years later and soon lost it once again to Seville.

The ruler of the Taifa of Toledo in the period 1044-75, al-Mumun, was a lover of gardens. He set up a royal botanic garden in the city, which contained a

Left. The 'Arab Walls' of Toledo.

pleasure section as well as an experimental area for plants brought from abroad. He gave patronage to experts who wrote treatises on agronomy, which were later translated and used in medieval Christian Europe. One book on agronomy had the marvellous title of 'Concision and Clarity'. Agricultural science flourished and al-Andalus was where the Arabic literature on agricultural topics burgeoned and developed.

Even during the chaos of the taifa times, agriculture continued and generally prospered. The Arab invaders of the Iberian Peninsula had brought many new plants with them, adding to produce like wheat and vegetable crops already introduced by the Romans. They brought plants found in the east of their Empire back to the west. From India came the Seville oranges, lemons, aubergines, melons and varieties of rice as well as sugar cane. Despite the prohibition on the drinking of alcohol, there were vineyards in al-Andalus. The Mozarabs and Jews provided a market for wine but many Muslim Andalusis also imbibed. Other crops introduced included pears, apricots, peaches and cotton. However, the planting of these crops presupposed that there was a ready supply of water. The Islamic rulers in the east had taken the established irrigation techniques of the Romans and earlier civilisations and adapted and improved them. They brought these techniques of storage of seasonal water supply and its distribution to Iberia, which already had a developed agricultural economy thanks to the Romans, albeit rundown during the Visigothic era. Al-Andalus became an even more fertile land where the cultivators, using the Islamic mastery of hydraulic technology, wrung the most out of the terrain. Lands then dry and unproductive were brought into production. Incidentally, with the expulsion of the Moriscos at the beginning of the seventeenth century, some land reverted

Below. Esenciero (essence bottle) in inscribed silver from Albarracín. Museo de Teruel.

Right. Woven silk from al-Andalus, dating from the twelfth century. Luxury textiles were highly valued and often used as gifts for visiting dignitaries. Victoria and Albert Museum, London.

back to its original state and much intensive cultivation was discontinued. The Arabs developed a large network of irrigation channels, now called *acequias,* in Spain. Many of these are still in use in areas like the Alpujarras or the *huertas* (gardens) of Valencia. The Arabs also perfected the technique of lifting water to these channels, using techniques like the *noria* or waterwheel. Originally adapted by the Islamic conquerors of Syria from water wheels developed by the Romans, the technique was brought to Iberia by the Arab settlers. Dams and cisterns were established and the countryside and cities were kept supplied with water which flowed along a network of channels and aqueducts.

The rulers of Toledo, the Dhu l-Nunids, had built up an alliance with Alfonso VI of Castile and, in 1072, provided him with a temporary refuge in Toledo. At that time he was embroiled in a war with his brother over the Leonese throne, which he subsequently attained. His stay in the city made Alfonso aware of the importance of this, the ancient capital of Iberia. In 1083, al-Qadir, the unpopular ruler of Toledo, trying to brutally put down revolts, offered Toledo to Alfonso, in exchange for his support in acceding to power in Valencia. The inhabitants of Toledo thought differently and resisted the handover. After a long siege, Alfonso took over the city in May 1085. The surrender agreement allowed the Muslim inhabitants to continue with their religion and

Above. The taking of Toledo in 1085 by Alfonso VI. This event precipitated the Almoravid takeover of al-Andalus.

the use of mosques. They would have to pay a poll tax, a similar condition that the Mozarabs and Jews had had to fulfil under Muslim rule. One can speculate if it was in a fit of hubris that Alfonso VI, on taking over Toledo, saw himself as the potential ruler of the Iberian Peninsula and, with Muslim as well as Christian subjects, declared himself 'Emperor of all Spain' ('*Imperator totius Hispaniae*').

The capture of Toledo, the old capital of Iberia, one of the leading cities of, and right in the heart of, al-Andalus, by a Christian King, was traumatic to the Islamic commonwealth. By a creeping process, the Christians had already been advancing southwards on the borders of al-Andalus. However, that had been hitherto in relatively unpopulated territory. In contrast, Toledo was one of the largest and most important cities of al-Andalus. The Christians had now penetrated to the heart of the Peninsula and the Andalusi frontiers were left exposed. As it turned out, Toledo was never to leave Christian hands and it was to form the core of the rising domain later known as New Castile. As well as the strategic threat it posed, the taking of Toledo was an affront to the cause of Islam and to the by now battered concept of al-Andalus. These factors added up to form the tipping point that propelled the Almoravids to leave the Maghreb, cross the Strait and invade the Peninsula. As we shall see in the next chapter, by 1110 the Almoravids had taken over all the taifas, save for the Balearics which they did

Right. The Sinagoga del Tránsito in Toledo. This synagogue was constructed in the fourteenth century, nearly two centuries after the capture of the city from the Muslims. It was influenced by the Andalusi architectural style. The scallop shell motif is common to many religions.

Left. Column and capital in the Sinagoga del Tránsito.

not occupy until 1116. Al-Andalus was to be dominated by Berber rulers from North Africa for the next century and a half.

Was the taifa period a time of anarchy and incessant struggle and a disastrous end to the glories of the Umayyad Caliphate? Not totally. Surprisingly, some aspects of the taifas were positive. After the disruption caused during the civil war, commerce and industry carried on and prospered in many areas. The sophisticated agricultural methods introduced during Umayyad rule continued and allowed high productivity to be maintained and further developed. The cities grew, eclipsing Córdoba, no longer having to be beholden to a central power or remit taxes to it. Despite the later heavy burden of the Christian *parias*, many areas experienced prosperity for much of the taifa era. Valencia, with its surrounding fertile *huertas,* grew in importance and wealth. It turned out to be a prize worth taking, as we have seen, with its capture by El Cid. Granada grew to be an important city, laying the ground for future glories.

139

Seville, situated in the productive Guadalquivir plain, developed into the pre-eminent city of the taifas. Public buildings were built across the various taifas, no doubt fuelled in part by competition among the rulers. The Aljafería palace in Zaragoza is a jewel and testament to the architecture and decorative splendour of the taifa era. Not surprisingly, military defence was a high priority for the rulers and elaborate wall systems and alcazabas (castles) were built all over the taifa cities.

In the cultural field, the taifas sparkled. The eleventh century (as the preceding one) has been described as forming a golden age of Andalusi literature. Many of the rulers of the taifas proved to be cultured men, some of them writers or poets themselves. We have seen how Abd Allah of Granada wrote his memoirs, a fine history of the time. Several of the rulers of Seville were accomplished poets. Literature and poetry benefited from the support of the rulers through the taifas. Science also received patronage and vigorously developed in the eleventh century, continuing strong links with the scientists and new discoveries in the Muslim east. Al-Andalus at that time was a leader in some fields, particularly in agricultural science and astrology. Many astrolabes, still on display today, were manufactured in al-Andalus during the time of the taifas. Mathematics, including geometry and algebra were well advanced. Indeed, the ruler of Zaragoza, in the period 1082-1085, al-Mutamin, wrote a mathematical treatise (called '*al-Istikmal*' - 'the Perfection'*),* which was in use in Baghdad centuries later.

As the taifa era ended, the Christian taking of Toledo in 1085 was to have a consequence of enormous significance for western civilisation. Scholars flocked to the city, encouraged by the sagacious new archbishop, Raimundus. In the newly-captured city they tapped into the great trove of books in Arabic from al-Andalus and the Islamic east. Not only did these include Arabic translations of ancient Greek works, but also the learning embodied in the works of Islamic scholars. The works translated covered medicine, science, literature and philosophy. In addition to learned men from the Iberian Christian kingdoms, foreign scholars in the centuries that followed included Gerard of Cremona, Hermanus Alemanus and Abelard of Bath. One of the more colourful thirteenth-century visitors was the eccentric scholar Michael Scotus who translated work by Aristotle and Averroes, as well as treatises on astrology and alchemy. Incidentally, Scotus featured in Dante's Inferno, appearing amongst the magicians. As the Islamic works were translated from Arabic, they were in turn disseminated all across Christian northern Europe. Toledo became one of the most important conduits through which the vast fount of advanced knowledge of the Islamic world was transmitted to the west. For centuries the theory of mathematics was brought to the west: those of algebra, trigonometry and advanced geometry. The advanced techniques of Islamic medicine became the basis for that later used in Medieval Europe. Thus a stream of knowledge flowed to the less-advanced north, forming the foundation for later European scientific development as well as for the Renaissance.

Chapter 6
The Almoravids and the Almohads

As the taifas were being set up, events were occurring far away to the south of the Maghreb – events which were, in time, to greatly affect al-Andalus. Early in the eleventh century, the native people around the banks of the Niger put pressure on the Saharan Berber tribes, who, in turn, moved northwards. Many of these were Sanhaja, who were far-flung relatives of the Zirid Sanhajas, located in the north of the Maghreb. A branch of these, as we have seen, established the Taifa of Granada.

The lands in the south of present day Morocco are generally flat, arid and sparsely inhabited. The nomadic Sanhajas traversed the desert wastes, herding camels and surviving on camel meat and milk. A practical custom was the wearing of a veil by the men of the tribe, shielding them from the sun and dust of the desert. A major trade route passed through this area, from Sijilmassa (on the edge of the Sahara in the mid-west of Morocco), then south to a trading enclave called Awdaghast and onwards to the gold mines of West Africa. Gold was brought to the north; trade products and essentials like salt were sent southwards.

The tribes had converted to Islam after the Arab conquest dating from the end of the seventh century. Conversion was mostly nominal as many of the tribes had developed their own interpretation of Islam, adapting its tenets to their own native practices. One of the leaders of the Gudula tribe of these Berbers, a man of piety, made a pilgrimage to Mecca in the first half of the eleventh century. On his return and desirous that his people would observe the norms of Islam, he brought back one Ibn Yasin, with the task of educating his tribe and encouraging a more rigorous application of the religion. Ibn Yasin was a scholar trained in the Maliki legal interpretation of Islam. However, the Gudula disliked the rigorous regime established by Ibn Yasin. On the death of their leader, the Gudula promptly expelled Ibn Yasin who moved on to the neighbouring Lamtuna tribe. At one stage, Ibn Yasin and his followers had to seek refuge in a fortified monastery or *ribat*. The name 'Almoravid' that emerged is possibly derived from *al-murabitun* (or people of the *ribat*). The number of Ibn Yasin's followers grew rapidly. They began to spread their orthodoxy by military force on the neighbouring tribes. This militant policy proved successful and they spread outwards, capturing Sijilmassa and Awdaghast around the middle of the eleventh century.

Left. The view looking out: the Moroccan desert. Emerging from nomadic tribes of the southern desert, the Almoravids rapidly spread their rigorous message of orthodoxy.

Ibn Yasin was killed by an enemy tribe in 1058. A Lamtuna leader, Abu Bakr took charge of the Almoravid movement. With a cohesive tribal confederation, forged together by the cement of Almoravid rigor and orthodoxy, he continued the expansion. He founded their new capital, Marrakech, in 1071. This was a felicitous location, being at the southern edge of the fertile plains of Morocco and on the western side of the High Atlas Mountains, thus capturing the moist air of the prevailing westerly Atlantic winds.

The development of Marrakech marked a transformation for the Almoravids from their nomadic origin to a more sedentary way of life. Abu Bakr ordered the construction of a fortress in the city, which was to form the seat of Almoravid power. Soon the Amir had to leave Marrakech to deal with a serious revolt that had broken out in the Sahara. He left his cousin Yusuf bin Tashufin in charge. A shrewd, intelligent well organised man, Ibn Tashufin began to develop and consolidate an administrative system. By the time Abu Bakr returned several years later, his cousin was well established. Abu Bakr, whether it was his wish or not, accepted the de facto situation, ceded the leadership of the Almoravids to Ibn Tashufin and left for the Western Sahara. Ibn Tashufin, now Amir, continued the skilful direction of the Almoravid conquest. He assigned trusted lieutenants to lead the military expeditions, which were taking territory up through the centre and on to the north of present-day Morocco. The Almoravids reached the Strait, taking Tangier in 1079 and Ceuta in 1083. By that date they had reached as far along the Maghreb coast as Algiers. Ceuta was reportedly taken with the assistance of a Sevillian naval squadron, reflecting contacts the Almoravids had made with al-Andalus.

Back in the Iberian Peninsula, the taifas were in trouble. As we have seen, the Christian kingdoms were harrying them and extorting large *parias* (tributes). The beleaguered Muslims began to look southwards at the powerful new Islamic movement that was expanding and had taken over a large swathe of the Maghreb. The pressure intensified - Alfonso VI had mounted a raid deep into Muslim territory, even reaching Tarifa by the middle of 1083. The final straw came when Alfonso VI took the strategic heart of al-Andalus, the city of Toledo, in 1085. No longer able to rely on the frontier defences of the Upper and Middle Marches, al-Andalus was now wide open to attack at its very centre. The shock of the fall of Toledo resulted in a rare example of unity: the disparate taifas agreed to assemble a delegation of senior representatives, which travelled to see the Almoravid Amir and ask for help.

Ibn Tashufin, mindful of the danger posed to Islam in al-Andalus, agreed to help. The delegation established that it was to be a holy war against the Christians which would not involve any conquest of the taifas. The Amir made a condition that the port of Algeciras be handed to him (a condition reluctantly acceded to by its ruler, al-Mutamid of Seville) to form a disembarkation point for his troops. They commenced landing there in July 1086 and Ibn Tashufin followed in September. The army set out for the north and was joined by troops from the taifas. Alfonso VI, engaged in attacking Zaragoza, on hearing the news of the Almoravid intervention, broke off and headed south. The massed armies met at Sagrajas, about eight kilometres north-east of Badajoz, in October 1086. It was a hard battle, with the Christians initially gaining advantage. Eventually, the full power of the Almoravid troops was mobilised and the tide of battle changed. The Muslims won decisively, forcing the Christians to retreat. Ibn Tashufin returned to the Maghreb shortly afterwards. At this stage he did not seem to harbour much interest in extending his power in al-Andalus and he was probably pre-occupied by the death of his eldest son in the Maghreb. However, he left behind three thousand horsemen. Despite the heavy defeat of Sagrajas, the Christians soon reverted to their old and profitable ways of harassing the taifas and extracting *parias*. Their activity became particularly intense in the Levante. The Christians moved south and set up in the castle of Aledo, located between Murcia and Lorca. This was a strategic location on the way from Granada to the Levante). It was soon used by the Christians as a springboard to penetrate deep into the surrounding region.

Another delegation set out from al-Andalus, this time representatives of the Levante plus Seville. They requested help once again from the Almoravid Amir. He set out with his troops for the second time, landing in Algeciras in the middle of 1088. The Almoravid army, with forces from the taifas, moved towards Aledo and laid siege to the stronghold. However, they did not succeed in taking the castle, due to a large degree to the squabbles among the taifa rulers. On hearing that a large relieving army led by Alfonso VI was on the way, the

Muslims abandoned the siege. Ibn Tashufin, much displeased, returned to the Maghreb. He was to return within two years and achieve a more decisive outcome.

The interaction between the Christians and the Muslims settled down once more to its normal pace, that is, one-sided and extortionate. *Parias* were extracted by the Christians and the consequent extra taxes burdened the populace of the taifas. By now, Ibn Tashufin had lost patience with his wayward co-religionists in al-Andalus. Many of the Andalusi religious scholars and learned men made representations to him requesting assistance while complaining about the situation, particularly the excessive taxes, illegal under Muslim laws. The Almoravid ruler was also suspicious of the manoeuvrings of the taifa rulers vis-à-vis the Christians. He wrote to Abd Allah, ruler of Granada, reproaching him for what he perceived to be his scheming ways and false declarations. As the Amir decided to take over the errant land of al-Andalus, care was taken to clothe this in some form of legitimacy in the Muslim world. It is said that a petition from Andalusi *ulemas* (learned jurists) was sent to the Abbasid Caliph in Baghdad to recognise Ibn Tashufin as Amir of al-Andalus. In reality, the Abbasids now had scarcely any relevance to the affairs of al-Andalus, either spiritual or temporal. However, on being asked, the Abbasid Caliph was willing to confer on the Almoravids the right to take over al-Andalus.

And so, in the summer of 1090, Ibn Tashufin set out for al-Andalus for a third time, determined to secure al-Andalus for Islam and to put an end to the decadent taifas. Abd Allah of Granada was the first in his sights. The latter harboured the mistaken hope that his Sanhaja lineage would win him favour with the Almoravid leader of similar but distant tribal origin. The population of Granada welcomed the Almoravids when they arrived in September 1090. Abd Allah was summoned to Ibn Tashufin and sent into exile in the Maghreb. As we have seen, once there, he wrote his enlightening memoirs. Málaga was taken next, then Tarifa. Some taifa leaders cravenly congratulated Ibn Tashufin on his success but they later became the target for his forces. The Almoravid army set off in separate contingents: one for Córdoba, which was taken in March 1091, another headed for Seville which was taken in September 1091. The ruler of Seville, al-Mutamid, was exiled to the Maghreb. The ruler of Badajoz tried to enlist the help of the Christians, handing over Cintra, Santarém and Lisbon in return for support. However, this was to no avail. The Almoravids eventually entered Badajoz in spring 1094, took revenge and killed the ruler and some of his sons.

To the east, the Almoravid steamroller had moved on towards the Levante. Murcia, Aledo and Lorca were taken in 1091. Dénia and Játiva were captured in 1092. By autumn 1092, the advance had continued to within a day's ride of Valencia. This sparked the overthrow of the compromised and ineffectual ruler al-Qadir (the former ruler of Toledo) by a pro-Almoravid faction. Rodrigo Díaz Alvar, El Cid, who looked on the city as his protectorate, set up his siege of the city in July 1093. It is reported that the Almoravids, at the time focused on the conquest of Badajoz, sent out a relief party, but did not engage El Cid's forces. El

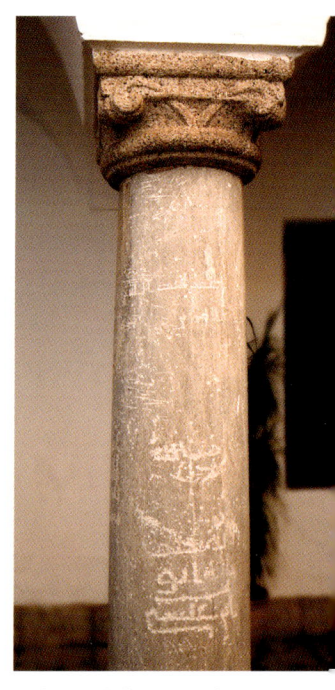

Above. Column in the Parador de Turismo, Mérida, a former convent. A series of columns was found in excavations, originally used in a fifth-century Christian church. The inscriptions in Arabic indicate that these may have been re-used in a mosque.

Right. The castle at Aledo, between Murcia and Lorca. The Christians set up here at the end of the eleventh century, using it as a springboard to penetrate deep into Muslim territory.

Cid took the city in June 1094. At the end of that year this redoubtable adventurer and military leader defeated an attacking Almoravid army at Quart de Poblet, just outside the city. He continued to rule the city, in effect, as his private taifa. On El Cid's death, in 1099, his widow, Jimena, took charge but the Almoravids captured the city in 1102.

Ibn Tashufin died in the fortress in Marrakech in September 1106. This gifted ascetic military leader and outstanding administrator had achieved much in his lifetime. Through his efforts, the Almoravids had become masters of al-Andalus (all save Zaragoza), a wide swathe of the Maghreb and part of Ifriqiya. A renowned eastern Islamic mystic theologian, al-Ghazali, had written admiringly to Ibn Tashufin that his country 'extends in distance for five months on the march, truly its northern limit adjoins the lands of the Franks, next to Zaragoza, of the land of Aragón, while its southern extremity is next to the country of Ghana'.

In al-Andalus, the Almoravid presence constituted a thin (mainly military) layer. The Governors were part of the Almoravid select few. However, most of the administration was left to the existing Andalusi leaders and officials. The Maghreb, by contrast, began to benefit from the more advanced culture of al-Andalus. A steady stream of Andalusi administrators, craftsmen, engineers and architects went south and gave of their expertise in North Africa.

Ibn Tashufin was succeeded by his designated heir and son Ali bin Tashufin who was proclaimed 'Amir of the Muslims' in Marrakech. Aged only twenty-two, this young man was to face many obstacles during his reign. Ascetic, pious and somewhat detached, he was not as engaged in the running of the Empire as his father had been. Over in al-Andalus, the Almoravid offensive was maintained. The Christian conquest of Toledo still rankled with them. An

Left. Mgoun in the High Atlas mountains. At 4071 metres, it is the second-highest peak in Morocco. The Almohads originated in the harsh landscape of the High Atlas.

Almoravid army attacked Uclés (on the eastern approach to Toledo) and took it in 1108. They moved to Toledo where they mounted a siege but this well fortified city was able to resist. Completing their conquest of al-Andalus, the Almoravids took Zaragoza in 1110 and the Balearics in 1116.

However, the great expansion of their Empire soon began to run out of steam. On the Iberian peninsula the Christian kingdoms were, understandably, vexed by the Almoravid invasion: up to now, the taifas of al-Andalus had been a ready source of easy income. In many cases, this had formed the greater part of their revenues and was now cut off. Aragón, a small kingdom, began an initiative to expand its borders and began to attack Muslim territory. The energetic King of Aragón, Alfonso I, the *Batallador* (Battler), took the emblematic northern bastion of Zaragoza in December 1118 and moved on to take the region around the Ebro. Alfonso I continued south and he decisively defeated the Muslim forces north of Teruel in July 1120. The frontier was pushed south of such places as Calatuyud and Daroca. Over the rest of the decade, Alfonso continued the offensive and made a triumphal pass deep through southern al-Andalus.

As the Christian pressure built up, a change occurred in the relationship between the Andalusis and the Almoravids. Originally, the North Africans were seen as upright, powerful saviours of the faith who were capable of acting as a bulwark against the severe and costly depredations of the Christians. When it turned out that the Almoravids couldn't actually hold back the Christians, the halo slipped and Andalusi opinion swung against the Almoravids. This disaffection was manifested in 1121 in a revolt in Córdoba which lasted for several months. To exacerbate the problems of the Almoravids, a rebellion by Ibn Tumart and his Almohads (which later proved fatal for the Almoravid Empire, as we will see) broke out near the capital of Marrakech. This conflict increasingly distracted Ali bin Tashufin from the affairs of the Iberian Peninsula.

When Ali died in 1143, he was succeeded by his son Tashufin, who was the third and last of the Almoravid Amirs. Tashufin had extensive experience of al-Andalus, having held positions of governor and led many expeditions there. He is reputed to have been valorous as well as possessing the family tendency to asceticism. However, his inheritance was clouded: he inherited an empire in peril. One of the problems was a structural one: the Almoravids were hobbled by the requirement not to introduce additional (non-Islamic) taxes. Thus, they simply could not afford to sufficiently fortify, garrison and repel the enemies of their far-flung Empire. By now, the Almohad threat had intensified: these rebels had moved out from their mountain strongholds and captured the plains of Morocco. The end was swift for the Almoravids: the Almohads captured their capital of Marrakech in March 1147.

Over on the Iberian Peninsula, as Almoravid power faded, Andalusi leaders and notables in the various regions emerged to seize power. Thus, for a second time, taifas began to emerge, albeit for a brief time, until they were extinguished by the Almohads. A leader with Sufist tendencies (Sufism is a more mystical interpretation of Islam), Ibn Qasi, took over Mértola in the Algarve region in 1144. He soon had recourse to the Almohads, emerging in the Maghreb, for help. This did not go smoothly and he turned to the Portuguese for assistance. The population of Silves, outraged at the prospect of coming under Christian control, murdered Ibn Qasi in 1151. The Almohads eventually took over the area. Fragmentation was now widespread in al-Andalus. Local notables set up in many places, including Jaén, Carmona, Ronda, Málaga, Dénia and Almería. One Abu Ya'afar bin Hud (of the Banu Hud who had been rulers of Zaragoza) emerged, with the early support of the Christians. Seizing the moment, he tried to seize power in various places and ended up taking charge of Valencia and Murcia in 1146 and demonstrated his ambitions by proclaiming himself Caliph. However, he lasted only a few weeks before being killed in a battle against his erstwhile allies, the Castilians. Another family, the Banu Mardanis, held out in the Levante, dominating it from Murcia, and survived until 1172, when, as we shall see, the Almohads took over.

Above. Village in the High Atlas mountains. Living in this rugged terrain, the Berbers irrigate and intensively cultivate the area around the villages.

Left. Mule transport in the Mgoun Gorge in the High Atlas mountains. With no roads, the Berbers here use mules and live much as in the time of the Almohads.

    Amid all this disintegration, the Almoravid influence was continued by the Banu Ghaniya, relatives of the first Almoravid Amir. They had been Almoravid governors of Murcia and Valencia. They held onto power there until the Valencians rose up in 1145. The peripatetic Banu Ghaniya made a series of transfers and displacements. They took over Seville and Córdoba and were eventually displaced from there. They went to rule in Granada and remained in power there until the Almohads took it in 1154. Other members of the Banu Ghaniya, who were governors of the Balearics, continued to keep the Almoravid flame alive there until the Almohads took the islands in 1203 and even fomented a major uprising in Ifriqiya, as we shall see.

    We now look at the rise of the Almohads. Many fundamentalist religious or political movements face a problem: the maintenance of fundamentalism is difficult. Pure rigour ends up being adulterated by compromises and temptations that arise when power is achieved. As the pattern of life and society becomes more relaxed, there is a danger that a new preacher or leader, displeased with the relaxation of morals or principle, emerges from the wings to begin cleansing afresh. And so it was with the Almohads who emerged to deal with, amongst other things, the slippage of morals represented by the Almoravid rulers.

The beginning of the Almohad dynasty dates from when a Berber, called Muhammad bin Tumart, from the Souss valley in the south of Morocco, returned around 1117 from studying in Córdoba and Baghdad. Puritanical and ascetic, he became convinced that the Almoravid State was misguided and decadent. He expounded that the Almoravid interpretation of the Koran was wrong; that it was misguided to say God had human aspects. In danger of being executed for his activities in Marrakech, he fled and eventually set up in 1224 in the remote location of Tin Mal, on the western side of the High Atlas mountains, about eighty kilometres south of the city. Ibn Tumart continued to develop his interpretation of Islam: he rejected the Maliki interpretation of the Almoravids. He saw the need to proclaim the unity of God and proclaimed himself the *Mahdi* (the divinely guided saviour*).* He began to build a community of believers, which he called *al-muwahhidun,* 'those who pronounce the unity of God', from which came the name 'Almohad'. In line with religious development, he began to construct a stratified social and political hierarchy. There were many layers in this new society: the top leadership, or 'Assembly of Ten'; the 'Group of Fifty', representing the Berber tribes which constituted the Almohad movement; specific groups such as servants and military. The military dimension was very important and the Almohad forces increasingly began to attack the Almoravid regime. The Almoravids, perhaps reflecting their nomadic origins in the plains, were not able to operate successfully in the mountains against this threat. They embarked on a policy of containment with the construction of strongholds along mountain edges.

While the Almoravids were of nomadic origin, by contrast, the majority of the Almohads came from settled mountain tribes, many of them Masmuda. In the arid High Atlas mountains the Berbers still live in similar fashion today in villages, nestling in deep valleys. They have efficient irrigation systems (the *acequias* of the Alpujarras are similar), which serve the verdant, terraced cultivation around the villages. These people are self sufficient. They grow cereals and cultivate fruit trees. Goats are herded over the rugged slopes, seeking out nourishment from the scrubland vegetation. Many villages are accessible only by foot and along mule tracks – mules are the form of transport. Life in these remote valleys in today's Morocco has not changed much from the time of the Almohads.

Ibn Tumart died in 1130. However, the Almohad leaders decided to keep his death secret for two years, probably due to a succession struggle. His successor was Abd al-Mumin, a close and trusted disciple, one of the Assembly of Ten, who was sworn in at the mosque in Tin Mal in 1132. Just as the Almoravids had the inspired leadership of Ibn Tashufin at the beginning, the Almohads had Abd al-Mumin as their gifted leader, who propelled them to greatness. He began by ruthlessly stepping up the war against the Almoravid enemy. Operating in mountainous terrain, they captured, in turn, the areas of the High Atlas, the Middle Atlas and the Rif Mountains. The Almoravid Amir was killed in battle at Oran in 1145, around which time the Almohads moved to the plains. Fez

Left. In the distance, the castle at Alarcos, near the river Guadiana. After a close-run battle the Almohads defeated the Christian forces here in 1195.

and Meknes were taken in 1146. They succeeded in seizing the capital, Marrakech, in 1147, putting the Almoravids there to the sword.

Al-Andalus was not the principal priority for the Almohads in their first years of power. Abd al-Mumin was principally preoccupied with Maghrebi affairs for more than a decade after the fall of Marrakech. He had had to deal with a major uprising in the heartland which he put down ruthlessly. There was the territory of present-day Algeria to capture. He then had to deal with dissension within the Almohad ruling circle. In 1158 he moved against Normans from Sicily who had set up in the coastal cities of Tunisia. The Almohads took Tunis in 1159 and eventually took over Tripoli.

Over on the Iberian Peninsula, we have seen how the fragmentation into the second taifas began as the Almoravid State evaporated. An early adaptation to the new power situation occurred in Cádiz, where the Almohad Caliph was recognised in a Friday sermon in 1145. According to one account, it was in 1147 that detachments of Almohad troops landed in the Peninsula, followed by their taking of Seville early the following year. The Almohads expanded progressively in al-Andalus until, by around 1160, most of the west and centre had declared allegiance to them. Amid all this expansion, enemies remained on many fronts. In the Levante, Ibn Mardanis remained independent and continued to resist the Almohads. As we have seen, the Almoravid influence had been continued by the Banu Ghaniya. They maintained power in various locations in mainland al-Andalus until 1154 and remained in power in the Balearic Islands until 1203. They even fomented a major uprising in Ifriqiya from 1184, as we shall see. The Christians, sensing weakness during the interregnum following the collapse of the Almoravids, had increased their attacks. The Count (later King) of Portugal emerged as a strong new Christian force, attacking Muslim strongholds to the west of the Peninsula. However, it was not all bad news for the Almohads.

Right. The Torre de Espantaperros in Badajoz was built during the Almohad era.

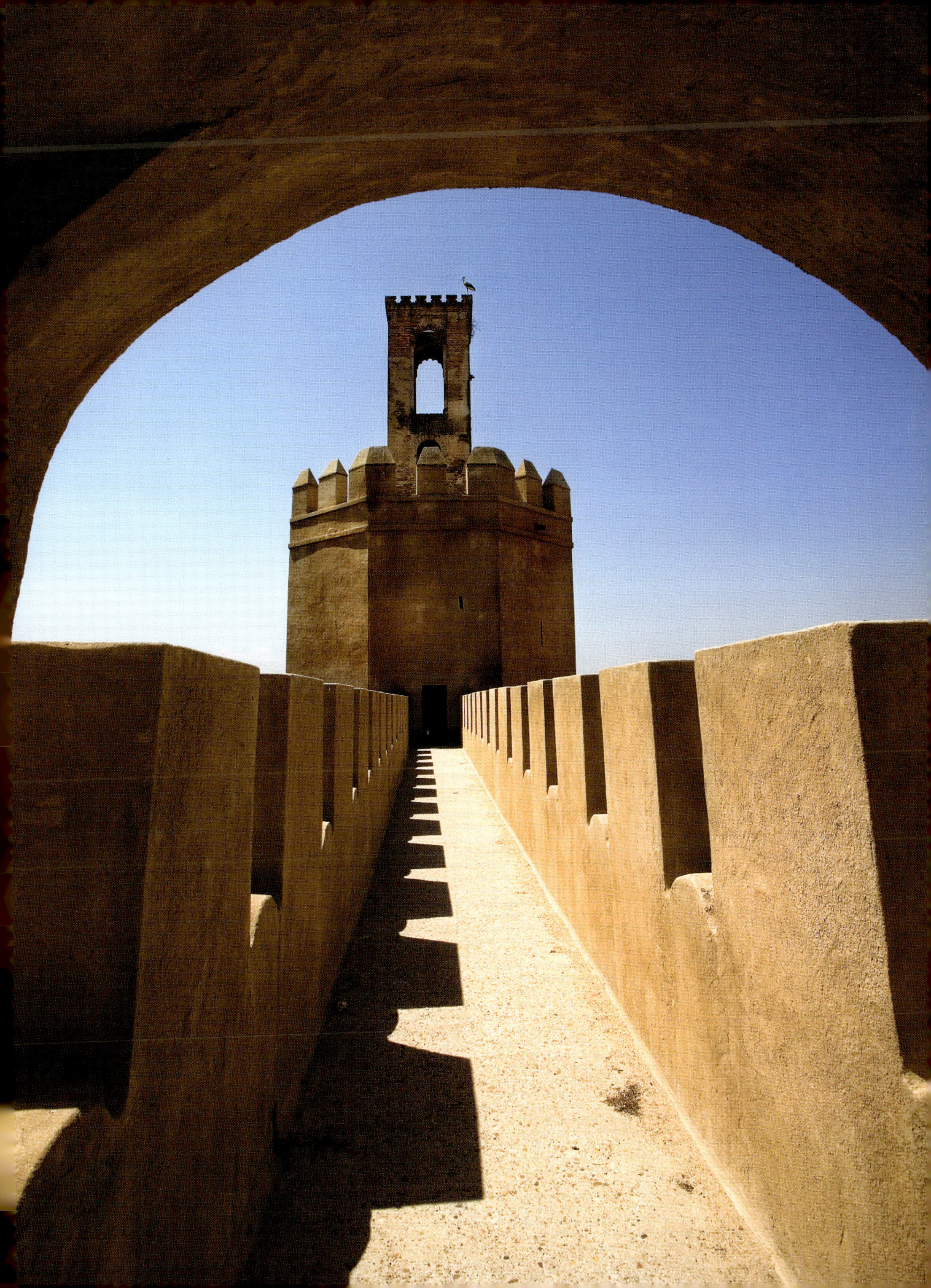

Left. The Torre de Espantaperros, Badajoz. This albarrane or advanced fortification is an octagonal tower connected to the Alcazaba by a walkway. Constructed around 1170, it predates the similar Torre del Oro in Seville by fifty years.

There was a respite from Castilian pressure when Alfonso VII died in 1157 and Castile and León reverted to two separate and disputatious kingdoms.

Abd al-Mumin had been engaged in campaigning against the Normans who had occupied the coast of Ifriqiya. He achieved a significant victory when, after a long siege, Mahdya fell to the Almohads in January 1160. Thus, with his campaign against the Normans successfully over, the Almohad leader was able to pay more attention to al-Andalus. Orders were sent out that Gibraltar be prepared as a suitable base for a visit by him. A palace and fortifications were swiftly built and Abd al-Mumin travelled there at the end of 1160. In an elaborate ceremony, representatives from the parts of al-Andalus, that had recognised the Almohads, came and swore an oath of allegiance. The Caliph confirmed his son Abu Ya'qub Yusuf as governor in Seville. Abd al-Mumin did not stay long and returned two months later to the Maghreb.

Abd al-Mumin did not live long. This first Caliph of the Almohads died in 1163. His son Abu Ya'qub Yusuf, Governor of Seville, was nominated to succeed him. Even though he was only twenty-five, he had much experience in al-Andalus of governing and leading armies. However, he did not fully inherit his father's qualities and tended towards indecision, an attribute demonstrated in his later military campaigns. There are accounts that he was a cultured and learned man who collected books. He returned to Marrakech to be confirmed

Right. The Almohad Torre del Oro by the banks of the Guadalquivir in Seville. Of dodecagonal shape, the name comes from the gilt tiles which once clad the tower. There may have been a similar tower on the other side, allowing a defensive chain to span the river.

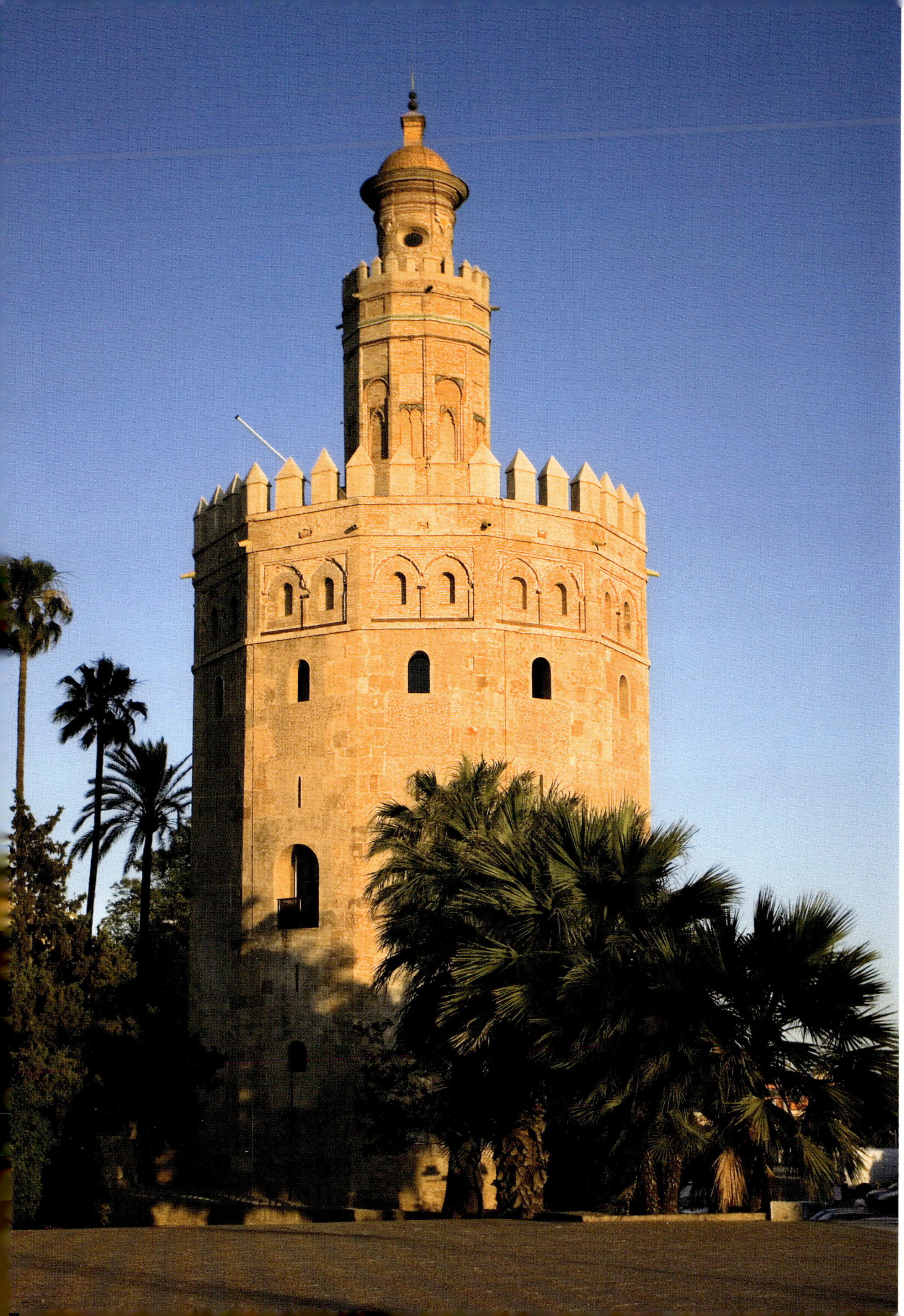

Left. The Koutoubia Mosque was constructed in Almohad Marrakech around 1158. The seventy metre-high minaret is one of the most significant examples of Almohad architecture.

there. He gathered an army and dispatched it to al-Andalus in early 1165 to deal with the many threats to Almohad rule. On arrival, the troublesome rebel Ibn Mardanis was first on the agenda. The Almohad army moved up to the east of Córdoba and began to harry the rebel. It succeeded in pushing Ibn Mardanis back but did not succeed in taking his city of Murcia. The Almohad army claimed victory and returned to Marrakech in some triumph. This was a feature of the Almohad era: the early (and usually premature) loud claims of victory and the constant shuttle back and forth of armies and leaders between the Peninsula and the Maghreb. Ibn Mardanis remained independent in the Levante from

Right. The Giralda tower of the Cathedral in Seville was the minaret of the Great Mosque bult by the Almohads. Its style was influenced by the Koutoubia in Marrakech. Construction of the mosque started in 1172. It is a vivid demonstration of the the purity of form and decoration of the Almohad style.

where he continued his resistance. The Almohads kept up the pressure on him, making incursions through Ibn Mardanis' territories. The Almohads also faced pressure on their west flank: the Portuguese 'El Cid', an adventurer called Giraldo Sempavor ('the fearless'), attacked in 1165, taking Cáceres, Évora and Trujillo. Later, in 1169 Giraldo was on the point of taking Badajoz but it suited the King of León, Fernando II, to deny the city to the Portuguese. He allied with the Almohads and Giraldo's forces were ejected.

The Caliph had set out for al-Andalus in 1171 with a large army. In June he arrived in Seville. He had two objectives: the seemingly never-ending resistance of Ibn Mardanis and the Christian threat. An expedition was mounted against

Left. A passageway in the Giralda tower. There are thirty five of these ramps to the top and it is said that they are wide enough to allow two mounted horsemen to pass.

Christian Toledo and harassment of Ibn Mardanis continued. The Caliph and his army wintered in Seville. There he ordered the construction of a new grand mosque. Fortune smiled on the Caliph as Ibn Mardanis died in Murcia in March 1172. His son and followers submitted to the Almohads and were embraced into the ruling elite, some gaining high positions. With the Christian enemy now in his sights, the Caliph launched an expedition from Seville in June 1172. Their destination was Christian-held Huete (about ninety kilometres south-east of Madrid), supposedly an easy target. The Almohad army captured several fortresses, eventually arriving at Huete about a month later. It mounted a direct assault on the position. This was unsuccessful and it settled down for a siege which lasted only a few weeks. The Caliph, seemingly fearing a counterattack by the king of Castile, Alfonso VIII, ordered a withdrawal. The army headed to Muslim Cuenca. The Christian army was spotted but the Almohads declined to engage it. They meandered back home in a confused manner via the Levante. The army was badly provisioned and arrived in Murcia in a poor state. The Caliph eventually returned to Seville in September 1172. The abortive Huete expedition was an indictment of the confused and poorly-planned leadership

Right. Reflections of the Giralda. The Christan bell tower was added in the sixteenth century.

Right. View of the cathedral from the Giralda. The cathedral was bult over the previous mosque, of which some traces can still be seen in the adjoining Patio de los Naranjos.

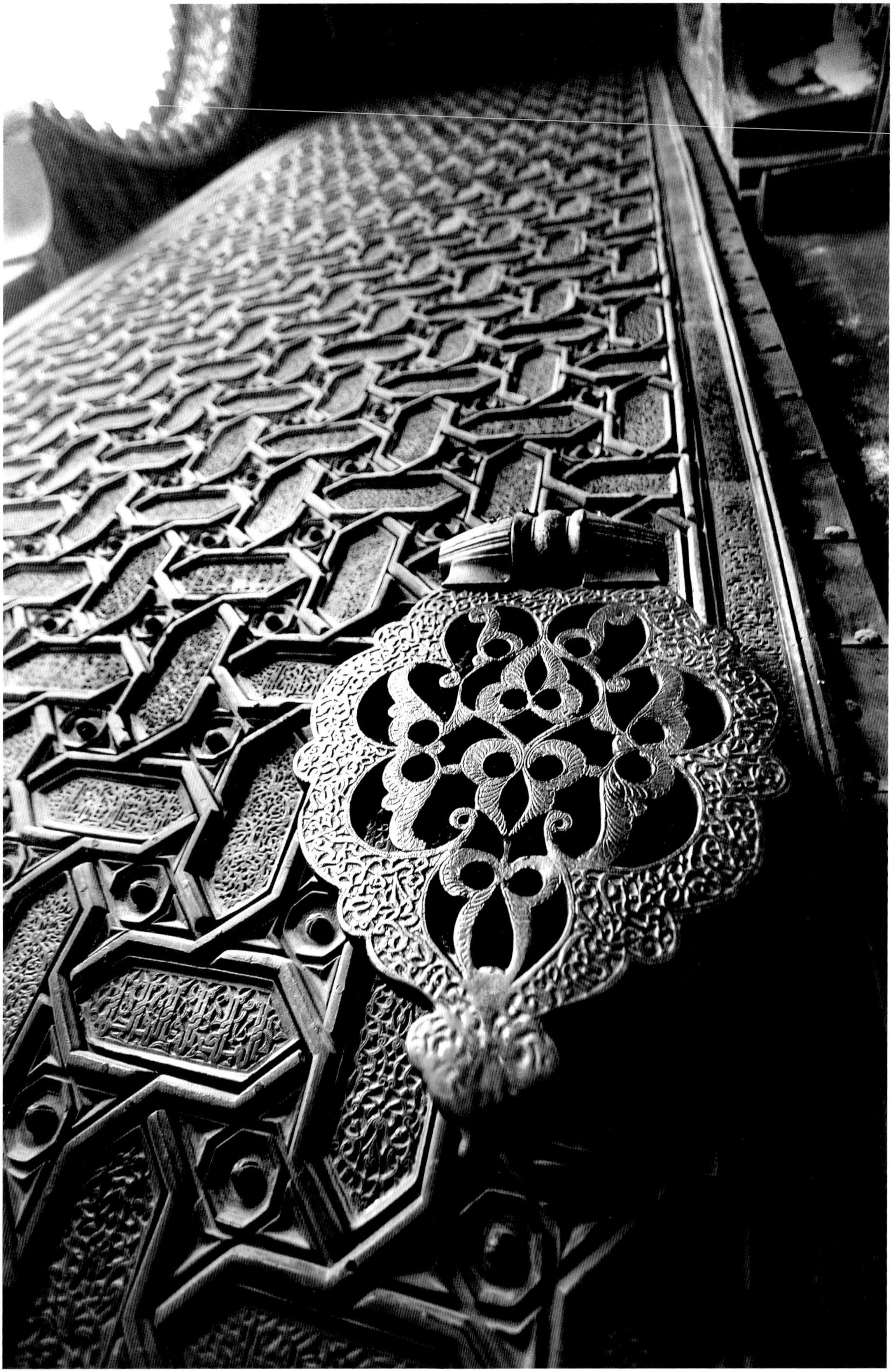

Left. Bronze door at the Puerta del Perdón at the entrance to the Patio de los Naranjos of the Cathedral in Seville.

Right. A former minaret, now a church tower, at Archez in the Axarquia. Built in Nasrid times, it is clearly influenced by Almohad architectural style of panels with a lozenge pattern.

Below. The construction of the minaret. Detail from plaque in Archez.

(particularly that of Abu Ya'qub) of Almohad military campaigns at that time. The Caliph remained in al-Andalus until 1176 when he departed, leaving his brothers in charge of Seville and Córdoba.

For al-Andalus, in the years that followed the Caliph's departure, it was a case, literally, of 'onward Christian soldiers'. Alfonso VIII kept up the pressure from Castile. The Portuguese also continued their attacks, on occasion coming within sight of Seville. Anguished requests for help were sent to the Caliph in Marrakech from al-Andalus. His response was slow and he assembled his forces in a measured way. Eventually, the army set off for al-Andalus in 1184. Once there, the first target was Santarém, which had been taken by the Portuguese. With Abu Ya'qub at their head, they arrived in June at the city which is on the right bank of the Tagus and about seventy kilometres north-east of Lisbon. A familiar chain of events ensued: an attack was made across the river. The Caliph then heard that a Christian army was on the way to relieve the defenders; he

Left. The Almohads were prodigious builders. Reflecting the conflicts of the time, many fortifications were built. Here, in the Macarena district, a section of the great ring of defensive city walls that the Almohads built in their Andalusi capital of Seville.

ordered a retreat back across the Tagus. In the disorganised withdrawal, he was stranded on the right bank of the river without sufficient guard. A Christian detachment attacked; the Caliph was wounded and died shortly thereafter. The appointment of Almohad rulers was usually surrounded by murkiness: the death of the Caliph was not announced in Seville until the succession was decided. His son, Abu Yusuf Ya'qub, was then proclaimed successor. The new ruler headed back immediately to Marrakech to be installed there and consolidate his position.

However, Abu Yusuf immediately had to face a new threat from an old enemy that emerged in North Africa. The neo-Almoravid Banu Ghaniya had continued ruling Majorca over the years, in a kind of uneasy coexistence with the Almohads on the Andalusi mainland. However, a new member of the family, who took power in 1184, made contact with rebels in the Maghreb and led a force down to join them at Bougie (around 180 kilometres east of Algiers). This caused a conflagration across North Africa as far as Tunis. Abu Yusuf had to concentrate on putting down this insurrection. Despite some serious reverses, the Almohads finally seized the rebel headquarters in 1188.

In al-Andalus, the Christians in the meantime had been keeping up the pressure, particularly in Portugal, where they took Silves in 1189. The taking of Silves was an important event in the gathering Reconquista: a large group of northern European crusading knights had arrived and joined with the local

Above. Part of the fortifications, now in ruins, at the Alcazaba of Reina in Extremadura, to the north of Seville. It was one of the important Almohad fortifications, being constructed during the second half of the twelfth century. It was captured by Christian forces in 1246, as part of the campaign to take Seville. It was later entrusted to the Order of Santiago.

Christian forces. And so the familiar pattern began once again: Abu Yusuf unhurriedly assembled a large army and, in 1190, set out once more to al-Andalus. On arrival, the Almohads headed for Silves and the west with the intention of pushing back the Portuguese. The army ranged up and down the frontier lands, ravaging the territory. However, it did not take any substantial strongholds and, through the characteristic bad management of provisions, the army began to suffer shortages. It headed back to Seville and broke out the banners, proclaiming a great victory. The army wintered in Seville and the next summer ventured out, this time succeeding in retaking Silves. The Portuguese signed a truce and, gratified, the Caliph headed back to Marrakech. There he set in train large building projects, including the commencement of the great mosque in Rabat.

Truces with the Christians expired and once again there was conflict. The Caliph returned in the summer of 1195. He assembled his forces and, in June, led his army from Seville to Córdoba onwards to meet the Christian threat. Heading for Castilian territory, the army went north through the pass of the Despeñaperros (a location that was to prove disastrous for the Almohads seventeen years later, as we shall see). Alfonso VIII, on hearing the news of the enemy advance, gathered his troops in Toledo and headed south. In July 1195 the armies met on the southern frontier of Castile near the Castle of Alarcos, (seven kilometres south-west of Ciudad Real) close to the river Guadiana. The battle

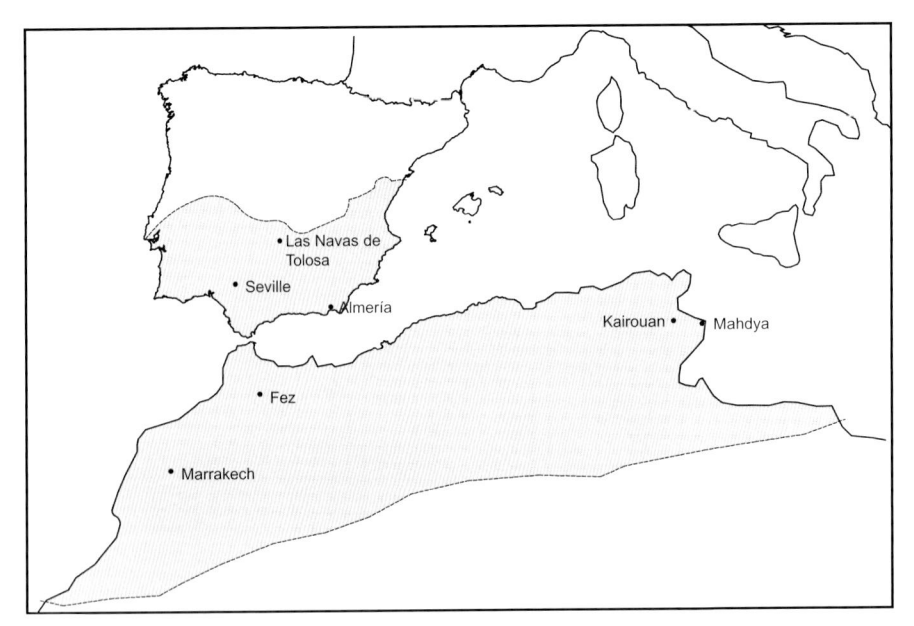

Left. Extent of the Almohad Empire around the beginning of the second half of the twelfth century.

was fierce and the Castilians initially gained the upper hand. However, eventually the Almohads won the battle. Large numbers of Castilians were killed (including nobles and bishops) and Alfonso had to flee back to Toledo.

This era was probably the most successful period for the Almohad Empire. The Almohads controlled roughly the lower half of the Iberian Peninsula, and they ruled in North Africa from Morocco all the way across to Tripoli. It was a time of general prosperity, albeit against the background of continuous strife on the frontiers. In prosperous times, states can afford to construct great buildings. The Almohads indeed were responsible for a prodigious number of buildings, both in the Maghreb and in al-Andalus. Reflecting the conflicts of the time, a multitude of fortresses and defensive walls was either built or reconstructed. The walls built by the Almohads can be seen in the Macarena district of Seville. Equally in Seville, can be see an example of the polygonal style of fortified tower: the Torre del Oro. An earlier example is the Torre de Espantaperros in Badajoz. Reflecting their origins as religious reformers, the Almohads built many mosques. Beginning with the simplicity of Ibn Tumart's mosque in Tin Mal, as their empire developed they began to build outstanding grand mosques. The Koutoubia mosque in Marrakech was built around 1158. Its minaret was an inspiration for a similar one in Seville and formed part of the new grand mosque, which, as we have seen, was commenced there in 1172 by the Caliph Abu Ya'qub. The place of the mosque is now occupied by Seville Cathedral but the minaret still exists. It is called the Giralda and is now topped by a Christian bell tower. Another minaret, of similar style, was begun in Rabat during the building works initiated by Abu Yusuf around 1196 but was never finished after the Almohad dynasty fell. The Almohad mosques were significantly less opulent than, for example, that of the Great Mosque in Córdoba of the Umayyads. In each of the minarets in Marrakech, Rabat and Seville, the ascetic tendencies

Right. Remains of the fortifications at Calatrava la Vieja. On the route from Córdoba to Toledo, it was a symbol of Umayyad power in the upper Guadiana region. It was captured by Alfonso VII in 1147. Shortly afterwards, the first Spanish military order, the Order of Calatrava, was founded here. After their victory at Alarcos in 1195, the castle was retaken by the Almohads and became a strategic base in their struggle against the Christians in Toledo to the north. It was finally captured by the Christians as part of the campaign that culminated in the decisive battle of las Navas de Tolosa in 1212.

of the Almohads can be seen in the simplicity of the plain **geometric decoration in raised brick**.

The ruling circle of the Almohads was based on the family of Abd al-Mumin, as well as descendants of the leading hierarchies formed during the time of Ibn Tumart. This gave stability to the Almohad dynasty and ruling clique but with the disadvantage that they remained a closed group, remote from the people of their Empire. As in the time of the Almoravids, the Almohad influence in al-Andalus was superficial; the Andalusis were broadly able to continue their way of life as before. While the Governors there were Almohad, the administrators and functionaries under them were Andalusi. Again, as with the Almoravids, the Andalusi influence on the Maghreb continued, with a steady absorption there of the more sophisticated culture, architecture and technology from the Peninsula.

The early Almohads originated in the Berber tribes based in the harsh terrain of the High Atlas. However, many of the subsequent caliphs and leaders, now urban dwellers, were learned and cultured men, who had a high regard for architecture, philosophy and literature. Two men, who were prominent in Almohad

Left. Averroes, described as the greatest intellectual figure of al-Andalus. Born in Córdoba, he rose to prominence but temporarily fell foul of Almohad intransigence. He moved to Marrakech and died there in 1198.

times, are portrayed by James Joyce in his book 'Ulysses' as 'Averroes and Moses Maimonedes, dark in mien and movement, flashing in their mocking mirrors the obscure soul of the world'. Averroes or Ibn Rushd was a philosopher and physician of an eminent Cordoban family. Described as the greatest intellectual figure of al-Andalus, he produced a prodigious output of learned texts, commenting on early Greek works, particularly the works of Aristotle. He was appreciated and encouraged by the Caliph Abu Ya'qub but the local religious leaders later denounced him and he was banished by the next Caliph, Abu Yusuf. He came back into the favour of the Caliph who brought him to Marrakech, where he became his physician and died there in 1198. Moses Maimonedes was another distinguished Cordoban, one of the most illustrious Jewish scholars. It must be said that Maimonedes rose to prominence despite the Almohads, as they persecuted the Jews in al-Andalus. He moved to the less

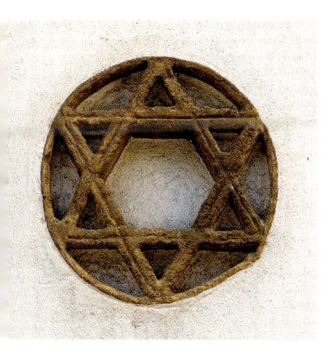

Above. Star of David set in the wall of a house located in the winding streets of the old quarter of Jaén.

Right. Maimonedes, a Cordoban and one of the most illustrious Jewish scholars. He moved to the less restrictive Fez to avoid the Almohad persecution of the Jews. He studied medicine there and died in Egypt in 1204, where he had been physician to Saladin.

Right. Bronze door of the Kairouan University, Fez, on which the shape of a Star of David can be seen. Maimonedes studied here for several years.

restrictive Fez, spending a few years there and studied at the Kairouan University. He eventually went to Egypt where he became court physician to the Sultan, Saladin and died there in 1204. Maimonedes' great work on philosophy bears the superb title of 'Guide for the Perplexed'. Waves of persecution of the Jews during the Almohad era forced a large number of Andalusi Jews to flee to Christian Spain and countries around the Mediterranean.

After the battle of Alarcos, Caliph Abu Yusuf remained in Seville. He and his father before him enjoyed their sojourns in their Andalusi capital and spent as much time as they could there during their reigns. At this time, the Almohads were in the ascendant and were generally dominant in the military offensives against the Christians. Having concluded truces with the Christians, Abu Yusuf returned to Marrakech in 1198. He died there the following year and was succeeded by his son who became the fourth Caliph, taking the honorific title of *al-Nasir*. In the first years of his reign the Almohads had to deal with the continuing threats originating from the neo-Almoravid Banu Ghaniya in Ifriqiya, who were also still in power in Majorca. The Almohads mustered a large number of ships and troops to attack them in their Majorca stronghold and succeeded in finally taking the island in 1203. However, remnants of these fled to North Africa and joined forces with the rebels there. The rebellion intensified in Tunisia and it took another three years for the Almohad forces to stamp it out.

There was relative peace in al-Andalus arising from the truces with the Christians but storm clouds were gathering. Alfonso VIII had not forgotten the bitter defeat of Alarcos. By around 1209, the Castilians and Aragonese recommenced their attacks on Muslim lands. Caliph al-Nasir, responding to pleas for help from al-Andalus, set out with a large army from the Maghreb. In June 1211 the Almohad army attacked the fortress of Salvatierra, an advance position of the Order of Calatrava and took it successfully. The Caliph and his army returned to Seville and wintered there. However, in an unprecedented move, the Christians began to form a coalition against the Muslims and plan a major attack. The struggle had escalated from mere conquest of land into a crusade. Since the middle of the twelfth century a series of papal bulls had equated the struggle against Islamic al-Andalus with the crusades in the Holy Land. This bolstered the idea of the Reconquista. This, the concept of recovery of the lands taken by the Muslims, now appeared achievable and came to the fore. Alfonso VIII secured a declaration of a crusade against the infidel in al-Andalus from Pope Innocent III. Detailed preparations were put in train from the spring of 1212. Christian knights from northern Europe came to Toledo for the crusade. The armies of Castile and Aragón assembled there. Alfonso IX of León, in dispute with Castile, refused to join the crusade and did not send his army. However, there were also individual detachments from León as well as from Portugal. The combined Christian forces headed south on the twentieth of June 1212 and moved towards the Muslim frontier. They retook castles lost after the defeat of Alarcos, including that of Calatrava la Vieja (twelve kilometres to the north-east of Ciudad Real). Around this time, the foreign knights abandoned the campaign. in discontentment, Apparently one of the causes was the exceed-

Right. Castle at Alcalá de Guadaira, near Seville. It was constructed by order of the Almohad Caliph Abu Ya'cub around 1172. The castle was enlarged several times after being captured by the Castilian forces in 1247.

Right. Symbolism: arrow hole at Alcalá de Guadaira, crowned by a cross.

Left. The Pass of Despeñaparros, a strategic point on the route from the Guadalquivir plain to the Meseta Central.

Left. Small castle near the site of the Battle of las Navas de Tolosa which took place in July, 1212.

Above. The Battle of las Navas de Tolosa. Francisco de Paula Van Halen. Patrimonio Histórico-Artístico del Senado, Madrid. Photography: Oronoz. This battle was a seminal event as the Almohads never recovered militarily from this decisive defeat.

Right. Monument to the victory of las Navas de Tolosa at La Carolina. In the front, in bronze, is the shepherd who, according to legend, guided the Christians through a hidden defile to gain advantage over their enemy.

Left. Victors at las Navas de Tolosa: Alfonso VIII and other Christian leaders, including the Kings of Aragón and Navarra.

ingly hot summer weather. However, the Christian army was reinforced by the King of Navarra and his forces who arrived shortly afterwards.

The Caliph promptly moved to meet the threat and led his forces out of Seville at the end of June. They went to Jaén and from there up to las Navas de Tolosa (around sixty-four kilometres north-east of Jaén). The army camped on a hill that faces the pass of Despeñaperros. This pass allows passage from the Meseta Central to the Guadalquivir plains and the Christian army was expected to descend through it. Legend has it that a local shepherd guided the Christians through a winding and hidden route through the defile, allowing them to avoid the well-defended main pass. They emerged and set up their encampment facing the Muslim lines. The Christians attacked the Almohads on the sixteenth of July 1212. The Christian heavy cavalry cut through the more lightly-armed Almohad troops. The Muslim army was decisively defeated and it scattered. The Caliphs of the later Almohad dynasty did not display any outstanding military brilliance and al-Nasir was no exception. Abandoning his troops, he fled to Baeza and retreated back to Seville. The Christians took Baeza and Úbeda and other enclaves in the region. Epidemics and lack of supplies impeded the Christians from pressing their advantage in the short term and they made only minor advances. However, the battle was to prove a seminal event. While the Almohad presence continued in the Peninsula for two more decades, their military capability was severely damaged and this defeat sounded the death knell for their rule.

Al-Nasir returned to Marrakech. He was poisoned there in December 1213. His son, Yusuf II, only ten years of age, was sworn in as the new Caliph. Guided by Almohad elders, the young man had a relatively uneventful reign until he died in January 1224, leaving no heirs. In the Iberian Peninsula, the rulers of Aragón and Castile had died in 1213 and 1214, respectively and the successions were complicated due to the fact that both heirs were very young. Fortunately for the Muslims, this diverted the Christians and al-Andalus enjoyed a relative respite from Christian pressure for a decade. However, back in the Maghreb, the Almohad dynasty now began the process of disintegration. On the death of Yusuf II, his great-uncle was chosen to be Caliph. Shortly afterwards a nephew of his, Abd Allah, the governor of Murcia, rose up in opposition and declared himself Caliph (taking the honorific of *al-Adil*). Most regions of al-Andalus

Above. Castle of Zuheros, south-east of Córdoba. Zuheros was an administrative centre of the Cora of Elvira during the Córdoba Caliphate. It was conquered by King Fernando III in the thirteenth century.

declared for al-Adil, save for the governor of Valencia, a *sayid* (or lord) Abu Zayd, known as Ceyt Abu Ceyt. A great-grandson of the first Almohad Caliph, he remained loyal to the ruler in Marrakech. Al-Adil was also opposed by Ceyt's brothers, one of whom seized power in Baeza (henceforth he was known as al-Bayyasi and declared himself as vassal of Fernando III of Castile). Al-Bayyasi cooperated with the Christians in their campaigns and set up in Córdoba. However, the citizens there were outraged at his collaboration and rose up. He fled and was killed in October 1225. Over in the Maghreb, the Marrakech Caliph had not ruled for long, being assassinated in September 1224. The claimant in al-Andalus, al-Adil, had spent time inconclusively fighting al-Bayyasi. In the west he also repulsed the attacks of the Portuguese who were pressing strongly and succeeded in advancing within sight of the Seville city walls. Eventually, at the end of 1225, al-Adil returned to Marrakech to be recog-

Left. Morning sky over the castle of Zuheros.

nised there as Caliph, leaving behind the precarious mess to his brother, Abu-l-Ala, governor of Seville.

In winter 1227 the intrigue among the Almohad ruling elite continued when al-Adil was assassinated. His brother in Seville, Abu-l-Ala (who took the honorific title of *al-Ma'mun*), proclaimed himself Caliph. He agreed a truce with Fernando III of Castile without delay and paid him a large sum. Having thus gained a temporary halt to the Castilian pressure, he gathered his Almohad troops and went to Marrakech in October 1228. Al-Ma'mun's departure signified the end of significant Almohad military power in the Peninsula. The new Caliph established his primacy in Marrakech but afterwards abandoned the tenets on which the Almohads had been founded and embraced Sunni Islam. He died in 1132 and a further four caliphs ruled up to the fall of Marrakech over thirty years later. The Almohad Empire in the Maghreb descended into oblivion: three separate rebellions broke out. To the east, the Hafsids had set up in Ifriqiya in 1228 and established their dynasty centred in Tunis, a dynasty that was to continue for centuries. The Zayyanids were active in north-western Algeria and set up in Tremecen in 1236. Their dynasty lasted over three centuries. Finally, emerged the power that later exerted significant influence in the Iberian Peninsula: the Banu Marin, or the Marinids, a nomadic Zanata tribe of

Right. The castle at Monteagudo, near Murcia. Now crowned by a statue of Christ, this was once the palace of Ibn Mardanis, who set up after the demise of the Almoravids and resisted the expansion of the Almohads.

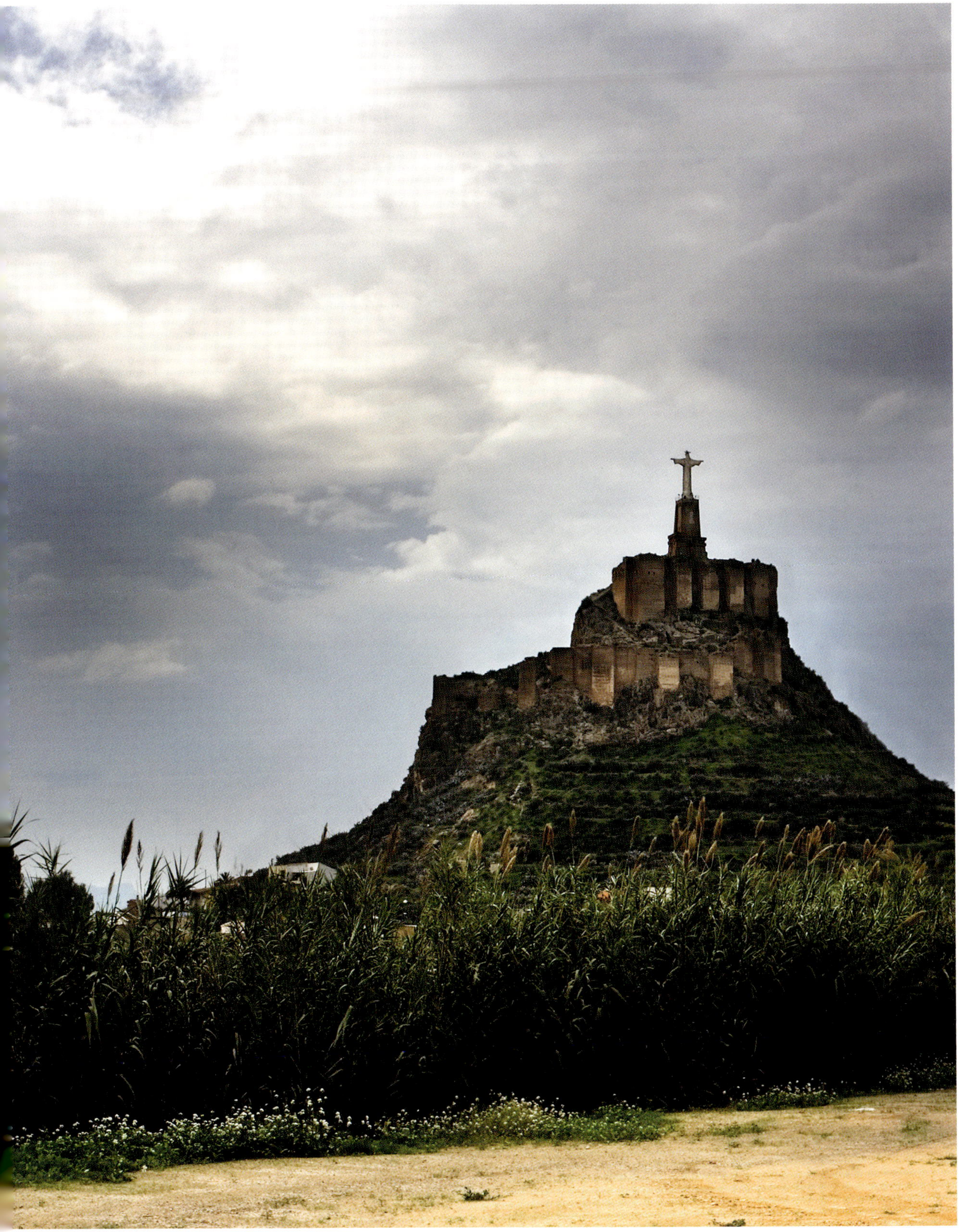

Left. Head of al-Azraq at a fountain in la Vall d'Alcalá in the Marina Alta, south of Valencia. Born around 1216, this local ruler in turn pacted with and rebelled against Jaime I of Aragón. He lost his life at a battle in Alcoy in 1276.

the plains. They had maintained a long struggle against the Almohads and took Fez in 1248, making it their capital. In 1269 they eventually captured the Almohad capital of Marrakech and gained mastery of Morocco.

By the time al-Ma'mun left al-Andalus, the local Andalusis were greatly disillusioned with the Almohads who had not been able to carry out the primary requirement of an Islamic ruler: to protect the population from external (Christian) attacks. History repeated itself. Just as they had done in the twilight of the Almoravids, the Andalusis rose up against North African rule. This led to the development of the 'third' taifas, all but one of which was to have an ephemeral existence. Like the pattern of previous taifas, local leaders stepped forward to take power, against the backdrop of the decline in central power. In 1228 one Ibn Hud of the Banu Hud, former rulers of Zaragoza, set up in Murcia and proclaimed himself 'Amir of the Muslims'. Seeking to enhance his legitimacy, he recognised the Abbasid Caliphs in Baghdad and, thereafter, flew the Abbasid black standard. He struck a chord across al-Andalus. All the main cities (including Seville, Córdoba, Granada and Almería), with the exception of Valencia, recognised him. However, the Christians also took advantage of the vacuum in Muslim power and launched vigorous offensives. Ibn Hud failed the litmus test of being able to defend Muslim lands against the Christians: in 1230 he suffered a serious defeat in a battle with the King of León, Alfonso IX, at Alange, near Mérida. The Christians continued their advances and took Mérida and Badajoz in 1232. The way was now open to the south and the Guadalquivir valley. On the death of Alfonso IX in September 1230, Castile and León were reunited and thus the Christian advance proceeded with even more energy. Fernando III (now of Castile and León) put Córdoba under siege and it surrendered in 1236. Córdoba had been the capital during the glory of the Umayyad

Right. The triumphal entry into Valencia by Jaime I of Aragón in 1238. Valencia had a chequered history, being captured from the Muslims by El Cid in 1094. After the death of El Cid it was seized by the the Almoravids in 1102.

Below. Bust of Jaime I. Museo Histórico Municipal, Valencia.

Caliphate and this was deeply demoralising for the Andalusis. The inhabitants were ordered to leave. The Great Mosque of Córdoba was consecrated as a Christian cathedral. The bells of Santiago de Compostela, seized by Almanzor in 997, were taken from the Mosque and returned to the Galician shrine. The Christians continued their traverse along the Guadalquivir valley, seizing territory and strongholds. Ibn Hud moved to Almería where he was assassinated in January 1238.

In Valencia, the Almohad Governor, Ceyt Abu Ceyt, was deposed by a Zayyan bin Mardanis (of the family of Ibn Mardanis, who had resisted the initial advent of the Almohads). He proclaimed himself Amir in February 1229. Ceyt Abu Ceyt fled to the frontier with Aragon and this staunch Almohad, surprisingly, later converted to Christianity, taking the name of Vicente. The Reconquista continued with the King of Aragón, Jaime I, concentrating on the seizure of Majorca, which he achieved by 1231. His sights now fell on Valencia and his forces steadily advanced towards the city. In April 1238 he mounted a siege of the city. In September of that year, Valencia, jewel of the Levante, capitulated to Jaime I.

Seville, the wealthy capital of the Almohads in al-Andalus, underwent a dizzying change of rulers as the Christian behemoth appeared on the horizon. Leadership of the city revolved from Ibn Hud to local leaders, then back to a recognition of the Almohads, ending up under a local council. The behemoth finally arrived and the Castilian Fernando III prepared by taking the cities around Seville like Carmona and Alcalá de Guadaira. He then commenced the siege of the city in July 1247. The Christians employed a squadron of ships from Cantabrica to sail to the south. The ships repulsed an Islamic fleet in the Gulf of Cádiz and then sailed up the Guadalquivir. The northern fleets managed to break through a bridge of boats over the river, which spanned from the city

Left. Statue of Fernando III in Seville Cathedral. He gave impetus to the Reconquista and conquered large swathes of al-Andalus. He captured Seville in 1248.

across to Triana on the other side. This was an era of changing allegiances and ruthless self-interest, as witnessed by the help the Christian besieging forces had received from troops dispatched by Ibn al-Ahmar (of whom much more later), founder of Nasrid Granada. Seville, running out of food, capitulated in December 1248. As was normal practice, the Muslim inhabitants were banished from the city.

    Most of the rest of al-Andalus was taken over by the Christians, either directly or indirectly, with submission by the rulers as vassals until the final takeover. Murcia lasted under Muslim rule until 1266, Minorca until 1287. Thus, in this turbulent thirteenth century, the Christians made enormous gains and the Reconquista was in full ascendance. They now controlled three-quarters of the former Almohad al-Andalus. Only the lands of the new kingdom of Granada (approximating to present-day Andalucía) remained under Muslim control.

Chapter 7
Nasrid Granada

As the Almohad star waned rapidly in al-Andalus, the Christians advanced and took over most of the territory. Only one small section remained: the Nasrid kingdom of Granada, which was to maintain Islamic rule in the Iberian Peninsula for another 250 years. The first of the Nasrids was Muhammad bin Yusuf bin Nasr, also known as Ibn al-Ahmar, who came from the town of Arjona, around thirty kilometres to the north-west of Jaén. He was from an established land-owning family of Arab origin. He was reputed in the earlier years to have had an ascetic and religious nature, verging on the mystical. Later, after forming his kingdom, he subscribed to the rigid Maliki tradition (a useful attribute, as it was to garner a lot of religious support from the *alfaquis* of Granada).

In the era of Almohad decline, Ibn Hud who, as we have seen, had set up in most of al-Andalus, had been originally looked on by the Muslims as a saviour. However, they soon lost confidence in him: he was defeated in several battles and he raised taxes to pay *parias* to the Christians who were in the ascendant. Under Fernando III the Kingdom of Castile had a new dynamism since its union with León in 1230. As the Castilian raids increased along the frontier region, Ibn al-Ahmar, then aged around thirty-seven years, came to prominence and established a reputation as an able defender. He took the initiative, rising up in Arjona against Ibn Hud and was proclaimed as leader in the local mosque in 1232. Ibn al-Ahmar soon expanded his domain in the surrounding region towards Baeza and Guadix. The people of Jaén invited him to be ruler in 1233 and he set up there. Saviours were in short supply and his reputation preceded him. In the same year he was invited to rule in Córdoba and, some time later, in Seville. In each case, his rule lasted only a few weeks. These big city dwellers did not take to the style of the man from Arjona and reverted back to Ibn Hud. Ibn al-Ahmar took the decision in 1234 to recognise Ibn Hud who conceded to him the lordship of Arjona and Jaén. This was an early manifestation of the essential skills of Ibn al-Ahmar that allowed him to survive and establish the Kingdom of Granada. All through his career, he demonstrated his capacity as a master tactician, combining pragmatism, shrewdness and a touch of deviousness.

It was common practice in those times to treat with the Christian enemy. Ibn al-Ahmar soon negotiated a treaty with Fernando III. One consequence was that he facilitated the Christian seizure of Muslim Córdoba in 1236. One wonders how that sat with his Islamic mysticism. However, it must be seen against the background of those dangerous times as the remaining Muslim enclaves around the Peninsula were being captured progressively by the Christians. Survival was a sensible choice and we later see Ibn al-Ahmar allying with the Christians anytime it suited. Whatever his mix of attributes, it appealed to the people of Granada who now requested him to be their ruler. He travelled there in May 1238 and set up his headquarters in the old Zirid Alcazaba. Shortly afterwards, news came of Ibn Hud's assassination in Almería. Ibn al-Ahmar seized the moment, headed there and took the city in mid 1238. Málaga submitted to him in the same year. Over the space of six whirlwind years, he had moved from being the leader in small-town Arjona to Amir of the Kingdom of Granada, in command of a significant part of the south-east of the Peninsula.

Ibn al-Ahmar's treaty with Fernando III expired in 1242. Christian accounts claim that he made attacks on Christian lands which provoked retaliation. In any case, the Castilians advanced and devastated the countryside around Jaén. They began a siege of the city in August 1245. Dominated by a castle on a hill over the city, it presented a difficult target. As the siege wore on, Ibn al-Ahmar made an attempt to send relief supplies to the defenders but was not successful. Finally, in 1246, he decided to resolve the conflict and signed a treaty with Fernando III. The conditions were hard. Jaén was to be handed over to Castile as well as a tribute of a huge sum of money every year. Ibn al-Ahmar was to be

Above. The castle of Santa Catalina overlooks the city of Jaén. In 1233 the people of this city invited Ibn al-Ahmar, founder of the Nasrid dynasty, to be ruler.

Right. The walls of Jaén, descending the hill, from the castle to the city. These are reportedly of Almohad origin. In 1246 Ibn al-Ahmar concluded a treaty with Fernando III which included the handing over of the city. However, it bought time for the Nasrid founder to consolidate his new Kingdom of Granada.

Castile's vassal and give military support when required. However, the positive feature was that the treaty was of twenty years' duration. Thus, Ibn al-Ahmar, now Muhammad I of Granada, bought himself time to consolidate his rule and set up all the necessary administrative structures for his new kingdom. The treaty also brought him protection, as a vassal of Castile, from the attacks of Aragón on his Levante frontier. On a strategic level, the excision of the Jaén region from his domain marked a retrenchment to a more defensible line. The Christians had proved that they held the advantage in open warfare across the plains of the Guadalquivir. The mountainous territory of the Baetic Cordillera formed a spine along the length of the Kingdom of Granada, which, coupled with the series of frontier fortresses that were constructed, now presented a more secure barrier against Christian attacks. In addition, the ports along the Mediterranean coast allowed access to support from the Islamic kingdoms of the Maghreb. Apart from the ports of the Strait which it was to lose at an early stage, the Kingdom of Granada was now in the shape it was to retain for most of the course of Nasrid rule. It comprised, more or less, the present-day provinces of Málaga, Granada and Almería and ranged in the west from Tarifa along the Mediterranean coast to the eastern frontier with Murcia.

Soon after he first established himself in Granada, Ibn al-Ahmar ordered the construction of the Alhambra, on a spur of the Sierra Nevada, the hill of the Sabika, which dominates the city. This was a palace-city, similar to the Madinat al-Zahra of the Córdoba Caliphate. One of the first buildings constructed was the great fortress of the Alcazaba, which faces the Granadan Vega. In addition, there were palaces and buildings for administration, baths and a great mosque. This was to be the heart of the Nasrid dynasty: it was the residence of the Amirs through the years as they continued their expansion of the Alhambra. As the Reconquista continued, a stream of Muslim refugees came to the Kingdom of Granada. The city grew rapidly, absorbing the flow of people from the lost terri-

Left. Parade helmet in steel, gold, silver and enamel, dating from Nasrid times. Metropolitan Museum of Art, New York.

tories of al-Andalus. The walls of the city were strengthened and were extended to incorporate the Albaicín district (named after refugees from Baeza who settled there).

Ibn al-Ahmar's assistance to Fernando III in sieging Muslim Seville represented the Faustian aspect of his pact with Castile. As vassal of Castile, he sent 500 horsemen to take part in the siege of Seville, which was taken at the end of 1248. This was a less than honourable part of early Nasrid history but one could argue that, had Ibn al-Ahmar been more principled, it is likely his Granada kingdom would not have survived for the two and a half centuries that it did.

The Marinids, who had set up in Fez, were eager to help their co-religionists in Granada against the Christian threat. This began their involvement in the Peninsula, which was to last for around eighty years. It commenced around 1263 when the Marinid Amir sent a detachment of *Guza*, or 'fighters of the faith' to Granada. Ibn al-Ahmar was strengthened by these new arrivals, which may lend weight to suggestions that he encouraged the uprising of the Mudéjars (Muslims living under Christian rule) in Christian territory, which erupted all along the frontier. He sent troops to aid them in Jerez in 1264, but the Granadan troops were repelled. More troops were sent to Murcia, but Jaime I of Aragón eventually ejected them. A fresh wave of refugees flowed into Granada as the Mudéjars were expelled by the Christians. Thus, Ibn al-Ahmar's brief attempt to roll back the Reconquista failed.

Trouble now broke out on the internal front. The Banu Asqilula family had been close supporters of Ibn al-Ahmar and had been prominent during his rise to power. This family was related by marriage to the Granadan Amir; one of the Banu Asqilula was head of the army. The family had built up expectations of sharing power that were frustrated by Ibn al-Ahmar's naming of his sons as heirs.

Above. The 'Arab Baths' in Ronda, which are of the Nasrid era and date from the thirteenth or fourteenth centuries.

Right. Ceramic bowl from Málaga. Even though it was made in the period from 1425-1450 when Málaga was under Nasrid rule, the ship has the arms of Portugal on its sail. It is speculated that this was commissioned by a Portuguese maritime merchant. Victoria and Albert Museum, London.

The Banu Asqilula were also perturbed by the presence of the Marinid *Guza*, who they perceived as displacing their control of the army. In 1266 the Banu Asqilula rose up against the Amir in two strategic locations to the east and west of Granada: Málaga and Guadix. The rebels looked for help to Alfonso X of Castile who sent to their aid a detachment of cavalry led by Nuño González. Despite his best efforts, Ibn al-Ahmar was not able to put down the rebels. He then turned to the disaffected nobles of Castile, the '*Ricos Hombres*', now led by the same Nuño González who had decided to oppose Alfonso X. With their help, the Nasrid forces attacked and took Antequera from the Banu Asqilula in July 1272. The political situation moved to equilibrium: the opposing power on each side allied with the dissident forces of its enemy. The conflict was still ongoing when Ibn al-Ahmar tumbled from his horse and died in January 1273.

He was succeeded by his son, Muhammad II. Aged thirty-eight, he was very experienced, having occupied senior positions of state. On his accession, the immediate task that faced him was that of suppressing the Banu Asqilula uprising. He first tried to treat with Alfonso X on this problem but the Castilian proved to be demanding and difficult. Muhammad II now looked further afield to the Marinids in Fez who had sent an earlier detachment of troops, the *Guza*. The Marinids agreed to give substantially increased help. In addition to the *jihadi* instinct, this reflected the hegemonic desire of the Marinids to reconstitute the old Almohad Empire, as well as to control the Strait of Gibraltar. The

Above. The Alhambra sits on the Sabika hill above Granada, in the shelter of the Sierra Nevada.

Right. Part of the ramparts of the castle at Tarifa. A strategic port during the battle for control of the Strait of Gibraltar, this was the scene of much conflict during the Nasrid era.

Marinid Amir, Abu Yusuf, made plans to lead a large army to the Peninsula. Thus a new and potent dynamic was added to the competing forces in the Peninsula and it was the beginning of a bewildering tableau of ever-changing alliances. The Marinid advance troops landed in Tarifa, setting up there and in Algeciras by May 1275. Abu Yusuf followed in August, leading the main force. Once installed, he convened a meeting attended by Muhammad II and representatives of the Banu Asqilula. This was a failure, with Muhammad II storming off at what he perceived as the pro-Asqilula attitude of Abu Yusuf. The Marinid army then embarked on a series of raids on Castilian lands, sacking the regions of Córdoba, Seville and Jaén. With Algeciras and Tarifa still under Marinid control, Abu Yusuf, laden with booty, returned to the Maghreb. However, the genie was now out of the bottle: the Marinids proved to be as much a danger to the Nasrids as were the Castilians. Without prior consultation with the Nasrids, the Marinids mounted another expedition to the Peninsula. Abu Yusuf led this new campaign, making several raids against localities from Jaén to Cádiz during the second half of 1277. Fearful of being attacked by the Nasrids, the Banu Asqilula ceded Málaga to the Marinids. Muhammad II, now alarmed by the danger the Marinids posed to his kingdom, made an arrangement with Alfonso X to join forces and eject the Marinids from the peninsula. He also reached an agreement with one of the other Maghrebi dynasties, the Zayyanids in Tremecen.

Events moved swiftly: in February 1279 the Castilians besieged Algeciras (in Marinid hands) from the sea but were beaten back by the Marinid fleet. Around the same time, Muhammad II manoeuvred, by bribery it is suggested, the takeover of Málaga. The Marinids then agreed peace with the Castilians and the swirling dance continued, with the protagonists rapidly changing partners. In 1280, the Castilians, the Banu Asqilula and Marinids now embarked on attacks on the Nasrids who succeeded in fending them off. Fortunately for the Nasrids,

Left. Statue of Sancho IV at Tarifa. In alliance with the Nasrids, he seized this port from the Marinids in 1292.

there was dissension within Castile: Alfonso X fell into dispute with his son Sancho who entered the fray on Granada's side.

Alfonso X died in April 1284 and was succeeded by Sancho IV. In 1285 the Marinids mounted another military campaign in the Peninsula, this time against Sancho. The Marinid Amir Abu Yusuf died in Algeciras in March 1286. At this time his kingdom was still in control of Algeciras and Tarifa. However, the priorities had changed for the Marinids. They now just wanted to maintain the status quo on the Peninsula: new challenges had emerged in the Maghreb and they wanted to concentrate their efforts there. In any case, the vicissitudes of dealing with the wily Nasrids and the quicksands of the ever-changing peninsular power alliances did not present an attractive prospect. Abu Ya'qub, the new Marinid Amir, signed a peace agreement with the Nasrids. In 1288, the Banu Asqilula faded out of the history of the Peninsula, as they emigrated to the Maghreb, where they were granted lands by the Marinid Amir. They set up a small dynasty in Ksar el-Kabir (around eighty-five kilometres south of Tangier).

Muhammad II, who wanted control over the Strait, signed an accord with Sancho IV in May 1291. The understanding was that the Castilians would take Tarifa, which they would then swap with Granada for some frontier fortresses. Sancho IV began the siege of Tarifa with the help of the Aragonese navy, which blockaded from the sea. Muhammad's' troops came from Málaga and joined the siege. The city fell in October 1292. However, Muhammad may have been too clever by far in his manoeuvring, as the deal ended up with a loss for him.

Right. Guzmán 'the Good', defender of Tarifa, which the Marinids attempted to retake in 1294.

Sancho reneged on the agreement, refused to hand over Tarifa and, at the same time, seized the promised frontier fortresses.

For Muhammad II, understandably angered, it was time to switch partners. He reverted back to the Marinids. The agreement that he now reached was that he would get Algeciras and Ronda, with the Marinids having possession of Tarifa. In the opposing corner were the Castilians, along with the Aragonese but now in an alliance with the Zayyanids in Tremecen (in the Maghreb), enemies of the Marinids. So, in April 1294, the Marinids started the siege of Tarifa. Although the Granadans were their allies, they gave only nominal support. Then the famous event happened, when the leader of the Castilian defenders Alfonso Pérez de Guzmán or 'Guzmán the Good' was confronted by the demand of the besiegers; surrender or they would kill his son whom they had captured. He defied them and legend has it that he threw his dagger down at them to do it, whereupon the son was killed. This event had poignant later resonances for an event in the twentieth-century Spanish Civil War when Colonel Moscardó, Nationalist commander of the besieged Alcázar in Toledo, was confronted with a similar proposal by the Republican forces. They had captured his son and threatened to shoot him unless the Alcázar was surrendered. It is recounted that he told his son, over the telephone, to die bravely.

The siege of Tarifa lasted just four months – it was lifted when Aragonese ships came to the rescue. After the failure of the siege, the Marinids decided to leave the peninsular stage. The two Amirs met to discuss this in Tangier in 1295 and, as a result, Granada was able to finally incorporate Algeciras and Ronda. Sancho IV died in April 1295. Castile was weakened by internal dissension, as

Left. A gold bracelet from the Nasrid era, from Bentarique in Almería. Archivo Fotográfico, Museo Arqueológico Nacional, Madrid.

the new successor to the throne was only ten years of age. Granada was now in a position of strength. As the Aragonese wished to avoid a pact between the Castilians and Nasrids, they signed a treaty with the latter. When Muhammad II died in April 1302 he was succeeded by his son Muhammad III (one source suggests that the Amir was poisoned by his son). The new Amir signed a pact with the Castilians, which gave him confidence to begin his new adventure. Desirous of total control of the Strait, he cast his sights on Ceuta in the Maghreb. For more than two centuries, the dynamic of invasion had come from the Maghreb to the Peninsula. This marked a reversal of that pattern. The Granadans fomented a revolt in Ceuta and subsequently took it over in 1307. This Nasrid venture proved to be a step too far: it propelled the Marinids, Castilians and Aragonese to form a triple alliance against Granada.

This external threat caused popular unease in Granada and resulted in Muhammad III being forced to abdicate in March 1309. He was replaced by his brother Nasr. (Muhammad was assassinated in January 1314). The situation facing the new Amir was bleak: Granada stood alone against three kingdoms. The Marinids attacked Ceuta, with the assistance of an Aragonese fleet and ejected the Nasrids. In July 1309 the Castilians began the siege of Algeciras and eventually seized nearby Gibraltar in September 1309. In August the Aragonese attacked Almería by land and sea.

The members of the Nasrid dynasty seemed to inherit the ability to skilfully negotiate their way out of dangerous situations. Nasr behaved adroitly: he took the difficult decision to negotiate with the Marinids and hand over to them the enclaves of Algeciras and Ronda. In exchange, the Marinids sent an army to his aid. On the Castilian side, internal dissent broke out among the nobles. Against all this the Castilian Fernando IV decided to raise the siege of Algeciras in January 1310 and sign a treaty with Nasr. It involved the usual vassalage and the handing over to Castile of two border towns and tribute. The Granadans sent a

Below. Stucco decoration in the Alhambra. The central inscription reads 'the only conqueror is God'. This was the motto of the Nasrid dynasty and is displayed in many places in the Alhambra.

Above. Castle of the Estrella at Teba. Legend has it that the Scottish knight James Douglas threw the embalmed heart of Robert the Bruce into the fray during a battle here with Nasrid forces in 1330.

Right. Dome of the Madrasa in Granada, built in 1349 during the reign of Yusuf I.

Left. This woven silk dates from the fourteenth century and is an example of the sublime craft skills found during the Nasrid era. Victoria and Albert Museum, London.

relieving force to Almería and the siege by the Aragonese was lifted, also in January 1310.

Fernando IV of Castile died in 1312 in Jaén. His heir Alfonso was a child of only one year of age, which led to dissension in the kingdom. In the same year an uprising broke out against Nasr with the Amir's nephew, Isma'il, at the head of the rebels. Eventually, in 1314, Nasr was forced to abdicate and Isma'il I took power in the Alhambra. Nasr headed for Guadix and set up in opposition there. The Castilians supported Nasr and various encounters took place between these and Isma'il's forces. Eventually Isma'il's army decisively defeated the Castilians in what was termed the Battle of the Vega in June 1319. Isma'il spent some time recapturing lost fortresses and consolidating his kingdom but was assassinated in July 1325, following a dispute with his cousin. Isma'il's son, only ten years of age, succeeded him and became the new ruler, Muhammad IV. Initially, he was under his Vizier's tutelage but eventually grasped the reins of power. Over in Castile another young sovereign, Alfonso XI, reached his majority. The Castilian now planned to take the initiative and avenge the great defeat of the Vega of less than a decade before. Imbued with a crusading spirit, he tried to organise a coalition of the Iberian Christian states, together with support from the northern European kingdoms, against Granada. It did not work as he had planned and it was only the Castilians, with some European knights, that eventually set out on the offensive. They began their assault and took several frontier fortresses, including that of Teba (around thirty kilometres north-east of Ronda), which fell after a long siege in 1330. James Douglas, a Scottish knight and lieutenant of Robert the Bruce, had joined Alfonso's forces. In the course of the battle for the castle, he was killed along with his retinue. Legend has it that, having been entrusted to take on crusade a casket with Robert the Bruce's embalmed heart, Douglas threw it into the fray during the battle.

Muhammad IV asked for help from the Marinids and together they attacked Gibraltar, which they took in June 1333, after several months of siege. With the

Below. Part of the tiled mosaic decoration in the Alhambra.

Right. Yusuf I embarked on major construction works throughout his Kingdom. View from the ramparts of the castle of Gibralfaro in Málaga, built on his orders.

Marinid troops once more in the Peninsula, Alfonso XI saw it as wise to sign a truce in August 1333. Shortly afterwards, Muhammad IV, still only eighteen years old, was assassinated near Algeciras by sons of the leader of the *Guza* (the fighters for the faith stationed in Granadan territory). Muhammad's brother, another young man (only fifteen years old), Yusuf I, succeeded to the throne. He immediately accomplished the first essential task: that of expelling the family of his brother's assassins to the Maghreb. He then signed peace treaties with the Christian kingdoms. However, rivalry over control of the Strait led to an arms race between the Marinids and the Castilians, with both sides building up their navies. This came to a head when the Marinid navy struck at the Castilian fleet near Algeciras in April 1340 and soundly defeated it. Emboldened by this, the Marinid Amir crossed the Strait with a large force and laid siege to Tarifa in August 1340. The Christian forces (led by Alfonso XI of Castile and supported by his brother-in-law, the King of Portugal) set out to attack the Marinid army, which had the support of Nasrid troops. The Christians met the Muslims at the Rio Salado (near Tarifa) and inflicted a crushing defeat. The Muslims suffered huge losses and fled, leaving behind arms, treasure and, according to one account, slaves and concubines. The Marinids hurried back across the Strait and the Nasrids to Granada. Capitalising on this great victory, Alfonso seized Granadan frontier fortresses. He mustered a substantial force of northern European soldiers and began the siege of Algeciras in August 1342. Despite a strong defence by the Muslims, including their use of cannon, this strategic port surrendered in 1344. The technology of gunpowder and cannon was absorbed by the Christians and it is reported that English knights who had been at the siege brought this knowledge back to England. Later we shall see how the Castilians achieved a sophisticated mastery of artillery, which hastened the end of the Kingdom of Granada.

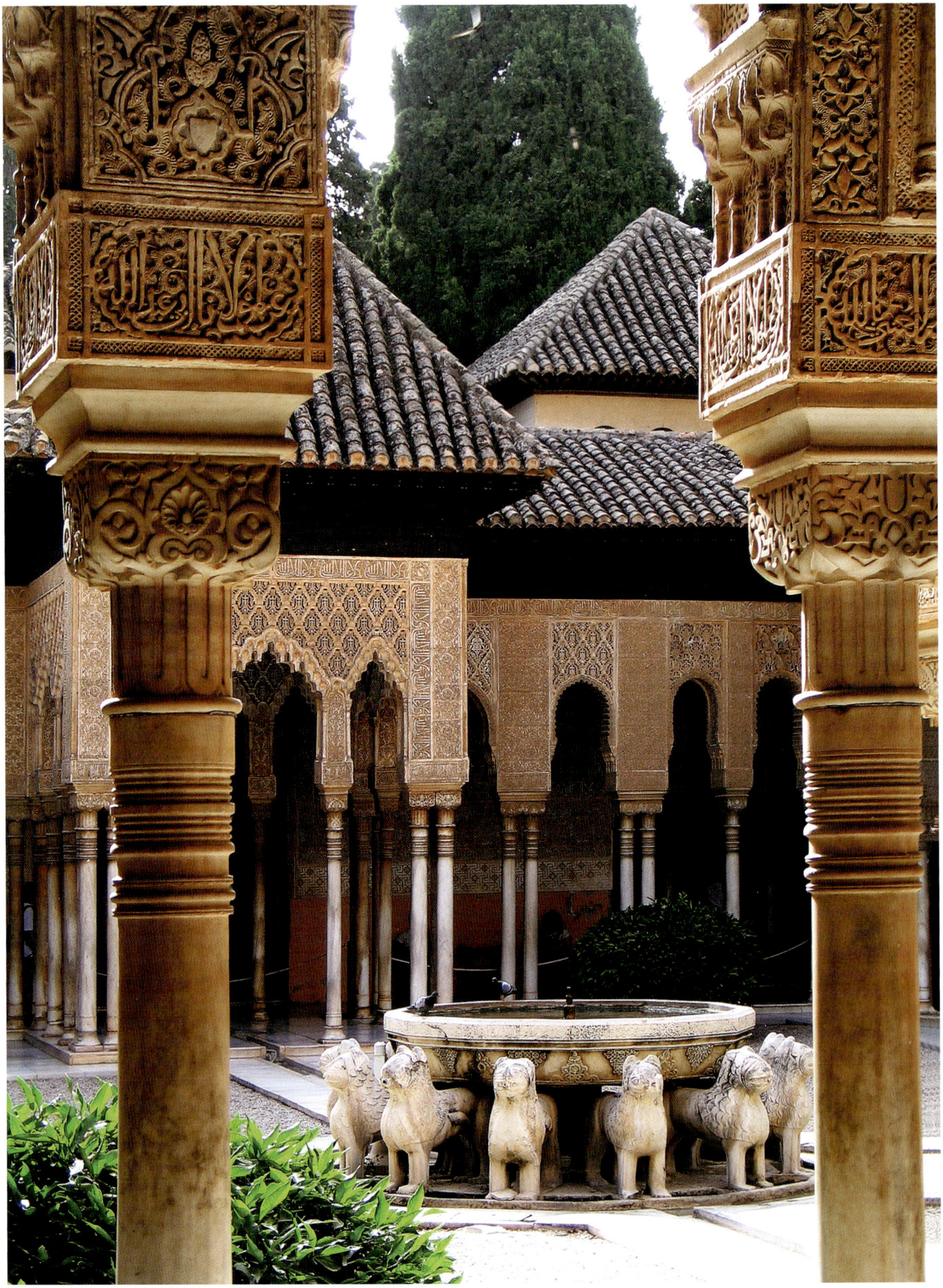

Right. The Mirador of Lindaraja in the Alhambra. Two windows look out on the garden. The walls have beautiful intricate stucco decoration with a lower level of tiled mosaics.

Left. Court of the Lions in the Alhambra. constructed by Muhammad V, whose reign marked an acceleration in the development of architecture, art and literature.

    As part of the handover of Gibraltar, Yusuf I concluded a ten-year truce with the Castilians. This peace and the resulting external stability led to a period of prosperity which fostered a flourishing of architectural, cultural and literary development in Granada. However, it did not escape the Black Plague, which had spread to Europe at this time. This pestilence was generally more virulent in cities than in the countryside. From 1348 onwards it passed through the Kingdom and had an impact on the economy due to the reduction of population. This did not stop Yusuf I from embarking on major construction works in the city and throughout his Kingdom. In the Alhambra, he built three imposing gateways as well as the towers of Machuca and Comares. The latter includes the main reception area, the Hall of the Ambassadors, which leads onto the Myrtle court. In 1349 Yusuf I built in the city itself the *Madrasa*, a theological semi-

Left. A German philosopher wrote that 'architecture is frozen music'. Never was this more exemplified than in this stucco decoration of exquisite delicacy in the Alhambra.

nary and law school. In Málaga he built the Gibralfaro castle which still dominates the city. Yusuf's reign marked the beginning of Granada's golden age and this continued during the reign of his son Muhammad V.

Alfonso XI of Castile had no scruples about breaking the truce with Granada. He began a siege of Gibraltar, but the Black Plague struck and he died there in March 1350. He was succeeded by his young son Pedro I, who gained the soubriquet of 'Pedro the Cruel'. He maintained good relations with the Nasrids and soon signed a peace treaty with them. However, the energetic Yusuf I was not to enjoy the peace for long. He was cut down in his prime at only thirty-six years of age by a demented slave, while he prayed at the mosque in the Alhambra, in October 1354.

He was succeeded by his son, Muhammad V. The new ruler was nearly sixteen years old but had the support of a talented and powerful group of court advisors, including the Vizier-historian Ibn al-Khatib. When personal energy and ability is combined with a long reign, external peace and a certain amount

Below. Polychrome decoration with inscription in the Comares Tower.

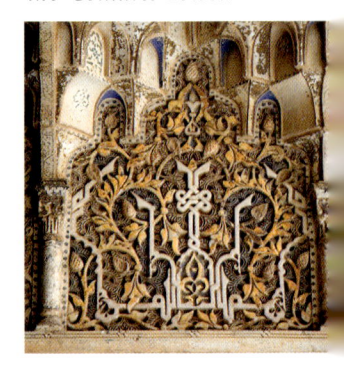

Right. In the Alhambra, column and capital against a decorated stucco background.

Right. Sublime beauty in the Alhambra: stucco frieze above a tiled mosaic.

Left. The ceiling of the Hall of the Abencerrajes, in the Alhambra.

Left. The Partal in the Alhambra. Shimmering water, set among luxuriant vegetation, a hallmark of the pleasure gardens of al-Andalus.

Right. The sound of water, sparkling in the fountain court of the Generalife, the summer residence of the Nasrid rulers.

Below right. Decoration of the Puerta del Vino.

Below. Marble, wood and tile: detail at the bottom of a door in the Alhambra.

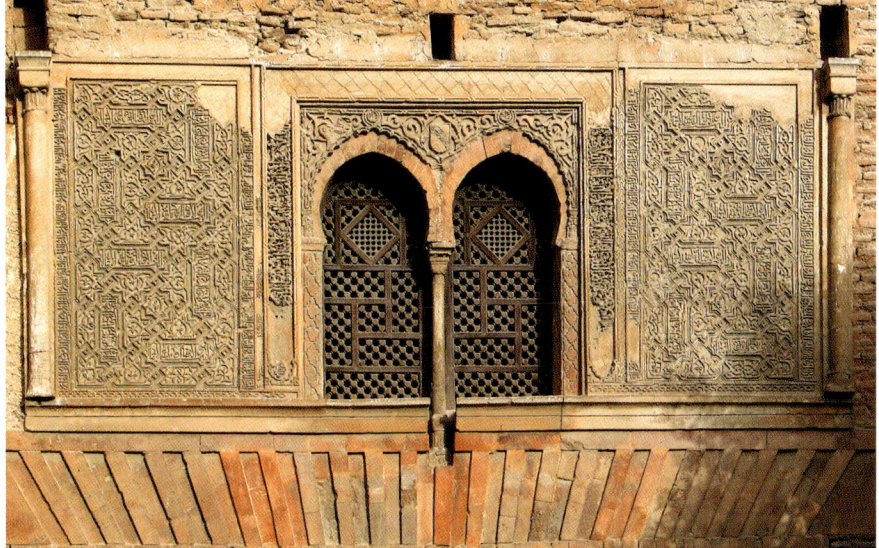

of luck, extraordinary things can be achieved. This was the case with Muhammad V, whose rule spanned thirty-seven years, albeit including an unplanned interruption of three years. This enlightened Amir presided over a period of stability and prosperity, which included the construction of some of the finest buildings in the Alhambra. In short, it was to represent the apogee of the Kingdom of Granada's splendour.

At the beginning of his reign, Muhammad V and his phalanx of advisors set about to copper-fasten the peace that he desired with the main powers that surrounded Granada. He signed new peace treaties, initially with Castile and later with Aragón. Not forgetting his co-religionists in the Maghreb, he sent Ibn al-Khatib to Fez in 1354, with the aim of establishing good relations with the Marinids. However, the peace was broken when, in 1358, Pedro I of Castile went to war with Aragón. Granada was sucked into the fray by virtue of its vassalage and had to send ships and land forces to support the Castilians. Domestic issues suddenly intervened when there was a takeover of the Alhambra in August 1359 by discontented palace plotters. Muhammad's stepbrother was proclaimed as the Amir Isma'il II. Muhammad managed to flee to Guadix and eventually headed to the Maghreb and found refuge with the Marinids in Fez. Back in Granada, the new ruler was reputed to be weak, indolent and dominated by his ambitious mother. He ruled for less than a year, his rule ending as suddenly as it had commenced. In July 1360 he was assassinated and replaced by his ambitious second cousin, Muhammad VI. This new ruler decided to establish

Above. Hand carved into the keystone of the outer arch of the Puerta de la Justicia, at the Alhambra. One explanation is that the five fingers represent the five pillars (or precepts) of Islam.

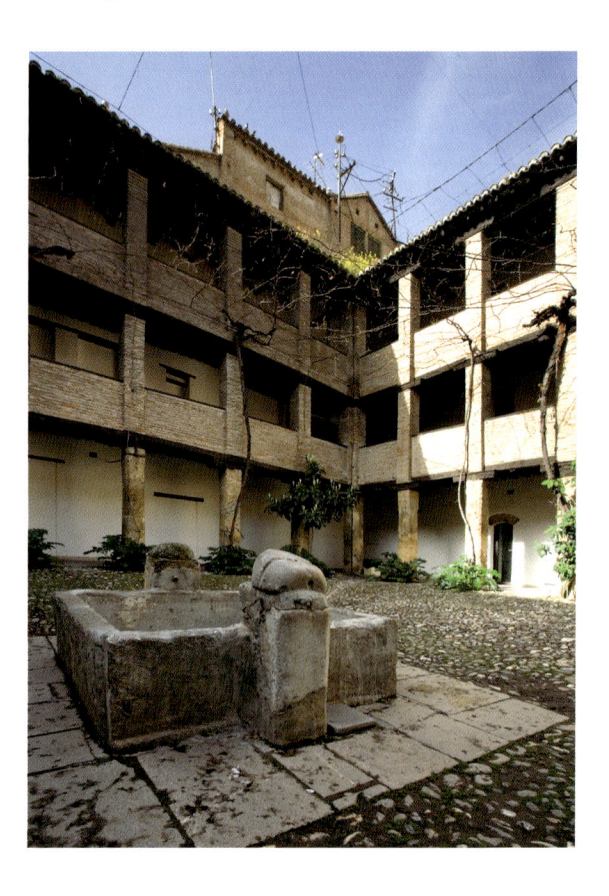

Left. Corral del Carbón in Granada. This was a funduq (or type of inn) where visiting silk merchants could lodge, as well as store their wares.

Right. Puerta de la Justicia, one of the principal entrances to the Alhambra.

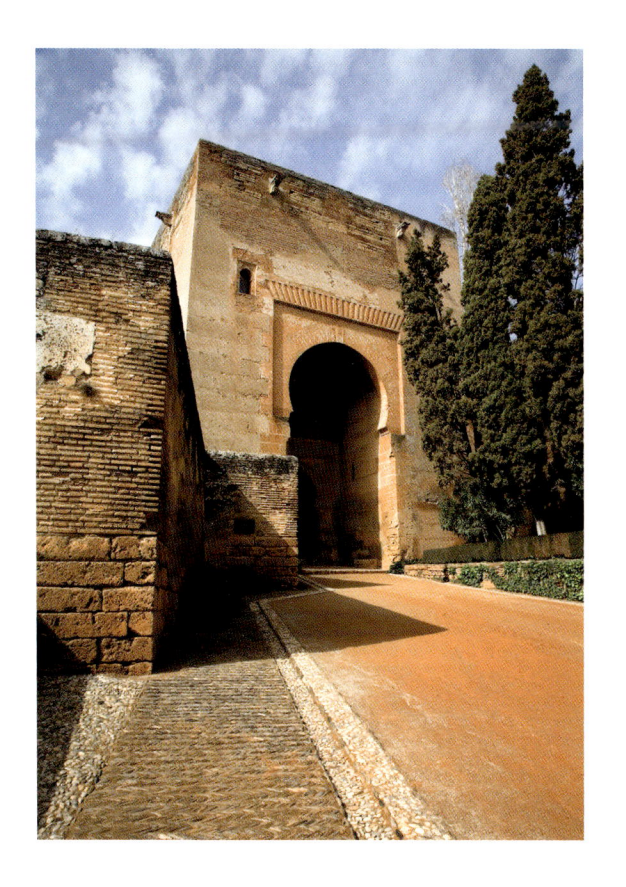

Right. The entrance gate of the Corral del Carbón.

Left. Statue of Pedro I of Castile, who was given the soubriquet of the 'Cruel'. Archivo Fotográfico, Museo Arqueológico Nacional, Madrid.

Left. Pedro I appreciated Muslim architecture. Employing Muslim craftsmen, some from Granada, he constructed the extraordinarily beautiful Real Alcázar in Seville, begun in 1364.

Right. Overlooking the fertile plain of the Guadalquivir, the Alcázar at Carmona, now a Parador. In the middle of the fourteenth century, Pedro I restored the former Islamic fortress and strengthened it.

close relations with Aragón. This proved to be a bad tactic, as, in consequence, Pedro I of Castile, engaged in conflict with Aragón, gave assistance to Muhammad V to reclaim his throne. Muhammad V returned in 1361 and established himself in Ronda. With Castilian assistance, he began a campaign to reclaim his Kingdom. After a slow start he eventually managed to take the important city of Málaga in 1362. This proved to be the tipping point and the other cities of the Kingdom declared for him. Muhammad VI, unwisely as it turns out, fled with his supporters to Castile to seek refuge. Pedro, displaying his appellation of 'the Cruel', executed them and sent their heads to Muhammad V, now reinstalled in Granada.

Following this episode of inter-family intrigue, Muhammad V now enjoyed an uninterrupted reign of nearly thirty years. After an initial period of conflict, this was to prove the longest and most peaceful period of rule in the history of the Kingdom of Granada. Muhammad, consistent with his first time on the throne, continued his skilful diplomacy, with the objective of achieving peace. As part of this, he maintained good relations with the Marinids, keeping a wary eye on any possibility that they might re-establish themselves in the Iberian Peninsula. He also maintained connections throughout the Maghreb and beyond, from the Zayyanids in Tremecen and the Hafsids in Tunis to the Mamelukes in Egypt.

As we have seen, Pedro I of Castile had assisted Muhammad V to regain his throne. Pedro I was fascinated by the exceptional Muslim architecture, considered by many to be the most brilliant of the time. This appreciation was demonstrated by Pedro's construction of the extraordinarily graceful Real Alcázar in Seville, which he began in 1364. This was built on an earlier Almohad building in the Islamic style, using Granadan master craftsmen. It was constructed during the same era as the Alhambra buildings – many of the styles and techniques are

Left. The Mediterranean, seen from the ramparts of the castle of Salobreña. This served as a royal prison during the dynastic intrigues of the Nasrids.

similar. However, Pedro had to concentrate on arms, not architecture. A war of succession flared up when Pedro was challenged by his half brother, Enrique II of Trastámara, who now stepped up his attempts to seize the throne. One of the accusations made against Pedro was that he was too pro-Muslim. In the midst of this civil war, Muhammad V backed Pedro and sent a detachment of troops to fight on his behalf. However, with the aid of French mercenaries and the support of Aragón, Enrique managed to seize the Castilian throne in 1366. Muhammad V, mindful of the danger of attack and with the Nasrid facility for survival, switched sides.

Skilful diplomat that he was, Muhammad V negotiated a tripartite peace treaty involving Granada, Aragón and the Marinids in Fez. However, in 1367 Pedro returned to regain his throne, this time with the aid of the English royal adventurer, Edward, the Black Prince. Muhammad V once again reverted to allying with Pedro. He used the dissension in Castile to attack anti-Pedro enclaves like Priego, Jaén, Úbeda and Baeza. However, in March 1369 Pedro was defeated and murdered by his half-brother. As Enrique II was still preoccupied with consolidating his kingdom, Muhammad V took advantage of this situation and ranged along the frontiers with Castile: he conquered Cambil and Rute in April. He gained major advantage when he seized the strategic port of Algeciras in July. Muhammad, by now in a strong position, signed an eight-year truce with Enrique II in 1370. This brought peace to Granada, which continued when Enrique died in 1379, as his successor Juan I was preoccupied with conflict with Portugal and England. Muhammad also further improved his command over the

Right. Zahara, to the north-west of Ronda, was on the frontier between Granada and Castile. Having fallen into Christian hands, the Granadans retook it by stealth. This unleashed the fury of the Castilians, who responded by seizing the important centre of Antequera in 1410. Zahara was temporarily seized once more by the Nasrids in December 1481, during the last decades of the Kingdom of Granada.

Right. Torre del Moral in Lucena, where Boabdil is said to have been imprisoned after being captured following his unsuccessful raid through the region in 1483.

Left. Málaga is well fortified: the defensive curtain wall snaking down from the Gibralfaro castle to the Alcazaba.

Strait when he retrieved Gibraltar from the Marinids in 1374. On taking Algeciras earlier, he had demolished its strong defences in order to deny it to the other powers that coveted the Strait.

The fruit of the peace was prosperity. It allowed a flourishing of art and literature as well as the construction of great buildings. Muhammad V continued work on the Alhambra, enhancing its unequalled splendour. His Vizier (and successor to Ibn al-Khatib), the great poet Ibn Zamrak, eulogised the palace-city thus:

'The Sabika hill sits like a garland on Granada's brow,
In which the stars would be entwined
And the Alhambra (Allah preserve it)
Is the ruby set above that garland'.

Muhammad V added to his father's work in the Comares Palace. One of his outstanding buildings is the Court of the Lions, a complete palace which includes royal pavilions. It is arranged around a court with colonnades, which surround a central fountain with twelve stylised stone lions. In the city of Granada, he built civic structures such as the *maristan* or hospital.

The effect achieved in the decoration of the buildings of the Alhambra is enthralling. The use of delicate and beautifully carved, moulded and painted surfaces of wood and plaster achieves a stupendous result. This breathtaking accomplishment in human art was achieved at a relatively little cost. The materials used were not expensive. The necessary inputs were imagination, inspiration and many skilled hands, which were obviously available in abundance during the Nasrid era. The Kingdom of Granada, while it achieved wealth and prosperity, did not encompass a large territory in comparison to that of the Córdoba Caliphate, many times its area and population. In contrast to Granada and the

Above. Olvera, to the north-west of Ronda. This stronghold was captured by the Castilians in the fourteenth century, and was an advance position for the Christians during the Reconquista. Olvera was attacked in 1482 by Nasrid forces, after their second (but ephemeral) recapture of nearby Zahara.

Alhambra, the unprecedented wealth flowing from what encompassed most of the Iberian Peninsula, in the tenth century, allowed Abd al-Rahman III to spend vast amounts of money on importing luxury materials, such as marble from Ifriqiya, from far and wide for the construction of his palace-city Madinat al-Zahra.

And so the peace continued, to come to an abrupt end when the Amir died in January 1391 at the age of fifty-two. He was immediately succeeded by his son, Yusuf II. His reign marked the beginning of the turbulent era which lasted for a century and ended with the demise of the Nasrid dynasty and the final remnant of Muslim rule in the Peninsula. Yusuf harshly stamped out the conspiracies which emerged. He reigned for little more than a year and a half and died of mysterious causes in October 1392. The art of assassination had reached high levels in those times: there is an allegation that he died after donning a poisoned tunic received as a gift from the Marinid ruler.

Yusuf II's younger son, Muhammad VII seized the throne, in contravention of the rules of primogeniture. This sixteen-year-old promptly had his elder brother locked up in the fortress of Salobreña. This location proved very useful as a royal prison during the next century of Nasrid dynastic intrigue. It was in this era that the Abencerraje family (or Banu Sarray) emerged highly influential at the top levels of Nasrid power and exerted a dark influence in upheavals and intrigues up to the end of the Granadan kingdom. Muhammad VII, forgetting the skilful husbandry of peace by his grandfather Muhammad V, rashly provoked the Castilians. Taking advantage of internal squabbles in the court of

Left. The Minaret of San Sebastian in Ronda, which originally graced a mosque, dates from the fourteenth century.

Left. The walls of Ronda. In 1485 the Castilian forces, having mastered advanced artillery techniques, systematically destroyed the walls of the town. It surrendered within a few weeks.

Above. The castle at Jimena de la Frontera. This was one of the Nasrid fortesses on the frontline during the battles with the Christians, hence the sobriquet 'de la frontera'. The aljibes (cisterns), seen in the foreground, are thought to date from the Almohad era.

Right. The narrow streets of the Albaicín in Granada. This was a stronghold for Boabdil's supporters during the civil war during the final decade of the Kingdom of Granada.

Left. The cape of Boabdil. Right. Boabdil's sword. Museo del Ejercito, Madrid.

Enrique III of Castile, he launched attacks across the frontier. A series of frontier raids by both sides followed and continued for well over a decade. One significant Granadan reverse was the loss of the stronghold of Zahara (to the northwest of Ronda). The Granadans came under pressure (not least because of growing Castilian mastery of artillery) and requested a truce with the Castilians. This was agreed at the beginning of 1408.

Muhammad VII was not to savour the peace as he died in May 1408. His brother was freed by supporters from his royal incarceration in Salobreña and seized power, becoming Yusuf III. The new ruler sought peace and a new truce was achieved with the Castilians, which lasted until April 1410. Shortly after the truce expired, the Granadans retook Zahara by stealth and sacked it. This tweaked the tail of the mightier Castile. The Castilians responded by besieging the strategically important centre of Antequera, taking it towards the end of 1410. The victory reflected the fact that the Castilians had grown rapidly in strength over the years. In comparison to Granada, Castile comprised a much larger territory with vastly greater resources and larger population. A prime factor in the demise of Granada was the significant Castilian superiority in artillery. To properly deploy artillery, large numbers of skilled artillerymen and support personnel were needed, together with the smooth delivery of large quantities of gunpowder and projectiles. The Castilians had mastered these skills and set up the necessary support organisation. Now, bereft of the assistance of their coreligionists in the Maghreb, Granada was in a weak situation in comparison to its Christian neighbours on the Iberian Peninsula and this was to tell in the coming decades. The loss of Antequera and its fertile region was a blow to the Granadan economy and morale. In the face of this loss, Yusuf III negotiated a peace and Granada enjoyed a period of general external peace up to 1428. Yusuf himself died in 1417.

The period from now until the final decades of Granada is a bewildering one of internal conflict: it was a revolving door for rulers, with usurpations, abdications, murders and incarcerations. There were eight rulers between 1417 and the beginning of 1464 (the advent of Muley Hacén), with fifteen separate reigns. Usurpation was the order of the day: one ruler, Muhammad IX, possessing a certain persistence, enjoyed four separate reigns. All of these rulers had Nasrid blood, a few tending to the periphery of the family tree. As we have seen, Castile was on the ascent and took advantage of the internal dissent. At various stages, the Castilians took sides, trying to impose their favoured candidate as Amir. However, when Castile was riven by internal dissent on occasion, the Granadans also took advantage and attacked Christian territory. Within Granada, the influential Abencerraje family played a sinister role, achieving high positions, manipulating the throne and intriguing to place their favoured candidate as Amir. On one occasion, in 1462, the Amir Sa'd, who had initially been supported by the Abencerrajes, turned on them and had two leading members of the family assassinated in the Alhambra. In 1464 Sa'd in turn was overthrown by his son Ali bin Sa'd, popularly known as Muley Hacén, who was encouraged by the Abencerraje clan. Muley Hacén proceeded to strengthen his army and the economy. He consolidated his rule and, amongst other initiatives, distanced himself from the Abencerrajes. Despite some upsets, he broadly achieved an external peace up to 1481.

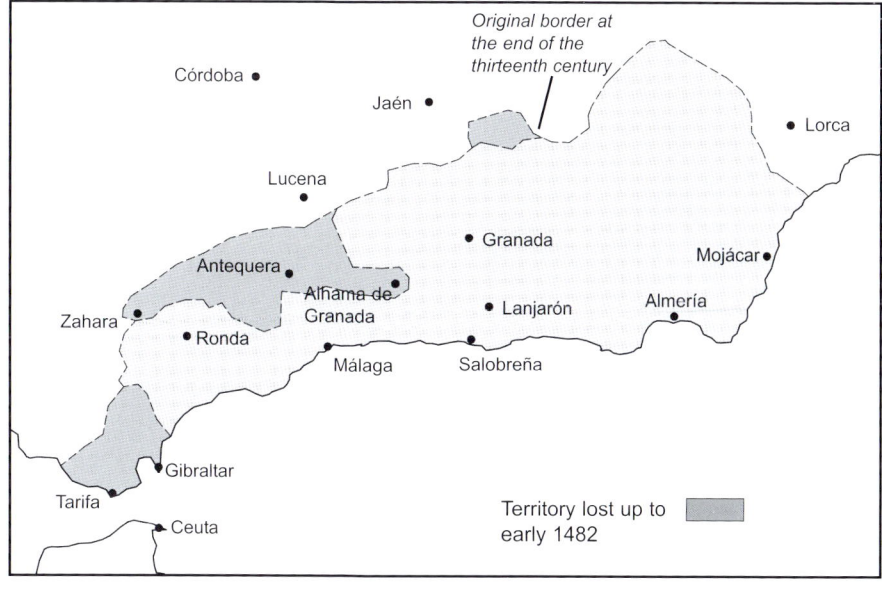

Right. The Kingdom of Granada. The Castilians captured territory over the centuries, a process accelerated in the 1480's up to the final surrender in 1492.

Left. King Fernando. The Catholic Monarchs, determined and able, conquered the Kingdom of Granada. Capilla Real, Granada.

An important event for the future of Granada occurred in 1474 when Isabel of Castile came to the throne on the death of her brother Enrique IV. She had married Prince Fernando of Aragón in 1469. Isabel, embroiled in a civil war over the Castilian succession, renewed the peace treaty with Granada. The two powerful states of Christian Spain became finally entwined in 1479 when Juan II of Aragón died and Fernando succeeded him. The internal dynastic problems had been resolved and the two monarchs were now able to pay full attention to the elimination of Islamic rule from the Peninsula, in final achievement of the Reconquista. Granada now faced an infinitely more powerful foe, with vastly greater resources and population. The Catholic Monarchs (the appellation of *Reyes Catolicos* or Catholic Monarchs was latterly conferred on the couple in 1494 by Pope Alexander in recognition of their capture of Granada) were an extraordinary couple, being imbued with religious fervour and steely determination. They proved highly effective in achieving their aims. The Catholic Monarchs allocated an enormous amount of money to the meticulously-planned campaign against Granada. The Christians had the will and the means to overcome Granada, which now entered the last chapter of its history.

Continuous attrition, due to Christian attack over the decades, meant that Granada's borders had shrunk. By the end of 1481, it comprised less than three quarters of the area of the early years of the Nasrid dynasty. The frontier now ran from just west of Estepona, looping inland to the north of Ronda, then

Right. The surrender of Málaga. This was the second city of the Kingdom of Granada. The Castilians began a siege in May 1487. After several months of heavy bloodhshed the defenders were reduced by starvation and the city fell.

south of Antequera, north of Granada, onwards to the east around Huéscar and to the coast east of Mojácar. The Kingdom of Granada still retained its mountainous spine and its Mediterranean ports. However, it had lost some of its fertile plains, which, coupled with the Christian policy of cutting down crops and fruit trees when raiding, resulted in the Granadan economy coming under severe pressure.

Although Granada was facing overwhelming odds, it still proved to be a formidable opponent. Even before the expiry of the current truce, the Granadans went on the offensive and once more took Zahara in December 1481. The Christians responded and struck deep into the heart of the kingdom: they took Alhama de Granada in February 1482 after a hard struggle. This was a severe loss. At only forty kilometres' distance, it was uncomfortably close to Granada. Alhama also controlled the main route from Málaga to Granada.

In July 1482 Muley Hacén was overthrown by his son Abu Abd Allah bin Ali (popularly known as Boabdil) who was supported by the perpetual intriguers, the Abencerraje. Muley Hacén left the capital and set up in Málaga and Ronda from where he was able to make successful raids against the Christians. Wishing to boost his prestige, Boabdil resolved to do the same. In April 1483 he mounted a raid north towards Lucena. The Christian forces reacted strongly and the Granadan forces were badly defeated. Boabdil was taken prisoner. Back in Granada Boabdil's star had fallen; a delegation went to Málaga and requested Muley Hacén to return to the capital, which he did. Meanwhile, after some consideration, Fernando had decided that backing

Left. The taking of Íllora (to the north-west of Granada). The defenders put up a stiff resistance. Once again, artillery proved decisive in securing the Christian victory here in 1486. Detail from a choir stall, Toledo Cathedral.

Boabdil represented his best chance to take Granada in the longer term. Following negotiations, a truce was signed. Boabdil was freed, with the payment by his supporters of a large sum of money and the handover of hostages. Boabdil set up in Guadix in October 1483.

Castilian attacks continued during 1484 and, with the skilful use of artillery, they began to steadily capture Granadan towns. In the midst of this, Muley Hacén was increasingly incapacitated by epilepsy and his brother, Muhammad bin Sa'd (known as al-Zagal), came to the fore. Al-Zagal headed for Almería, a stronghold of Boabdil, and captured it at the beginning of 1485. In the meantime, the Castilian advance continued. To the west of Málaga, Coin and Cártama fell in early 1485. In May the strategic town of Ronda was attacked. The Castilian artillery demonstrated its power and accuracy. The walls were systematically destroyed and the people within terrified. The town surrendered within a few weeks and the population was ignominiously expelled. Back in the Nasrid capital, al-Zagal consolidated his grip on power and Muley Hacén, a sick old man, was forced to leave the city and died a few months later. Al-Zagal repelled a Castilian attack on Moclín. However, the Christians managed to capture Cambil, and other enclaves to the north of Granada.

Boabdil, in the meantime, capitalising on the hunger for peace among the population and on the premise that he could secure peace with the Castilians, gathered support in the east of the Kingdom. Within Granada itself, his supporters spread this message in the Albaicín and an uprising broke out there in March 1486. The rebels were attacked by al-Zagal's forces, which didn't shirk from using artillery. After several months of struggle, reconciliation between uncle and nephew came about in May 1486, with Boabdil recognising al-Zagal. Boabdil was assigned Loja. The city came under siege by the Castilians and Boabdil headed there. Despite a strong resistance, the Christian artillery pre-

Below. One of the collection of Castilian flags and standards in the Capilla Real, Granada, final resting place of the Catholic Monarchs.

Right. 'The Surrender of Granada', by Francisco Pradilla. Patrimonio Histórico-Artistico del Senado, Madrid. Photography: Oronoz.

vailed and Loja was taken at the end of May. Boabdil once again submitted and made an arrangement with Fernando, which recognised him as ruler in the eastern Granadan territories, with vassalage and support for him in his endeavour to capture territory. An additional inducement was the offer of a three-year truce with the Christians for those towns and districts that rose up to support Boabdil. With this secured, Boabdil made a pass through the east, gathering support. Once more he headed for Granada, moving into the Albaicín in secret in October 1486. There he rallied his supporters. In January 1487 al-Zagal assembled his forces, entered the Albaicín and made a great effort to stamp out the rebellion. In the meantime, news came that the Castilians were marching on Vélez-Málaga to the east of Málaga. It was most likely that they were complicit with Boabdil, to relieve pressure on his uprising. Al-Zagal took the difficult choice to split his forces and, at the end of April, led a contingent across the mountains towards Vélez-Málaga. However, the town capitulated at the beginning of May 1487 and al-Zagal led his failed expedition back towards Granada. On the way, he received the news that, in his absence, Boabdil had prevailed and was now in control of the city. Al-Zagal had no choice but to divert to Guadix, where he set up.

Having gained control to the east and west of Málaga, the Castilians began the siege of the city in May 1487. This, in the second city of the Nasrid kingdom, was a key step in the campaign of the Catholic Monarchs. A major advantage of capturing this port city would be to deny the passage of reinforcements and supplies from North Africa to Granada. The Castilians opted for direct assault rather than a long-drawn out siege. However, the inhabitants, ably led and well organised, put up heroic resistance. The city was well fortified with natural defences, being dominated by the Gibralfaro fortress on top of a steep hill. It turned out to be one of the bloodiest encounters of the Castilian campaign. The defenders received no assistance from Boabdil, in compliance with

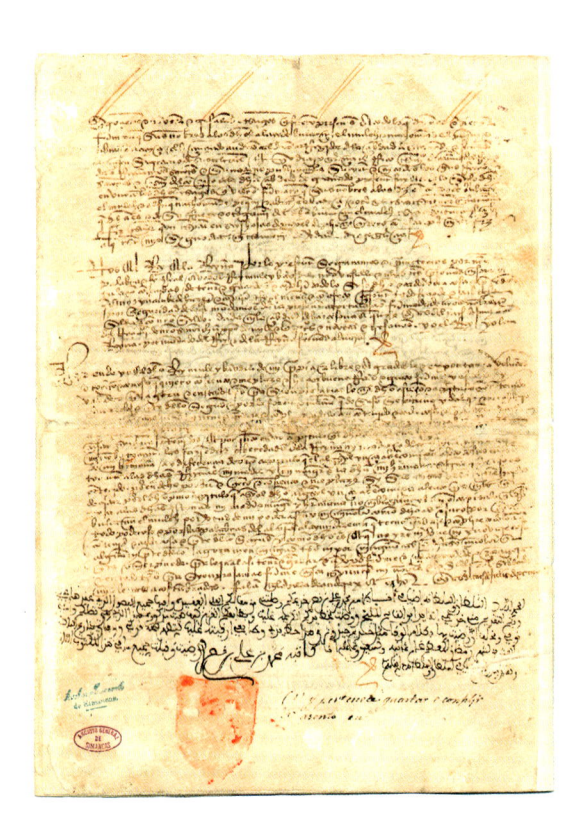

Left. Part of the Capitulations of Boabdil which set out the conditions for surrender of Granada to the Catholic Monarchs. Archivo General de Simancas, Valladolid.

his compact with the Castilians. He even went to the extent of intercepting reinforcements sent by al-Zagal. In Málaga, the initial Christian assault was held up and they changed tactics. The Christians now carried out an extensive exercise, building a ring of trenches and redoubts around the city. The battle changed to a static form, with both sides exchanging artillery salvoes. Castilian spirits fell to a low ebb at this stage and Fernando arranged for Isabel to join him at the siege to raise morale. Eventually, the defenders were reduced by starvation and the city fell after three and a half months of attack. The inhabitants now had to endure the ordeal of being reduced to slavery, as punishment for their strong defence of the city.

During 1488 the Castilians received the submission of strongholds to the east, from Galera to Mojácar. These were places promised to Boabdil and it broke the understanding the Christians had made with him. This takeover is likely to be one of the causes for Boabdil's subsequent strong resistance of the takeover of Granada. 1489 dawned; all that remained in Muslim hands were a few cities and their immediate hinterland. There was Boabdil in Granada and al-Zagal who held Almería, Baza and Guadix. The Castilians now turned their sights on the beacon of resistance, al-Zagal. It would be necessary to eliminate this irritant before the final assault on the Granadan capital. The Castilians advanced towards Baza and put this formidable stronghold under siege in June 1489. The Castilians assembled what were by now the usual ingredients: a large body of troops and heavy artillery, which required heavy logistical support. Al-Zagal, from Guadix, sent reinforcements to the defenders. As the siege dragged

Right. The Catholic Monarchs reconstructed the Aljafería in Zaragoza as their palace, using a team of Mudéjar craftsmen. Here the frieze at the base of the coffered ceiling in the Throne Room is decorated with an inscription: 'Fernando... victorious with God's help, having liberated Andalucía from the Moors, and having driven out the old and fierce enemy, ordered this work to be constructed in... 1492.'

on, once again, Queen Isabel travelled to the front to boost Christian morale. The defenders ran out of supplies, negotiations were entered into and the enclave fell at the beginning of December 1489. Events moved swiftly. Al-Zagal had had enough and was convinced that resistance was now futile. By the end of December 1489, he reached an agreement with the Castilians and surrendered his territories of Guadix and Almería. In return, he received a lordship in territory which encompassed parts of the Alpujarras and the valley of Lecrín.

Now, all that remained for Castilian attention was the city of Granada and its surrounding district. Christian envoys were sent to meet Boabdil's representatives at the beginning of 1490, with the intention of negotiating the takeover of the city. However, it was clear to Boabdil that his previous agreements with the Castilians had been torn up and this mercurial monarch reverted to fighting back on behalf of his Muslim people. He mounted an expedition, which fought its way through the Alpujarras and headed south to Salobreña on the coast. This most likely had the objective of establishing a supply line to the coast and possible reinforcements from North Africa. This expedition had a consequence for his estranged uncle. With Boabdil on the horizon, al-Zagal decided to vacate the Alpujarras. He headed for Almería and then decided to transfer with his family to Oran in the Maghreb, which he did in mid 1490.

Receiving the news that the Castilians were marching on Granada, Boabdil headed back to the city in August 1490. There was skirmishing in the countryside and the Castilians ravaged the crops along the Granadan vega. This proved an effective tactic and disrupted supplies to the city. At the beginning of 1491 the last piece of the Castilian plan was put in place: the siege of Granada. The massed armies set out for the city, attacking districts on the way. In April 1491 the siege began. The Catholic Monarchs set up their great fortified encampment in a location around ten kilometres to the west of Granada, which was given the appropriately inspirational name of Santa Fé. Skirmishes and attacks continued into the winter, with all the fortifications in the outlying countryside eventually being overrun. As the cold weather set in, the strategic route that brought supplies to the city on mountain tracks from the Alpujarras was cut off by snow. Food became scarcer and hunger intensified. Negotiations began in secret between the representatives of Boabdil and the Catholic Monarchs. By the end of November terms for the surrender of Granada were worked out in detail.

These terms or capitulations included: the entitlement for the Muslims to remain in the city under Christian rule, with freedom to practise their religion, customs and laws and to keep their property and belongings. They were also entitled, for a period of three years, to emigrate with their possessions, with free passage to the Maghreb ports. There have been suggestions that Boabdil was acting as a puppet of the Castilians and according to a predetermined script. This may have been the case. However, in the context of the times, the capitulations that he signed were fair. As we shall see, the fatal flaw was that there was no safeguard if these were broken, as they were by the Castilians later on. Boabdil, of course, did not neglect his own interests. He was to be allowed to set up in the Alpujarras and establish a statelet there under Castilian vassalage.

The deal being agreed, the end was orchestrated rapidly and clandestinely, so as not to inflame the passions of the citizenry. The Alhambra was vacated on the night of the first of January 1492 and, in secrecy, a detachment of Christian troops, led by Gutierre de Cárdenas, arrived at the city-palace. The next morning, in the Hall of the Ambassadors in the Comares Tower, Boabdil handed over the keys of the Alhambra to de Cárdenas. The Christian troops secured the palace. Later in the afternoon, Boabdil met the Catholic Monarchs at the gates of the city and rendered homage to them. Curiously, one account tells that the Catholic Monarchs had dressed in Muslim attire for this occasion. If true, it would have added a certain theatrical touch to the pathos of the fall of Nasrid Granada, the last vestige of al-Andalus and it marked the end of 780 years of Muslim rule in the Iberian Peninsula.

Chapter 8
Moriscos and Expulsion

By the beginning of 1492 the Iberian Peninsula was under full Christian control, with the Peninsula's kingdoms in a state of ascendance. To the west, Portugal with its Atlanticist outlook, was in a phase of great exploration and conquest across the Oceans. In the greater part of the Peninsula, the new and powerful land of Spain had arisen from the matrimonial union of Aragón and Castile. With lands across the Mediterranean and with a powerful army, battle-hardened in the Granadan conquest, the combined kingdoms of Aragón and Castile now had the critical mass to be a principal player on the European stage. The momentum and energy created in the final Reconquista was to continue and be channelled into new expansion. In the same year as the capture of Granada, Columbus, who had received his orders from the Catholic Monarchs in the city, set off and discovered the New World. This propelled Spain to become the international superpower of its time. It is significant that 1492 was also when the first Castilian grammar book was published. Not as epoch-making as the discovery of America perhaps but it was a key step in establishing Castilian as the underpinning language of the new Spanish Empire.

With strength came intolerance. The Catholic Monarchs were believers in a unified Christian State and had little tolerance for religious dissent. This had been manifested by the earlier establishment of the Inquisition in 1478, with the intention of maintaining the religious purity of Spain. The triumphal Catholic Monarchs, having conquered the infidel Muslims of Granada, now issued an edict on the Jews of Spain in March 1492: the choice offered to these was either conversion or exile. Around 150,000 chose exile and, in one stroke, Spain lost a dynamic and talented group of its citizens, many administrators and merchants who would have been invaluable in supporting the future growth of the Empire and its economy. A few months earlier, the Granadans had surrendered on the basis that they had the right to practise Islam. The expulsion of the Jews was not a good omen for the application of this agreement and so it was to be.

Immediately on the surrender of Granada, the hapless Boabdil headed for the Alpujarras and set up there, as per the terms of the surrender. Luis de Mármol, in his book written in the sixteenth century, which deals with the subsequent rebellion in Granada, recounts the tale of how, on passing through the foothills on his way to the mountains (at a point now known as Suspiro del Moro), Boabdil is supposed to have looked back at Granada and wept, whereby his

Left. Statue in Plaza de Isabel la Católica in Granada: Columbus presents his proposal to Queen Isabel.

mother brusquely said: 'You weep like a woman over what you could not defend like a man'. Boabdil spent some time in the Alpujarras, but at the end of 1493 he left and travelled to the Maghreb, settling in Fez.

The Muslims of Granada, just like their co-religionists centuries earlier in Castile, Aragón and other parts of Spain, had become Mudéjars, or Muslims who lived under Christian rule in the Iberian Peninsula. For a few years, life in Granada continued more or less as before. The new Christian administrators, soldiers and prelates operated at one level, beneath which the Granadan Muslims were able to continue their daily life. They enjoyed a respite from the recent strife of the Reconquista. Some of the Muslim leaders and *alfaquis* participated in the administration of the city. The Muslim population declined after the defeat of 1492. Many, particularly the upper classes, had taken the opportunity to emigrate to North Africa. In turn, Christian immigrants arrived in the city and the demographics began to change, with the Albaicín developing into the predominantly Muslim district.

However, storm clouds were gathering on the Granadan horizon. Little by little, intrusive new laws, such as that denying Muslims in the Vega the right to buy land, came into force to facilitate the settlement of Christians. The pressure was to increase sharply when, in 1499, the influential Francisco Jiménez de Cisneros, Archbishop of Toledo and former confessor of Isabel I, was invited to visit the city by the Catholic Monarchs to assist with conversions. This visit was to have grave consequences for the Granadan Mudéjars. Up to now the Archbishop of Granada, Fernando de Talavera, had adopted a benign attitude

Right. 'The Moor's last Sigh'. Legend has it that Boabdil looked back at Granada on the way to his exile in the Alpujarras and wept. This is a nineteenth century painting which reflects that century's perception of the Andalusis as dark, exotic and alien. Marcelino de Unceta y López, Museo de Zaragoza.

Right. The location around twelve kilometres south of Granada known as 'Suspiro del Moro' or the 'Sigh of the Moor'.

Left. The suburb of the Albaicín, Granada. The uprising here in December 1499 resulted in the forced conversion of the Muslim population.

towards the Muslims, attempting to convert them by preaching, even converting Christian religious material into Arabic but with little success. Cisneros took a different attitude to such gradualism. Austere and energetic, he targeted those Muslims who had converted from Christianity in the recent past and who thus had consciously rejected what he saw as the true faith. These were termed renegades and were not tolerated at that time. Despite a specific protection for these converts in the capitulations of Granada, Cisneros began to force them to reconvert to Christianity. He also ordered Islamic books to be gathered and burnt, all save a few medical works that he sent off to the library of the University of Alcalá de Henares. He continued by attempting to force Christianity on prominent members of the Mudéjar community.

In December 1499 the people of the Albaicín rose up in protest, outraged at this breaking of the capitulations. They seized the gates of the district and fortified them. The uproar was dampened down by the skilful negotiation of Archbishop de Talavera and the Captain-General of Granada. The rebels dispersed. However, Cisneros advised the Monarchs that the conversions should not stop; since the Muslims had rebelled, they merited death but their pardon should be conditional: convert or be expelled. The Monarchs duly consented. The baptisms were carried out speedily, en masse, with no time for any instruction in the faith.

News of these forced conversions spread to the Alpujarras. Alarmed, but trusting in the impregnability of their mountainous region, the Mudéjars there rose up in January 1500. In reality, these Muslim farmers and townspeople had no chance against the large numbers of experienced Castilian troops, which were

Right. Baptism of the Muslim men. Detail from the Altar of the Capilla Real in Granada.

sent rapidly to quell the uprising. The Castilians attacked the rebels, who had set up in various strongholds across the Alpujarras and put down the uprising with brutal force. To the east, the Count of Lerín led a force which attacked the Castle of Láujar. In the course of these hostilities, he ordered the nearby mosque of Andarax to be blown up, although full of women and children who were sheltering there. A large force of royal troops headed towards the west of the Alpujarras. Fernando himself led the assault on the Castle of Lanjarón, which he took at the beginning of March 1500. Against these onslaughts and with no prospect of any help from their co-religionists abroad, the rebels had to give up. Conversion (or the alternative of expulsion) was now imposed on them and the rest of the Mudéjars of the Kingdom of Granada. The conversions were effected in the period from August to October of 1500. Further rebellion flared up in the west, in the Serranía de Ronda and nearby Sierra Bermeja in 1501. After an initial reverse, the Castilian forces soon put this rebellion down.

The uprisings in the Kingdom of Granada and the consequent forced baptisms had now freed the conversion genie from the Castilian bottle. Given the desire for religious uniformity of the Catholic Monarchs and the Castilian establishment, the focus now fell on the settled Mudéjars in the rest of Castile. These, many of whom were speakers of Castilian, had been living peacefully and modestly under Christian rule for several centuries. A royal decree was proclaimed in February 1502, ordering that they convert.

The Mudéjars of all Castile (including Granada) had now been transformed into *Moriscos*, or Iberian Muslims who became baptised Christians, living under Christian rule. In reality, in reaction to the forced conversion, most were crypto-

Muslims. They had converted as they had no real alternative and to gain relief from the unbearable pressure. While they were nominally Christian, they continued to dress in Muslim attire, persisted with their cultural practices such as baths, maintained their diet, and practised their religion in private. The Granadans continued to speak Arabic. The Church made efforts to dispatch priests to instruct their new flock in the newly acquired religion, with the corollary that the converts would give up their Muslim dress and customs. However, very few priests could speak Arabic or had the desire to. Scarcely any headway was made with these reluctant converts. It was patently obvious that the conversion was not genuine and this became a source of irritation at the royal court.

The Muslims of North Africa looked on with sympathy at the travails of their co-religionists. In 1504 a *fatwa* was issued by a *mufti* (an expert on religious law) in Oran. This gave an interpretation of Islamic law in an effort to deal with the peculiar situation in which the Moriscos found themselves. In effect, it said that they could physically carry out Christian rituals and remain Muslims, so long as in their hearts they rejected these rituals and believed in Allah. As it became evident to the authorities that the Moriscos had not changed their ways, various restrictive proclamations were issued in 1511 to try to get them to change. These included: dress as a Christian; no tailor may make Muslim attire;

Above. Capileira in the Alpujarras, nestling in the folds of the Sierra Nevada. The high villages of the Alpujarras, set in this remote terrain, were at the heart of the Muslim uprisings against oppressive State impositions.

do not use the halal method of slaughtering animals; do not use the Muslim-style baths etc. These and other measures were applied in a disorganised and half-hearted way and had very little impact.

Fernando's domain, the Crown of Aragón, comprised Aragón, Catalonia and Valencia. The marriage of the Catholic Monarchs gave Castile and Aragón a unitary direction at high level. Nevertheless, the Crown of Aragón remained separate, was administered separately and its subjects jealously guarded their rights. The Kingdom of Valencia was home to the largest population of Mudéjars in the Peninsula. These had been living in relative peace there under Christian rule for nearly three centuries. As news came of the forced conversions in Castile, alarm spread among the Mudéjars of Valencia. However, they were productive tenants of the local *Señores* (lords). The latter wanted to preserve the status quo and made known their strong opposition to the conversion of their tenants. When Fernando acceded to the Crown of Aragón, a part of the royal oath that he swore included the obligation to protect the Muslims there. As it turned out, even though he had presided over the conversion in Castile, did not issue a similar decree in Aragón. L. P. Harvey in his 'Muslims in Spain 1500 to 1614' says of Fernando that 'the promises to protect Muslims made on his accession, he had repeated to the Cortes... in 1510, and he kept his word until his dying day.'

Some time after Fernando's death in January 1516, he was succeeded by his grandson Carlos V (known in Spain as Carlos I) who swore the same oaths of Aragón. However, the status quo was not to last. Tensions had built up over the years in the Kingdom of Valencia between the Mudéjars with their distinctive customs and those Christians who were at the lower end of the social scale. Discontent among these Christians was manifest in a revolutionary movement known as the *Germanía*. Conflict broke out in 1521 when the rebels attacked the forces of the Viceroy of Valencia. The rebels associated the Mudéjars with the Señores and the Crown. Mudéjar areas were attacked by the rebels. As the Crown forces fought back, in some cases the Señores engaged their Mudéjar tenants to fight on the side of the King. In some localities the rebel mob imposed mass conversion on the Mudéjars. By the end of 1522 the rebellion was defeated. However, in its aftermath, there were now large numbers of new 'Christians' whose conversion was, after some consideration, deemed by Christian theologians to be valid. Thus, there was no gratitude to the Mudéjars for their aid to the Crown during the rebellion. In fact, the reverse occurred. Carlos V issued an edict in November 1525 (thus breaking his coronation oath) that mandated the expulsion from the State of all Mudéjars of Aragón, Catalonia and Valencia, the alternative being conversion. As the conditions attached to leaving were impractical, most chose to convert. At the beginning of 1526 resistance to the decree broke out. The Mudéjars of Benaguasil (near Llíria) and those in the Sierra de Espadán (in Castellón, to the north east of Segorbe) rose up and set up in the mountains. Troops (including *tercios*, the elite and feared royal regiments from the overseas Spanish possessions) were swiftly sent and, by October 1526, all resistance was stamped out in the region. And thus, in theory, the population was now uniformly Christian and no Muslims remained on the soil of Spain.

For the next decades, the pace and intensity of pressure on the Moriscos (the Muslims converted to Christianity) reduced somewhat. The requirements for assimilation were applied only sporadically. Moriscos had found ways to moderate the advance of the Inquisition by the expedient of whole communities making regular payments to it. Also, any measures that might arise against their Morisco tenants were again moderated by the protective interest of the Señores. But Spain was changing, both within and abroad. In 1556 Felipe II succeeded his father Carlos V. He now commanded a vast empire. In addition to five-sixths of the Iberian Peninsula and the far-flung Indies, it dominated half the European Continent. However, as J. H. Elliot pithily notes in his book, 'Imperial Spain 1469-1716', the Empire of Felipe II was born under 'the double sign of bankruptcy and heresy.' Despite its power and size, this Empire was indeed in dire financial straits. It was also in battle with the heretic, both in Northern Europe (Protestantism) and in the Mediterranean (Islam). There was conflict in the Spanish Netherlands and also in the Caribbean. To the east, the Spanish were particularly sensitive to the rising power of the Ottoman Empire. To use a contemporary Russian phrase, Spain's 'near abroad', the Mediterranean, was in danger of becoming, in Spanish eyes, an Islamic lake. During the first half of the

Below. Castle in the Valle de Lecrín near Murchas. The Second War of the Alpujarras commenced after the meeting in nearby Béznar when Aben Humeya was elected King at the end of 1568.

Right. Tablate at the western frontier of the Alpujarras. There was a battle across this abyss, at the commencement of the Second War of the Alpujarras. This sixteenth-century bridge was built afterwards.

Below. Válor in the Alpujarras, the birthplave of Abén Humeya.

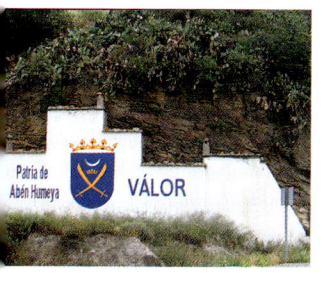

sixteenth century, the Spanish had established a series of *presidios* or fortified enclaves along the North African coast. The Turks had taken Tripoli in 1551, followed by the seizure of two *presidios*: Vélez de la Gomera in 1554 (this last to the south and dangerously close to the Spanish coast) and Bougie in 1555. A Spanish-Italian attempt to set up a base on Djerba Island to recapture Tripoli was crushingly defeated by the Turks in 1560. The sense of vulnerability was also reinforced by an increase in attacks by Turkish and Barbary corsairs on the coast of Andalucía.

Uneasy indeed lay the Crown of Spain and it was in this atmosphere that the Moriscos of Spain came to be increasingly mistrusted. In the State's eyes they were seen as an Islamic fifth column, ready to support an enemy attack. The

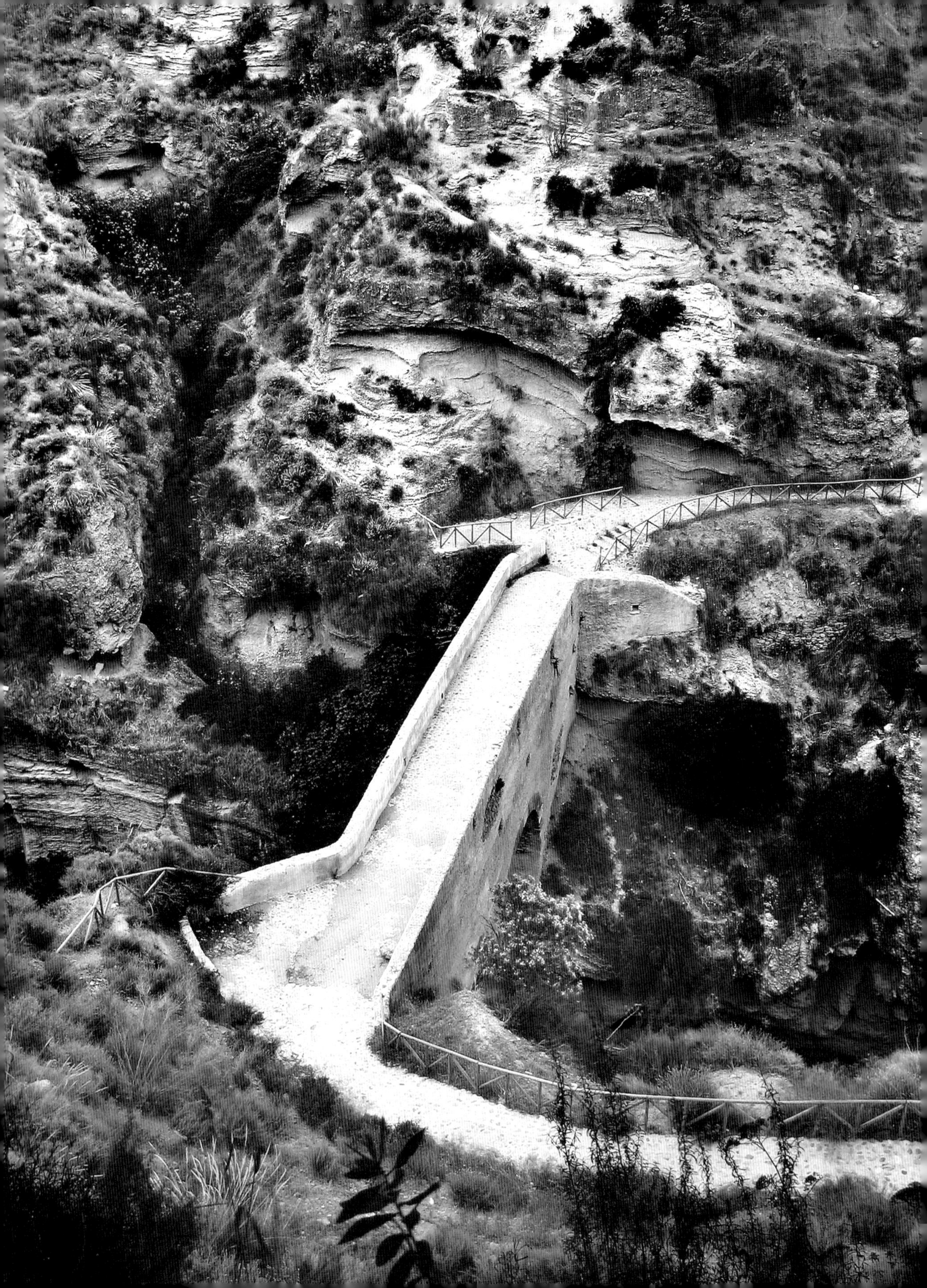

Above. Castle at Lanjarón. The royal army advanced from Tablate to Lanjarón and moved deeper into the Alpujarras.

Left. The bridge at Tablate. During the battle here in January 1569, a Christian friar heroically leapt across the defile, inspiring the royal army to follow and decisively defeat the Morisco defenders.

Moriscos had continued over the years to maintain their distinctive customs and dress and, in many cases, used Arabic or wrote in *aljamía* (Castilian written in Arabic script). Thus they were a very visible minority, obviously not adhering to orthodox Christianity. The general populace disliked the Moriscos and this hatred continued to mount. The Moriscos, in turn, resented their oppressive treatment, were alienated and harboured positive feelings towards the Turks, seeing them as potential liberators. Reflecting the climate of suspicion and dislike, increased measures were taken against the Moriscos. In 1560 the Moriscos of Valencia were prohibited from fishing, in order to deny them contact with pirates or Turks. Valencian Moriscos were banned from possessing arms. In Granada, at the end of the 1550's, punitive measures were enacted, which meant that Moriscos without land title were fined or had their land confiscated. Adding to the woes in Granada was the crisis in the silk industry. This had been a lucrative activity for the Moriscos in the Alpujarras and was depressed by a State ban on silk exports in the 1550s and sharply increased taxes after 1561.

In 1565 representations were made to the King by a synod of Granadan Bishops, requesting the enactment of the measures banning Muslim customs that were made in 1511. This gained consideration and finally, in January 1567, a document was published which laid down restrictions on dress, baths, religious

Above. Aljibe (reservoir), dating from Muslim times, by an old mule track high in the mountains of the Alpujarras.

observation, language and social gatherings. The Moriscos of Granada thought that they could buy off the enactment of these edicts by the payment of a large sum, a tactic that had worked in the past. Envoys were sent to negotiate but, by 1568, it was evident that there was going to be no change. With the economic losses due to the decline of the silk industry, coupled with years of ill-treatment, this tough new attitude of the authorities proved to be the last straw. Rebellion was in the air and secret meetings were held in the Albaicín and in the Alpujarras.

On Christmas Eve 1568, in Granada, Farax Aben Farax (said to be of the lineage of the Abencerrajes, plotters *par excellence* from Nasrid times) lit the flame of rebellion. He led a small group that tried to galvanise the residents of the Albaicín to rise up. This attempt failed and the rebels withdrew. However, in the Alpujarras, the real revolt began on the same day. Moriscos took over the towns and hamlets of the western Alpujarras. In the village of Béznar (less than thirty kilometres south of the city, in the Valle de Lecrín), a king was named by the Moriscos of the Alpujarras: one Aben Humeya, formerly known by his Hispanicised name of Fernando de Válor. As his Muslim name implied, he claimed to be descended from the Umayyad dynasty. The uprising in the Alpujarras released the pent-up anger of this persecuted people. This was initially focused on the unfortunate Christian clergy who had been inserted throughout the region and atrocities were widespread. Priests were tortured and slaughtered. Churches were destroyed. Christians in the districts took refuge in church towers and fortifications, many of which were burnt, with great loss of life. The rebellion spread rapidly across the Alpujarras and adjacent territories. This rising was to prove difficult to put down and developed into a hard-fought conflict, known as the Second War of the Alpujarras. Full of strategic danger for Spain, it turned out to be a major preoccupation for Felipe II.

The initial Government response was swift. The Captain-General of Granada, the Marques de Mondéjar, assembled his forces and set out from the city on the third of January 1569. He headed south to the strategic hamlet of Tablate, which was the entry point to the western Alpujarras. Here, entry would be gained across a bridge that spanned a deep ravine. The rebels, anticipating the arrival of royal forces, had destroyed the bridge, save for some ancient planks which spanned the void. Both sides began an exchange of projectiles. A Franciscan friar, Cristóbal de Molino, accompanying the royal troops, now undertook one of the few heroic acts of the war. It is said that, with his habit hitched up in his belt, a crucifix in his left hand and a sword in his right, he invoked the name of Christ and leapt across the rubble and planks and scrambled his way up the other side. He was followed by soldiers, emboldened by his example. They put the Moriscos, entrenched on a height above the bridge, to flight. The bridge was quickly repaired and the Marques de Mondéjar advanced to Lanjarón and onwards to Orgiva where he set up his headquarters. Over the following months, his forces ranged over the west and central Alpujarras, harrying the rebels, capturing towns and releasing Christian captives. By March the Christian forces had pushed back the rebels. Aben Humeya and other leaders had to flee, narrowly avoiding capture. Soon, negotiations on surrender terms began. The Marques de los Vélez had also set out with troops from Murcia at the beginning of January, blundering into the more peaceful eastern Alpujarras, causing commotion among the still-unrisen Moriscos. At this point, the Christians managed to snatch failure from the jaws of victory. The two Marqueses were long-time rivals and did not cooperate. Many of their troops were undisciplined and behaved in a brutal manner towards the local populace. This fanned the flames of revolt, more Moriscos flocked to the rebel cause and the uprising gained new strength.

Felipe II was conscious of these problems with the campaign, especially as Mondéjar's enemies were at his ear. In March 1569, he turned to his half-brother, Don Juan de Austria, (a mere twenty-two years of age) to direct his armies in suppressing the rebellion. The experienced Mondéjar and los Vélez were placed under this royal youth's overall command. The war, which initially had seemed like a local difficulty, had spread beyond the Alpujarras. The Christian forces were now strongly reinforced. They comprised infantry and supporting cavalry and artillery. These forces were a mix of seasoned veterans (including Italian *tercios*) of the regular army as well as militia forces raised from the cities, which were of variable quality. While the Christian forces had overwhelming might

Left. A fine tiled plaque, by M. Guillén, in the village of Genalguacil in the folds of the Sierra Bermeja, inland from Estepona. During the revolt in 1570, Christian soldiers sent to the Sierra Bermeja enraged the Moriscos by their brutality. In the midst of skirmishes, the Moriscos set the village church on fire, with Christian soldiers within.

and the advantage in conventional warfare, the rebels gained some advantage in the mountains. There they knew their terrain, were able to choose impregnable positions and were able to live off the land. They also had the support of latter-day fighters for the Islamic faith, some Turkish and North African soldiers who had landed on the Mediterranean coast. As always, the Spanish were very aware of the Turkish danger and placed a fleet to patrol the coasts and interdict any reinforcements.

The armies of Don Juan and his commanders fought hard through the Alpujarras and in the regions to the east, meeting fierce resistance. To the west, in the Málaga region, Moriscos in the Axarquia had also risen. In June 1570 the rebels had assembled from the surrounding districts and set up on the heights of the Peñon de Frigiliana. The Christian forces (including the feared *tercio* of Naples) moved to the area and launched an attack on the Moriscos, who lacked firearms and could only fight back with arrows and stones. The battle was intense and ranged over the nearby ridges and gullies. After many assaults, the Christian forces won, leaving two thousand Morisco dead, with the remainder put to flight.

As the war progressed, the Morisco ranks became riven by dissension. Aben Humeya had fallen out with his lieutenants. Personal differences arose along with suspicions that he was negotiating the handover of the Alpujarras to the Christians to further his own interests. In October 1569, a group of plotters, including one Aben Aboo, set out to intercept him at his headquarters in Láujar

Below. Genalguacil, with the church, long since rebuilt, to right of centre.

de Andarax. Luis de Mármol, in his contemporary account, hints darkly that Humeya was a sexual libertine; the assassins found him 'sleeping between two women.' Whatever the truth, the intruders strangled Humeya. Aben Aboo was named as the new king and continued the war against the Christians.

In October 1569 Felipe II ordered the waging of total war: in fire and blood. Don Juan demonstrated this amply when he attacked Galera (thirty-five kilometres north-east of Baza) in January 1570. This encounter resulted in the greatest atrocity of this sanguinary war. Galera was a medium-sized town in the Granadan altiplano, with tightly packed houses built around a small ridge. Contrary to the principles of guerrilla warfare, several thousand rebels had allowed themselves to be corralled within this fixed location, now under siege by a conventional army. Don Juan's army disposed of over 12,000 men. The Christians duly discharged their heavy artillery, to no great effect, as the walls of packed mud of the outer ring of houses were able to absorb the canon balls. It took weeks of fierce fighting to take the town, which fell at the beginning of February 1570. Thousands of Moriscos had lost their lives, including 400 women and children slaughtered by direct order of Don Juan after the capture of the town. The final punishment was biblical: the town was razed to the ground and the land was salted (under the direction of none other than our chronicler Luis de Mármol, who was present at the siege, in a quartermaster role).

The rebels continued to fight across the region, but by now the Christian forces had the upper hand. Some of the rebels began to negotiate surrender. Others retreated higher into the mountains using caves for shelter. The Christian forces used fire to smoke them out and many were asphyxiated. Resistance reduced rapidly and by November 1570, the war was effectively over. In the west, there were later instances of resistance around the Serranía de Ronda and the Sierra Bermeja, which were put down by the end of 1570.

The way was clear to complete the expulsion of all the Moriscos of Granada. There had been some expulsions during the course of the rebellion, as the Spanish forces captured territory. There had also been initial expulsions of the inhabitants of the Albaicín in June 1569. Now, the main wave of expulsion began in November 1570. This was aimed, not only at those who had rebelled and surrendered, but covered all Moriscos, including those who had peacefully carried on their daily life. The operation had been planned months before and the machinery of state swung into place with grim determination. The Kingdom of Granada was split up into seven zones. Moriscos in each zone were to assemble at designated points. They were then marched off in large groups, each escorted by a detachment of soldiers. They were dispersed widely, to Extremadura, other parts of Castile and western Andalucía (in other words, well away from the Mediterranean coast). The marches were cruel for the old and infirm, particularly as some of the refugee columns heading north encountered winter snows. On reaching the designated destinations, the intention was that the Moriscos were to be dispersed within the surrounding districts. In several cases, many stayed within the *morerias* (the Mudéjar quarter) of the Castilian

Left. Three heads floating in the sea. Carlos V awarded this sanguinary coat of arms to Almuñécar in 1526 after its local militia defeated Barbary pirate boats.

cities. The last Moriscos remaining in the Albaicín were ejected from there to meet their Castilian fate by the end of 1570. In all, it has been estimated that around 80,000 Moriscos were expelled from the Kingdom of Granada.

A few rebels still remained in the Alpujarras. Aben Aboo was at the head of a group of four hundred who hid in the heights of the Sierra Nevada. However, one of these, a disgruntled rebel, had negotiated with the Christians to secure his own safety and in March 1571, in a mountain cave, he killed Aben Aboo. The last 'King of Granada' had an inauspicious end. His body was salted and sent off to Granada where it was paraded in the streets. The head was posted on the gate of the city that faced the Alpujarras. Meanwhile, the victor of the war, Don Juan de Austria, went on to battle the infidel on the international stage. By 1571 the Turkish fleet had gained ascendance in the Mediterranean. The Holy League, an alliance of Spain, the Papal States and Venice, was formed to meet this threat. A large fleet under the command of Don Juan was assembled in September. It sailed to meet the Turkish fleet, which was in the Adriatic. The two sides met at Lepanto in October 1571. The Christians emerged victorious, defeating the Ottomans. This victory burnished Spain's reputation as the defender of Christianity. However, the victory was ephemeral, as the Turks regained their dominance in the Mediterranean soon afterwards.

As manifested in the Germanía uprisings in the early sixteenth century, there had always been tensions between the Moriscos and the Christian peasants, who were concerned that the Moriscos were competing for the same kind of work and driving down wage rates. With the dispersal of the Granadan Moriscos to new districts, tension and unease now became more widespread. While the original Muslims (now Moriscos) of Castile had had time to be at least partially absorbed into the Christian State, the new arrivals did not fit in so well. The situation for the settled Moriscos of Valencia had been relatively stable but a colder wind was blowing all across Spain. From the 1570's onwards, the Inquisition started to pay more attention to the Moriscos who now formed the majority of

Right. Watchtower near Sabinillas, Málaga province, which may date from Roman times. Fear of invasion of the Mediterranean coast was constant throughout history. The danger of invasion by the Ottoman Turks preyed on the Spanish Monarchs and was one of the drivers of the final decision to expel the Moriscos.

its victims. Added to the general dislike by the 'old' Christians (as opposed to the Moriscos, supposed 'new' Christians), was the fear of being swamped: the Morisco population was growing faster than the Christian one. The suspicion that the Moriscos would ally with any external enemy (Islamic or Christian) of Spain continued. This anxiety was exacerbated by the continuous threat posed by the Ottomans, as well as a plot at the beginning of the seventeenth century by Valencian Moriscos to enlist the help of the French, which was foiled. In the meantime, the Muslim corsairs continued their raids along the Mediterranean coast. The distrust of the Morisco minority was such that, when the English seized and sacked Cádiz in 1596, restrictions were placed on the Moriscos of nearby Seville.

In 1580 Felipe II managed to enforce his claim of inheritance to the throne of Portugal. He transferred to Lisbon, from where he administered his Empire.

As it happens, Portugal had expelled its Muslims and Jews in 1497. (Unusually, the Muslims had been allowed to take refuge in Spain!) It was perhaps an appropriate location, where the chief councillors of the King discussed the expulsion of the Moriscos from Spain. The dislike and fear of these unfortunates was manifested in the extreme remedies that were mooted, such as castration of the male Moriscos, along with expulsion of the entire group to remote areas like Newfoundland. It has been contended that a 'final' solution was even proposed: that of sending the Moriscos to sea and scuttling the boats. Whatever solution may have been put to him, Felipe II refrained from taking direct action and the 'Morisco Question' continued to be discussed for the rest of his reign up to his death in 1598. History has not dealt kindly with his son Felipe III, who then came to power. He is remembered as different from his authoritarian and hardworking father. He was described as weak, vacillating and rigidly pious. The vacuum in power was filled by the Duke of Lerma, Francisco Goméz de Sandoval y Rojas, a noble and courtier, who had become a favourite of the young sovereign. He effectively ran the Empire on the King's behalf, amassing great wealth on the way, in addition to the huge estates that he held in Valencia. There, like his fellow Valencian Señores, he had multitudes of Morisco vassals. Into the hands of Felipe III and the Duke of Lerma fell the fate of the Moriscos. The King and his courtier, as well as the Council of State, have to take the primary responsibility for the major exercise in ethnic cleansing of the seventeenth century: the expulsion of the Moriscos.

As the new century dawned, the pressures to proceed with expulsion were building with greater intensity. Within the church, there were those who argued that assimilation had not worked and expulsion was the solution. A particularly strident and influential voice was that of the Archbishop of Valencia, Juan de Ribera. At the end of 1601, he sent a letter to the King saying that it was impossible to convert the Moriscos, they hated the King and wanted to see themselves under Turkish domain. The King asked for a solution and de Ribera wrote again recommending banishment of the Moriscos. Curiously, in the expulsion debates, the Inquisition institution was not to the forefront of those pressing for expulsion. The Inquisition paid its expenses by means of fines on those that fell with-

Above. Painting in the Sala Dorada of the Palau Comtal in Cocentaina, south of Játiva in Valencia. This dates from the early seventeenth century and depicts the struggle between the Christians and the Muslim forces.

Right. Some of the estimated 6800 steps on a track, known as the 'Arab Steps,' dating from Muslim times, in the Vall de Laguart, south of Valencia. The Kingdom of Valencia contained the largest concentration of Moriscos in Spain.

in its grip and the Moriscos were a fruitful source. Perhaps some instinctively anticipated what in fact happened, that there would indeed be a severe drop in Inquisitorial income after the expulsion. However, genuine humanity was probably the motivator for the Inquisitors of Valencia, who declared that the Moriscos should not be expelled as 'they are Spaniards like ourselves.'

Pope Paul V was perhaps more sensitive to the norms of humanity than some of the pastors of his Spanish flock. A priest who came from Spain had made a proposal in Rome that the Moriscos be declared apostates and argued for their rapid and total expulsion. The Moriscos were theoretically part of the Christian community and this proposal was not entertained in Rome. After evil events occur in history, revisionism sets in and people are quick to deny involvement. A book appeared in 1611 claiming that the Papacy had approved the expulsion. However, it appears that the Pope was justified when he took particular care to ensure that that passage was excised.

The need to expel had been mooted by many and in many permutations over a long time. Finally, at a meeting in January 1608, the Council of State unanimously agreed to expel the Moriscos from Spain. The King had earlier set aside the more extreme solutions and decided that they would be deported to North Africa. The final obstacle to expulsion had also been overcome. The Señores of Valencia had opposed expulsion, being reluctant to lose their productive Morisco tenants, a valuable source of income. The Duke of Lerma, owner of enormous estates in Valencia, had previously been opposed to the expulsion, but had arrived at a formula that solved the problem. This was the expedient of including, in the decree of expulsion, the requirement that the Moriscos could only bring with them what they could carry. Their belongings and holdings would then be allocated to their respective Señores. Thus, the short term gain seemed attractive over what might be (and turned out to be) long term loss.

The concept of expulsion of the Moriscos had not exercised general public opinion across Spain - this decision to expel was taken by those at a high level. Ultimately, a consensus was arrived at by the King and those that surrounded him: the Duke of Lerma, the Council of State with the background support of some Church leaders. The Council of State represented the political and the military viewpoint of Spain. The Council members were swayed by the eventual decisive vote for expulsion by the Duke of Lerma. The principal reason as presented was the perceived threat to the security of the State posed by the Moriscos, who might give support to any enemy attacking Spain. The religious element, that of the expulsion of heretics, only ranked second. Paradoxically, Spain reached a twelve-year truce with the Dutch in 1609, a pragmatic agreement with 'heretical' Protestants. It is likely that the absence of such an external threat (there also had been earlier treaties with the French and English) was one more contributory factor that allowed Felipe III to arrive at the dangerous and risky resolution to expel nearly a third of a million of his subjects.

The decision to expel was kept secret. It took over a year to make the detailed preparations. It had been decided to expel the Moriscos of Valencia first. These were the most concentrated, the most populous, many living in mountainous regions and seen as posing the most danger during the expulsion exercise. A fleet of Italian galleys was assembled clandestinely in Majorca to await the call to Valencian ports. The army was put on alert and thousands of soldiers were placed ready for the Valencian exercise. The Castilian cavalry was deployed, as a reserve, on the borders of the Kingdom of Valencia. The galleons of the fleet of the ocean were put on watch off the North African coast. These preparations soon became public knowledge and a sense of alarm spread, not

Above. Snaking through spectacular terrain, the 'Arab Steps' pass through a cavern in the Vall de Laguart. The name comes from 'al-aguar' or cavern in Arabic.

least among some Señores of Valencia, who were not aware of Lerma's facilitation of their interests. They made representations to the Viceroy about the ruin they would face when their tenants were evicted. The specific clause incorporated in the decree was explained to them - the residual belongings of their soon-to-be-deported Morisco tenants would be entirely theirs. Many of the Señores immediately switched to supporting the expulsion.

The decree of expulsion was published by the Viceroy in Valencia in September 1609. The Moriscos in each locality were given three days to arrive at specific gathering points whence they would travel to the disembarkation ports. The ships would then transport them to North Africa. They could bring what they could carry. The remainder of their belongings could not be hidden or destroyed, under pain of death for all the people of the village in question. Six families out of every hundred had to remain behind. Their task would be to mind the irrigation system, rice fields and sugar mills and to instruct the future Christian settlers in their operation. Those who were licensed as communicants by their bishop were also exempt. Where a Morisco was married to an 'old' Christian woman, she and her children under six years could remain but the Morisco had to go. Children under four years of age might remain, subject to agreement of their parents. In a move designed to reduce fears of the unknown, ten of the first batch of the expelled Moriscos were to be allowed to return, in order to explain to their fellow Moriscos what awaited them.

Rebellion flared up in two regions of Valencia. One was in the region around the Valle de Cofrentes, around thirty kilometres south of Requena, where the Moriscos of the villages and valleys had rebelled. The insurgents then set up on the rugged massif of Muela de Cortés. A Morisco called Vicente Turixi was selected as leader. In November 1609 the rebels were defeated quickly by royal forces which included Italian *tercios*. Turixi and some accomplices were captured in a cave, brought to Valencia, quartered and executed. Some of the rebels had managed to escape. A bounty was put on them, (the head of a dead Morisco was worth half that of a live Morisco) and they were hunted down.

Another rebellion broke out in the densely populated Morisco region of Marina Alta, around twenty kilometres inland from Dénia. The Moriscos came from the valleys all round and assembled in the Vall de Laguart. As leader, they chose a local baker, Ahmed el-Mellini. The King's troops advanced to smash the rebellion and, again, Italian *tercios* were deployed. They were led by Agustin Mexía, a veteran of the harsh fighting in Flanders, who set up nearby at the beginning of November 1609. The Morisco rebels did not stand a chance when the royal troops attacked. After suffering huge losses, including the death of el-Mellini, the rebels retreated and took over the castle of Pop. As the Spanish army continued its bloody advance, the Moriscos retreated further up to the ridge of the Serra del Penyal de Laguart with its twin peaked mountain, now known as Cavall Verd ('green horse' in Valencian). The Moriscos had a legend that their hero, al-Fatimi, concealed under the mountain, would emerge, mount-

Above. The twin peaks of the Cavall Verd (green horse) mountain in the Vall de Laguart where the Moriscos of the region were defeated in 1609.

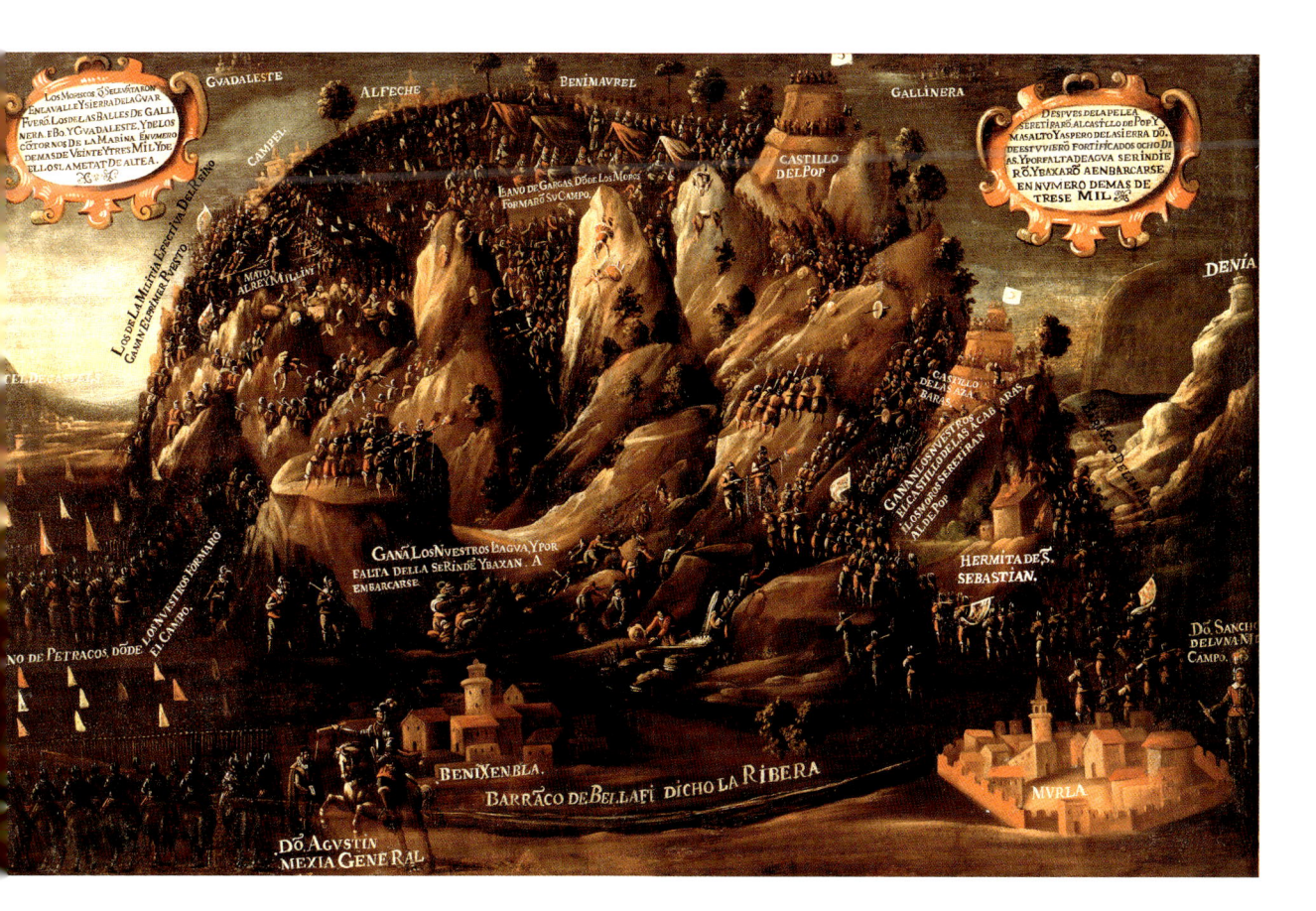

Above. The rebellion of the Moriscos around the Cavall Verd, where there was great loss of life. One commentator compared the scenes to Dante's Inferno.
Painting by Jerónimo Espinosa. Bancaja Collection.

ed on his green horse and save them. It is a similar theme to that of the Spanish fable of Saint James, the *Matamoros* or 'Moor Slayer', miraculously emerging on his horse at the mythical battle of Clavijo in 844 to smite the Muslim foe. No miracle occurred at Cavall Verd, and, suffering from thirst, the rebels had to come down from the mountain and surrender. The women and children were condemned to slavery. The men were transported to the ports where, one account darkly suggests, they were embarked on ships only to be thrown overboard.

However, most of the Moriscos of Valencia went to their exile quietly, stoically accepting the inevitable. A few were pleased to go, to a place where they thought that they would not be oppressed and be able to freely practise Islam. Most did not want to leave, many had developed an affection for their land and locality, the farmland developed and cultivated by their ancestors over many centuries. The belongings of the Moriscos, their crops, grain and oil, as well as the cattle - all of these were to be left to the benefit of the Señores. A few of these Señores behaved with humanity to their Morisco tenants: some accompanied them to the ports, protecting them from attack. The streets of the Valencian ports and the surrounding beaches soon became crowded with the deportees as they awaited transfer across the Mediterranean. Ships shuttled back and forth to Oran on the North African coast, an enclave under Spanish rule, carrying their cargo of Moriscos. On arrival at Oran, they were rapidly deposited across the frontier. The first transfers began at the beginning of October 1609.

Most went by sea but a few took the land route to France. By the middle of 1610, all the Moriscos of Valencia had been rounded up and expelled from the kingdom, an estimated number of around 120,000.

Now it was the turn of other parts of Spain. This posed less danger for the State than the expulsion in Valencia: there were fewer Moriscos and they were more dispersed and less likely to cause trouble. Several edicts of expulsion were published in January 1610 covering Granada, Andalucía and Murcia and parts of old and new Castile. The expulsion proceeded relatively smoothly. The State had gained experience and confidence in the undertaking. It also added to the restrictions. Now the Moriscos were not allowed to take any gold, silver or jewels, only the money they needed for their journey. Seville, Sanlúcar and Gibraltar were the main ports of embarkation in the south-west. The decree for Extremadura and other parts of the two Castiles was issued in July 1610. Many of these Moriscos headed north and departed across the French border. At an early stage of the expulsions, the French had maintained a lenient attitude and allowed the Moriscos to cross the frontier. Some were even allowed to stay if they converted to Catholicism. The policy changed temporarily when Henry IV of France was assassinated in May 1610. The Moriscos were then refused entry and access was allowed only from the following August. The decree of expulsion for the Aragonese Moriscos was published in March 1610. Most of these passed through the port of Alfaques on the Ebro delta (as did the Moriscos from Catalonia) but some went via France.

Above. The embarkation of the Moriscos at the port of Grau, Valencia. Painting by Pere Oromig. Bancaja Collection.

Right. The dusty town of Hornachos in Extremadura. The ruins of a castle overlook the town.

Right. The Fuente de los Moros at Hornachos. The tough Hornacheros were seen as a problem and their expulsion was dealt with as a special case in 1610. They later went on to excel in piracy, operating out of Salé in Morocco.

Left. Chefchauen in Morocco.

Left. Chefchauen, nestling in the Rif Mountains, still has an Andalusi quarter.

Right. Scene from the narrow streets in Fez.

Right. The Rif Mountains in Morocco, where many Moriscos went to live.

Left. Tetouan. Many of the expelled Moriscos settled here and there is a conscious Andalusi heritage in the city.

Left. Carved timber stepped crenellations in the Madrasa es-Sahriji, located in the Andalus quarter in Fez. This style of crenellation is widespread and, according to one source, originated in Umayyad Córdoba.

Right. Azulejos (tiles) in Fez. Andalusi influences in decoration and architecture flowed south to Morocco.

Below. Stepped crenellations atop a tower in Tetouan.

And so, over the years of the expulsion process, columns of Moriscos were seen on the highways and tracks across Spain as they headed to the ports or the French border. Old and young, men and women, sick and healthy, they set out from where, for most, their ancestors had resided for centuries. On carts, horseback, or on foot, these bedraggled groups made slow progress, carrying a miscellany of belongings. Most of these people were poor. The well-off minority smuggled gold, silver or jewels on their persons. On the way, they encountered a hostile reaction from many 'old' Christians. In a few cases they were attacked and robbed. The majority were burdened by despair, hopelessness and the fear of an unknown future, whether in North Africa or further afield.

The redoubtable people of Hornachos were dealt with as an exceptional case. This small town in Extremadura, around fifty kilometres to the south-east of Mérida, was predominantly Morisco with a population of around 4500 people. It was in the hands of the Order of Santiago, which garnered a healthy rent from its tenants. The independent folk of Hornachos had built up a reputation for being tough and prickly to deal with, all the more reason for the State to plan special treatment of what were perceived as difficult characters. Eventually, in January 1610, an individual decree of expulsion was published for the town. The inhabitants were given two weeks to assemble. Unusually, they were given the right to bring their arms with them, They travelled from Seville to Ceuta. Most eventually went en masse to the Atlantic port of Salé, just across the river from Rabat. Salé at the time was run-down but was revitalised by the arrival of the 'Hornacheros'. There, they set to the profession of piracy with gusto. Other Andalusis also came to the city, but the tough Extremeños dominated the city. Against the background of a weak central Moroccan state, they ran the city effectively as an independent Corsair republic. Piracy needed ships and shipyards were developed, building the sophisticated and swift vessels suited for this specialised trade. The city grew as more people came from afar, drawn by news of the rich booty that was being captured. The city was ideal for its new role, protected from the attacks of European navies by the new fortifications that were built. In addition, the shallow draught of the estuary of the Bu Regreg river meant that it was difficult for enemies to navigate into the port. The Hornachos

Left. The abandoned village, or despoblado, of Atzuvieta in the Marina Alta region, Valencia. Villages were abandoned when their Morisco inhabitants were expelled in 1609.

pirates proceeded to give a headache to the State that had expelled them and to the other Christian European maritime states. In England, the term 'Sallee Rovers' became a synonym for Barbary pirates.

One of the last cases involved the Moriscos living in the Valle de Ricote, around thirty kilometres north-west of Murcia. They had, at an early stage of the expulsions, been assessed as good Christians and were passed over for expulsion. At this time a report was commissioned which concluded that these were true Christians, consuming wine and pork and fully participating in Christian ceremonies. However, it was ultimately to no avail. These Moriscos were finally expelled in at the end of 1613, with most heading for France or Italy. By this stage, it was all over, save for a few stragglers spread around the country. In February 1614, the Council of State reported to Felipe III that the expulsion had been completed.

Where did the Moriscos go to? A small number settled in European countries. Of those who had travelled to France, most travelled onwards to other locations. The minority who converted to Catholicism remained in France. A few went to Italy and converted, although forbidden to stay in the domains there associated with the Spanish King. Many Moriscos made it as far as the eastern shores of the Mediterranean and settled in Salonika, Syria, Lebanon and Egypt. A great number went to Constantinople. However, the overwhelming majority of Moriscos went to the Maghreb. There had been a centuries-old tradition of emigration by Andalusis to the southern continent. The terrain in many parts of the Maghreb was similar, as was the culture and, of course, the religion. Many had gone there after the great expansion of Castile during the Reconquista of the thirteenth century. As the Christian pressure on al-Andalus

Right. Abandoned buildings at Queirola in the Marina Alta, originally Morisco.

was maintained, the steady stream of refugees continued. The fall of Granada resulted in a sharp increase in the number moving to the Maghreb. This was followed by another constant flow, as the miseries of the sixteenth century unfolded for the Mudéjars and then Moriscos of Spain. Then came the final wave.

Most of the refugees of 1609, who travelled via the Spanish enclave of Oran, went to Algeria. A lot of these Moriscos met a miserable fate as they crossed the border, as the local Berber nomads pounced on what they perceived as rich and alien interlopers. Typically, they robbed them of all their belongings, leaving them destitute. Quite a few Moriscos went to Tunisia, which was under the Turkish rule of the Dey Utman. He took an enlightened attitude, viewing this influx of capable people as an opportunity for development of the country.

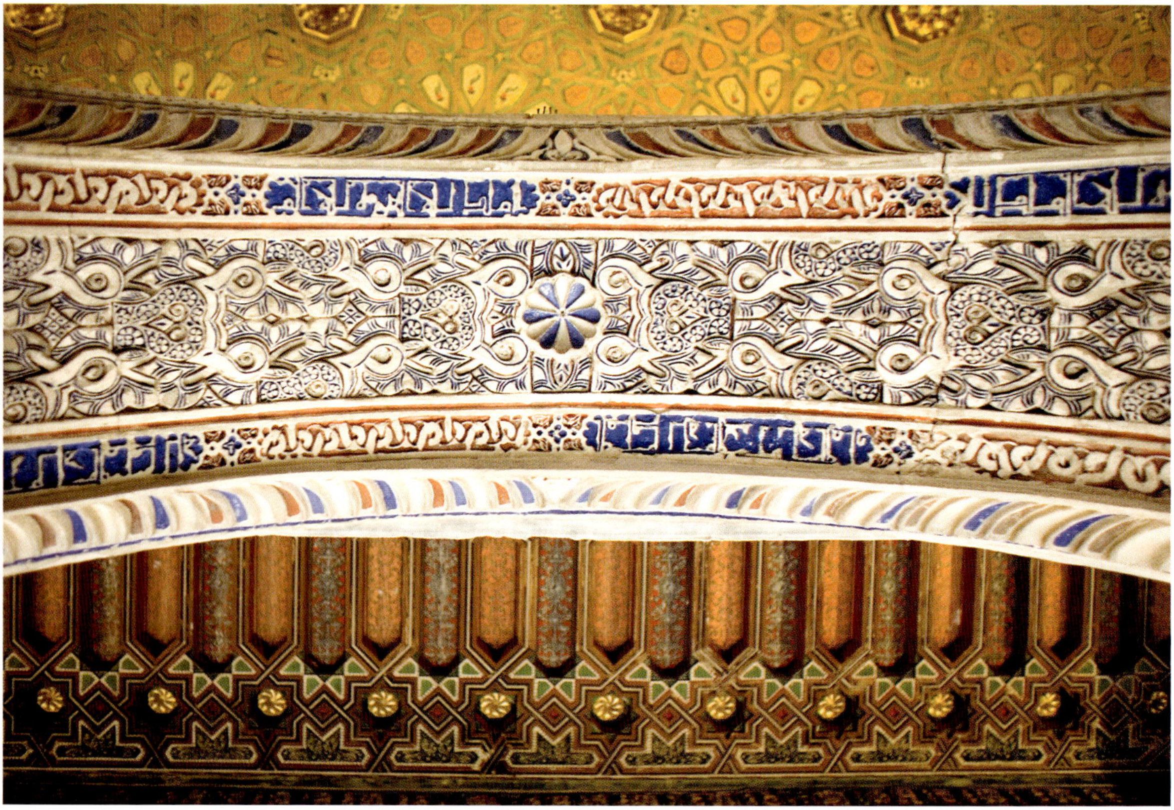

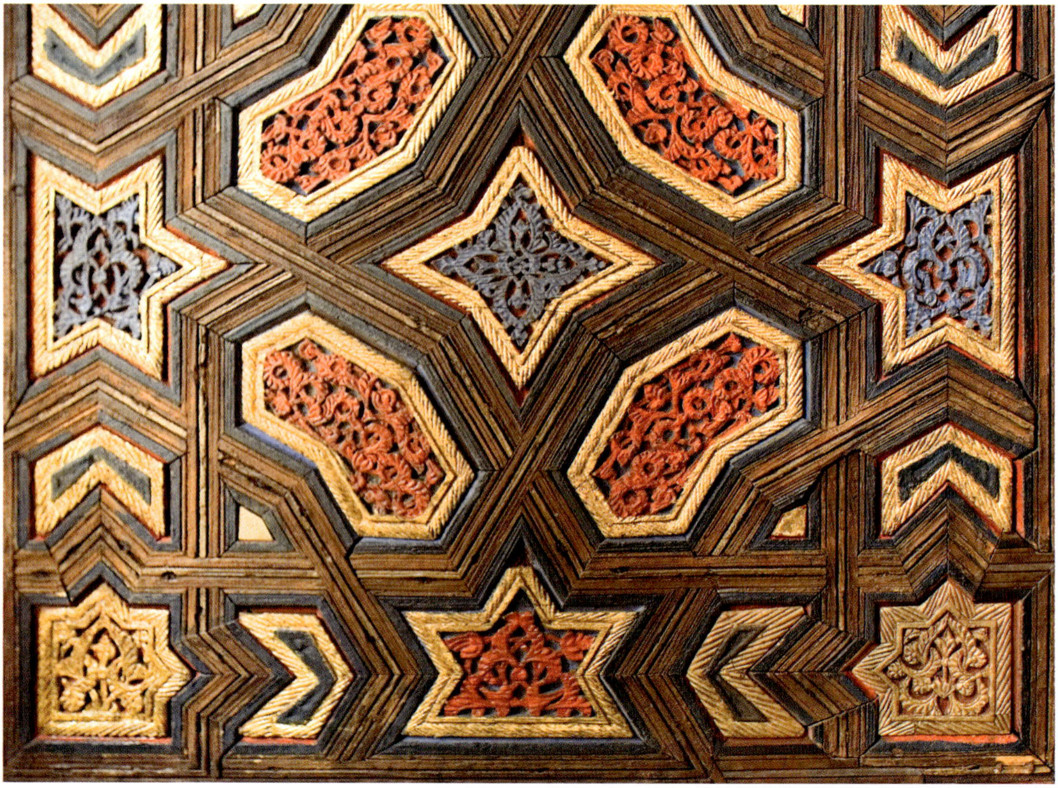

Right. Tower of the church San Pedro, one of several similar towers in Teruel. This dates from the thirteenth to the fourteenth century, and was rebuilt in the eighteenth century. It is decorated in the Mudéjar style. Inset in the brick facade are green and blue diamond tiles.

The heritage of Andalusi decoration survives in the Real Alcázar in Seville, constructed by King Pedro I in the 14th century.

Above left. Vertical view of arch.

Below left. Exquisitely decorated wooden shutter.

Below. Stucco and tile decoration in the Real Alcázar, Seville.

Moriscos of all types, artisans, craftspeople and merchants, settled in the cities and rural areas. This resulted in the rise of such industries as textiles and ceramics, as well as a big increase in agricultural production, due to great Morisco skill in cultivation and setting up irrigation systems.

A substantial number of Moriscos went to the territory of present-day Morocco. Many went to the cities and towns in the north of the country, such as Tangier, Tetouan, Fez and Chefchauen. We have seen how the doughty 'Hornacheros' fared in Salé. The Moriscos were highly talented and brought a great number of skills to the local economy. Their influence is remembered in today's Morocco, including its music, cuisine, ceramics, architecture, agriculture and irrigation. This reinforced the earlier influx of Andalusi skills and culture that had started during the Córdoba Caliphate, coming into full flow during the time of the Almoravids and Almohads. There is a strong Andalusi heritage, particularly in Northern Morocco, in such places as Tetouan. In Chefchauen, there is an Andalus quarter. Incidentally, it should not be confused with the Andalus quarter of Fez, which dates from an earlier wave of refugees from Córdoba, expelled by the Umayyad Amir during the early ninth century.

The Moriscos settled into their new life in North Africa and boosted the local economy in many areas. Some felt uneasy in their new location. Some may actually have been Christian: there are accounts of those who wanted to return to Spain, being afraid to declare that they were Christians and rightly fearing reprisals. There is a report that the Moriscos who came to North Africa were regarded as 'very white' by the indigenous population. There was probably an ethnic difference between most of the Moriscos and the native North Africans. The Andalusi population, particularly by the time of the Córdoba Caliphate, had developed into a mix of Arabs, Berbers and predominantly Muwallads, the original inhabitants of the Peninsula, who had converted to Islam. The memory of the Iberian Peninsula still tugs at the hearts of descendants of Andalusis across the Muslim Mediterranean world. In Tetouan, for example, there are accounts that some people there were in possession of keys, handed down over the centuries, from their ancestral houses in al-Andalus. This has resonances with the situation of some present-day Palestinian refugees in the Middle East who still possess the keys of their abandoned houses in such places as Haifa.

North Africa's gain was Spain's loss. As in the earlier expulsion of the Jews, Spain lost a host of industrious and skilled people. This was particularly marked in the parts of the country that had high numbers of Moriscos. The effect was especially harsh in the Kingdom of Valencia where the Moriscos comprised around a third of the population. Agricultural production dropped sharply. In Valencia, of a reported nearly 500 abandoned villages, only a little over half were repopulated by Christian settlers by 1638. Indeed, there are a few *despoblados* (abandoned villages) from Morisco times still to be seen to the present day. In Aragón, irrigated lands fell back into aridity and there was a shift in some places from more labour-intensive cultivation to the less skilled grazing of cattle. Silk production was affected in Murcia. In Castile, where the proportion of Moriscos was low, the effects were less severe. Ironically, earlier in the Alpujarras, the new Christian settlers found that the local authorities, used to exploiting the Moriscos by such means as tax, continued their extortionary practices on the new arrivals.

Most estimates of the total number of Moriscos that were expelled put the figure at 300,000. The expulsion was later described by Cardinal Richelieu as

Above. Symbolic of the new reality? Prominent over Almería: statue of Christ on the Cerro de San Cristóbal, with, in the background, the fortified wall leading to the Alcazaba.

Right. The view south from los Reales mountain in the Sierra Bermeja: Gibraltar and the Rif mountains of Morocco in the background. By 1614 Spain was entirely Christian, with most of the Moriscos settling in the Maghreb.

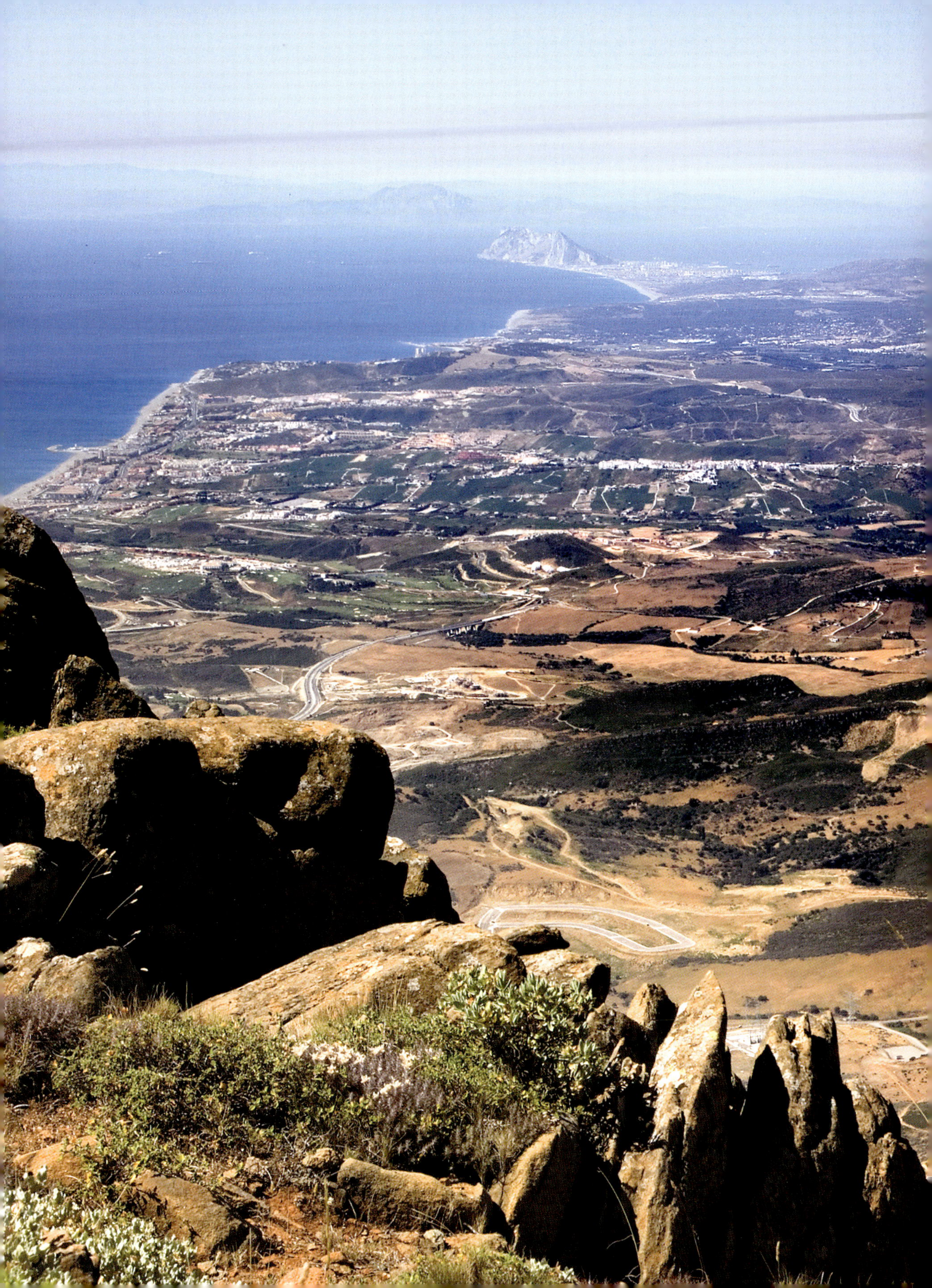

'the most barbarous act in human annals'. Humanity has managed to outdo this barbarity over the following centuries. Nevertheless, the expulsion truly was a savage finish to the long history of al-Andalus.

This history commenced in 711 with the swift invasion and dominance by Muslim Arabs over most of the Iberian Peninsula. Turbulence and conflict continued up to the establishment of the Umayyad dynasty in Córdoba and continued throughout its history. Medieval Europe, including Iberia, were harsh places but brilliance did emanate from Córdoba at the zenith of the Caliphate in the tenth century. It truly was 'the ornament of the world'.

Disorder reigned as the Caliphate disintegrated but the Andalusi achievements in science, arts and culture continued, despite the turmoil of the taifas and the later domination by the rigorous Islamic invaders from North Africa, the Almoravids and the Almohads. The Christian Reconquista made its 'great leap forward' during the thirteenth century by capturing most of al-Andalus. An incidental effect was that enlightened Christian scholars managed to translate advanced Andalusi works in science and literature and transfer them to Western Europe. Eventually, only Nasrid Granada remained as the rump of old al-Andalus. It, too, achieved brilliance and bequeathed such jewels as the Alhambra to posterity. Several centuries later, in 1492, it was snuffed out in the final vigorous phase of the Reconquista. The final century was cruel for the Mudéjars, who had to suffer an imposed faux-Christian existence as Moriscos and it culminated in their expulsion. It was an inglorious end to the curious mix of turmoil and peace, *covivencia* (coexisting cultures) and occasional intolerance, prosperity and intermittent pillage, high culture, civilisation, splendour and brilliance that was al-Andalus.

Did the brilliance die with the abrupt expulsion of the Moriscos? Not entirely. Western civilisation, as it developed and moved towards the glory of the Renaissance, did so based in part on the foundations of the developments in Islamic science and philosophy, transmitted in a significant part from al-Andalus. The quality of Andalusi art was evident from the way that the neighbouring Christian kingdoms eagerly collected its objets d'art. Islamic textiles were prized - Isabel of Castile occasionally dressed in Islamic clothes. Pedro the Cruel's Real Alcázar in Seville is a *te deum* to the beauty of Andalusi architecture. The form of architecture based on the Andalusi style, now known as Mudéjar, has continued in Spain up to present times. Early Mudéjar works like the towers of Teruel were executed by Muslim craftsmen. The Spanish language contains thousands of words derived from Arabic. A large proportion of the place-names of Spanish towns and cities are a constant reminder of their Islamic founders. The splendid Spanish cuisine and music (particularly flamenco) have roots in the Andalusi past. Much of the depth, richness, complexity and even darkness of this most fascinating country can be attributed to its 900 year-long heritage of al-Andalus.

Glossary

Al-Andalus: Islamic Spain and Portugal. Originally it extended over most of the Iberian Peninsula, but progressively was reduced so that by the middle of the thirteenth century it was confined to the Kingdom of Granada, more or less the territory of present-day Andalucía.

Alcazaba: Castle or citadel.

Alcázar: A fortress or palace.

Alfaqui: Person versed in Islamic law.

Amir: A ruler or commander.

Caliph: The successor (of the Prophet) and both spiritual and temporal ruler.

Jihad: Striving for religious and moral perfection. It can involve waging a holy war in the name of God against unbelievers.

Madrasa: Islamic school of learning.

Mahdi: Expected Messiah of Islam.

Maqsura: A sanctuary in a mosque reserved for the Caliph.

Mihrab: Niche in mosque indicating the direction of Mecca.

Moors: A term used, in the context of Spain, to denote Muslim inhabitants of al-Andalus. In common usage, it is inaccurate, as most of the Muslim Andalusis were descended from the original inhabitants of the Iberian Peninsula, with only a minority originating from the Maghreb or further to the east.

Morisco: Iberian Muslim who became a baptised Christian, living under Christian rule.

Mozarab: Iberian Christian living under Muslim rule.

Mudéjar: Muslim living under Christian rule, after the Reconquista.

Muwallad: Christian living in the Iberian Peninsula who had converted to Islam.

Noria: A waterwheel.

Qadi: Judge who adjudicates on the basis of Islamic law.

Wadi: Watercourse (usually dry). In Spanish, presented as the root 'Guad', hence the rivers Guadalquivir, Guadiana, etc.

Illustrations

The author is grateful to the institutions mentioned on page 5 which allowed him to use photographs. All photographs are by Michael Barry © 2008, with the exception of the following:

Images which have been kindly provided by the following (and are copyright of these):

Fundación Bancaja, Valencia. Pages 237, 238.

Metropolitan Museum of Art, New York. Pages 18, 102, 180.

Ministerio de Cultura, Archivo General de Simancas, Valladolid, PTR-LEG, 11, 3. Page 212.

Museo Arqueológico Nacional, Madrid. Pages 15r, 89, 134bl, 186l, 198t.

Museo del Ejercito, Madrid. Pages 206, 207.

Museo de Huesca. Page 135r.

Museo de Teruel. Page 136b.

Patrimonio Histórico-Artístico del Senado, Madrid. Photographs by Oronez. Pages 169, 211.

Victoria and Albert Museum, London. Pages 80tl, 99, 103, 108, 137, 181r, 188l.

Photographs on pages 6, 9, 21, 39, 69, 113, 141, 177, 186b, 188b, 190-195, 196a and 215, as well as those of the Alhambra on the jacket, were taken by Michael Barry, authorised by the Patronato de la Alhambra y Generalife, who reserve the copyright to those images. Similarly for the photographs on pages 208, 210b and 219, the copyright is reserved by the Capilla Real of Granada.

Bibliography

For those who wish to explore further the world that was al-Andalus, the following are recommended in the first instance:

Barrucand, M. and Bednorz, A., 'Moorish Architecture in Andalusia', Taschen, Cologne, 2002.

Collins, R., 'Early Medieval Spain', St. Martin's Press, New York, 1995.

Fletcher, R., 'Moorish Spain', University of California Press, Berkley, 1993.

García de Cortázar, F., 'Atlas de Historia de España', Editorial Planeta, Barcelona, 2005.

Guichard, P., 'From the Arab Conquest to the Reconquest, The Splendour and Fragility of al-Andalus', Legado Andalusí, Granada, 2006.

Harvey, L. P., 'Islamic Spain 1250 to 1500', University of Chicago Press, Chicago and London, 1990.

Harvey, L. P., 'Muslims in Spain, 1500 to 1614', University of Chicago Press, Chicago and London, 2005.

Kennedy, H., 'Muslim Spain and Portugal', Longman, Harlow, 1996.

Other sources:

'Andalusian Morocco, a Discovery in Living Art', Museum with No Frontiers, Vienna, 2002.

'Art and History of Jordan', Bonechi, Florence, 2007.

'Art and History of Syria', Bonechi, Florence, 2008.

'Córdoba in Focus', Edilux, 2001

'El Islam en Aragón', Caja de Ahorros de la Immaculada de Aragón, Zaragoza, 1995.

'In the Lands of the Enchanted Moorish Maiden, Islamic Art in Portugal', Museum with No Frontiers, Vienna, 2001.

'Itenerario Cultural de Almoravides y Almohades', Legado Andalusí. Granada, 2003.

'Ronda in Focus', Publicaciones Ronda, Ronda.

'Route of the Caliphate', Legado Andalusí, Granada, 1998.

'Route of the Nasrids', Legado Andalusi, Granada, 2001.

'Ruta de los Almoravides y Almohades', Legado Andalusí, Granada, 2006.

'Ruta de Washington Irving', Legado Andalusi, Granada, 1999.

'Sevilla, Siglo XIV', Fundacion Jose Manuel Lara, Seville, 2006.

'The Alhambra and Granada in Focus', Edilux, 2006.

'The Aljafería of Zaragoza', Cortes de Aragón, Zaragoza, 1999.

'The Encyclopedia of Islam', E. J. Brill, Leiden; Luzac, London.

'The Real Alcazar of Seville', Patronato del Real Alcazar de Sevilla, Seville, 2005.

Aranda Doncal, J., 'Los Moriscos en Tierras de Córdoba', Publicaciones del Monte de Piedad y Caja de Ahorros de Córdoba, Córdoba, 1984.

Arnaldez, R., 'Averroes, a Rationalist in Islam', University of Notre Dame Press, Notre Dame, Indiana, 2000.

Barbour, N., 'Morocco', Methuen, London.

Barton, S. and Fletcher, R., 'The World of El Cid', Manchester University Press, Manchester and New York, 2000.

Becerra, E., R., 'Igualeja Despues de la Expulsion de los Moriscos' Editorial la Serranía, Ronda 2005.

Brazales, J., C., Uzal, A., O., 'En Busca de la Granada Andalusi', Granada 2002.

Brett, M., Fentress, E., 'The Berbers', Blackwell, Oxford, 1997.

Burckhardt, T., 'La Civilizacion Hispano-Arabe', Alianza Editorial, Madrid, 2001.

Cebrian, J. A., 'La Cruzada del Sur', La Esfera de los Libros, Madrid, 2005.

Clevenot, D., Degeorge, G., 'Ornament and Decoration in Islamic Architecture', Thames & Hudson, London, 2000.

Cuenca Toribio, J. M., 'Historia General de Andalucía', Editorial Almuzara, Madrid, 2005.

De Aristegui, G., 'La Yihad en Espana', La Esfera de los Libros, Madrid, 2005.

De Mármol Carvajal, L., 'Historia de la Rebelion y Castigo de los Moriscos del Reino de Granada', Editorial Arguval, Malaga.

De Zayas, R., 'Los Moriscos y el Racismo de Estado', Editorial Almuzara, 2006.

East, W. G., 'An Historical

Geography of Europe', Methuen, London, 1966.

Ekin, D., 'The stolen village, Baltimore and the Barbary Pirates', The O' Brien Press, Dublin.

Elliott, J. H., 'Imperial Spain, 1469-1716', Penguin, London, 2002.

Encinas Moral, A., L., 'Cronologia Historica de al-Andalus', Miragueno Ediciones, Madrid, 2005.

Fanjul, S., 'La Quimera de al-Andalus', Siglo XXI de Espana Editores, Madrid, 2005.

Fletcher, R., 'The Quest for El Cid', Hutchinson, London.

Garcia-Arenal, M., 'La Diaspora de los Andalusies', Icaria Editorial, Barcelona, 2003.

Gerli, E. M., 'Medieval Iberia, an Encyclopedia' , Routelage, London, 2003.

Gomez Bayarri, J. V., 'La Valencia Medieval', Real Academia de Cultura Valenciana, Valencia, 2003.

Gonzalez Ferrin, E., 'Historia General de al-Andalus', Editorial Almuzara, Madrid, 2006.

Goodwin, G., 'Islamic Spain', Penguin, London, 1991.

Guichard, P., 'Al-Andalus frente a la Conquista Cristiana, los Musulmanes de Valencia', Biblioteca Nueva-Universitat de Valencia, Valencia, 2001.

Harvey, G., 'Gibraltar, a History', Spellmount, Staplehurst, 2000.

Haussig, H. W., 'Byzantine Civilisation' Thames and Hudson, London 1971.

Jacobs, M., 'Andalucia', Pallas Guides, London, 2006.

Janer, F., 'Condicion Social de los Moriscos de Espana', Ediciones Espuela de Plata, 2006.

Kamen, H., 'Spain 1469-1714, a Society of Conflict', Longman, London, 1991.

Kamen, H., 'The Spanish Inquisition, an Historical Revision', Phoenix, London, 2003.

Lacave, J. L, Armegon, M., Ontanon, F., 'Sefarid, Culturas de Convivencia', Lunwerg, Barcelona, 2002.

Ladero Quesada, M. A., 'La Guerra de Granada', Los Libros de la Estrella, Granada, 2001.

Levi-Provencal, E., 'Histoire de l'Espagne Musulmane", Vol 3, Maisonneuve et Larose, Paris, 1999.

Makariou, S., 'La Andalucía Arabe', Legado Andalusí, Granada, 2000.

Maranon, G., 'Expulsion y Diaspora de los Moriscos Espanoles', Taurus, 2004.

Menendez Pidal, R., 'Historia de Espana', Vols. III, IV, V, VIII (1,2,3,4), IX, Editorial Espasa Calpe, Madrid.

Moreno, E., M., 'Conquistadores, Emires y Califas', Critica, Barcelona, 2006.

Nicolle, D., 'Historical Atlas of the Islamic World', Mercury Books, London, 2003.

O' Callaghan, J. F., 'A History of Medieval Spain', Cornell University Press, Ithaca and London, 1983.

O' Callaghan, J. F., 'Reconquest and Crusade in Medieval Spain', University of Pennsylvania Press, Philadelphia, 2003.

Ortiz, A., D., Vincent, B., 'Historia de los Moriscos', Alianza Editorial, Madrid, 2003.

Perez Higuera, T., 'Objetos e Imagenes de al-Andalus', Lunwerg, Barcelona.

Perez, J., 'The Spanish Inquisition', Profile Books, London, 2006.

Robinson, F., 'Cambridge Illustrated History of the Islamic World', Cambridge University Press, Cambridge, 2005.

Sherlin, H., 'Oriental Treasures in the Mediterranean', White Star, Vercelli, 2005.

Smith, C., 'Christians and Moors in Spain', Vol. I, Aris and Phillips, Westminster, 1993.

Smith, C., 'Christians and Moors in Spain', Vol. II, Aris and Phillips, Westminster, 1998.

Trillo San Jose, C., 'Agua, Tierra y Hombres en al-Andalus', Ajbar Coleccion, Granada, 2004.

Valdeon Baruque, J., 'Abderraman III y el Califato de Córdoba', Editorial Debate, Madrid, 2001.

Valdeon Baruque, J., 'La Reconquista', Espasa Calpe, Madrid, 2006.

Vidal, C., ' Espana frente al Islam', La Esfera de los Libros, Madrid, 2004.

Ziegler, P., 'The Black Death', The Folio Society, London, 1997.

Index

Abbasid, 31, 32, 40, 42, 49, 51, 73, 87, 90, 144, 174
Abd al-Aziz, 23, 24, 123
Abd al-Malik, 104, 108, 109, 123
Abd al-Mumin, 149, 150, 152, 163
Abd al-Rahman I, 32-34, 36-40
Abd al-Rahman II, 40, 44, 46, 49-54, 63, 90
Abd al-Rahman III, 40, 57, 60, 67-69, 71, 73 -77, 81-93, 101, 106, 111, 112, 119, 121, 203
Abd Allah, 39, 40, 44, 57-60, 67-69, 84, 90
Abelard of Bath, 140
Aben Aboo, 228-230
Aben Humeya, 222, 223, 226-228
Abencerraje, 203, 207, 209
Abu Bakr, 17
Abu Ya'qub, 152, 159, 162, 164
Abu Yusuf, 160-162, 164, 166
Aftasids, 121
Agila, 21
Aglabids, 60
Agusta Emerita, 11, 12
Ahmed el-Mellini, 236
Al-Azraq, 174
Al-Bayyasi, 171
Al-Fatimi, 236
Al-Hakam I, 40, 41, 44
Al-Hakam II, 74, 84, 90-99, 101-104, 130
Al-Ma'mun, 172, 174
Al-Madina al-Zahira, 101, 102, 103, 108, 111
Al-Mughira, 99
Al-Mumun, 136
Al-Mundhir, 40, 54-57
Al-Mushafi, 96, 98-101
Al-Mustain, 120
Al-Mutadid, 118, 119
Al-Mutamid, 143, 144
Al-Mutamin, 121, 140
Al-Mutarrif, 57
Al-Nasir, 166, 170
Al-Qadir, 128, 137, 144
Al-Ribad, 41, 42
Al-Zagal, 210-212, 214
Alange, 54, 55, 174
Alarcos, 150, 161, 163, 166
Albaicín, 180, 205, 210, 211, 216, 218, 226, 229, 230
Albarracín, 121-123, 133, 136
Albolafia, 127
Alcalá de Guadaira, 167, 175
Alcalá de Henares, 218
Alcalá la Real, 49
Alcaudete, 59

Aledo, 143-145
Alexandria, 42
Alfaques, 238
Alfonso I, 42, 60
Alfonso II, 43-45
Alfonso III, 53, 54, 60, 63, 64
Alfonso VI, 121, 123, 128, 137, 138, 143
Alfonso VIII, 156, 159, 161, 166, 170
Alfonso X, 182-184
Alfonso XI, 49, 188, 189, 192
Algarve, 147
Algeciras, 55, 73, 97, 118, 130, 133, 135, 143, 183-186, 189, 200, 202
Algeria, 19, 72, 150, 172, 245
Algiers, 143, 160
Alhama de Granada, 207, 209
Alhambra, 179, 182, 186, 188, 191-197, 199, 202, 203, 207, 214
Alicante, 122
Aljafería, 120, 121, 132, 135, 140, 213
Almanzor, 95, 97, 103, 104, 106-108, 111, 113, 114, 119, 122, 123, 130, 175
Almería, 67, 68, 74, 84, 122, 133, 147, 162, 174, 175, 178, 179, 186, 188, 207, 210, 212-214, 248
Almohad, 147, 149, 150, 152, 154 -156, 159-167, 170-177, 179, 182, 199, 205
Almonaster la Real, 64, 65
Almoravid, 141-150, 160, 166
Almuñécar, 32, 230
Alpuente, 121, 125, 133
Alpujarras, 137, 213-220, 222, 223, 225-228, 230, 248
Andalucía, 31, 57, 71, 213, 223, 229, 238
Antequera, 182, 201, 206, 207, 209
Arabian Peninsula, 16, 17
Arabs, 21, 22-29, 31, 34, 37
Aragón, 145, 146, 166, 170, 174, 175, 179, 180, 196, 199, 200, 208, 215, 216, 221, 248
Archez, 159
Archidona, 57, 59
Arcos de la Frontera, 119
Arjona, 177, 178
Asturias, 29, 31, 46, 53, 54
Atienza, 93, 103
Atzuvieta, 244
Autun, 26
Averroes, 164
Axarquia, 159, 228

Badajoz, 54, 55, 118, 121, 125, 133, 143, 144, 150, 152, 155, 162, 174

Baetic Cordillera, 9, 179
Baetica, 11, 14, 21, 25
Baeza, 170, 171, 177, 180, 200
Baghdad, 40, 51, 61, 73, 87, 90, 144, 149, 174
Balearic Islands, 100, 122, 146, 148, 150
Baños de la Encina, 100, 101
Banu Asqilula, 180, 182-184
Banu Dhu l'Nun, 76
Banu Ghaniya, 148, 150, 160, 166
Banu Hud, 120, 147, 174
Banu Mardanis, 147
Banu Qasi, 39, 46, 48, 62-64, 76, 78
Banu Razin, 121, 122
Barbate, 22, 25
Barcelona, 25, 33, 44, 79, 93, 106, 120
Basques, 11, 16, 22, 27, 29, 34, 44, 61, 62, 95
Baza, 212
Beja, 58
Belmez, 53
Berbers, 19, 20, 26, 30-32, 39, 42, 47, 53, 63, 67, 73, 102, 104, 111-113, 116, 118, 119, 121, 125, 128, 130, 133, 135, 141, 147-149, 247
Béznar, 222, 226
Boabdil, 201, 205, 206, 209-217
Bobastro, 56-58, 69, 71-73, 75, 79
Bordeaux, 26
Byzantine, 16, 88, 90, 96

Cáceres, 155
Cádiz, 11, 22, 150, 175, 183, 231
Cairo, 94, 103
Calatañazor, 60, 104, 108
Calatrava la Vieja, 163, 166
Calatuyud, 76, 79, 109, 147
Cambil, 200, 210
Capilla Real, 208, 210, 219
Capitulations, 212, 214
Cardinal Richelieu, 248
Carlos V, 221, 222, 230
Carmona, 11, 61, 71, 118, 130, 134, 147, 175, 199
Cartagena, 23
Cártama, 210
Carthage, 11, 19
Castile, 63, 79, 82, 93, 95, 102, 103, 106, 111, 119, 120, 123, 128, 135, 137, 138, 152, 156, 159, 161, 166, 170, 171, 174, 177-180, 182, 184-186, 188, 189, 192, 196, 198-201, 206-208, 215, 216, 219, 221, 229, 230, 238, 244, 248, 250
Catalonia, 44, 221, 238
Catholic Monarchs, 208, 210-

216, 219, 221
Cavall Verd, 236, 237
Ceuta, 21, 25, 30, 73, 74, 93, 94, 103, 186, 207
Ceyt Abu Ceyt, 171, 175
Charlemagne, 33, 44
Charles Martel, 26
Chefchauen, 240, 247
Christianity, 29, 72, 218, 222, 225, 230
Chronicle of 754, 22
Cintra, 144
Ciudad Real, 161, 166
Coimbra, 121
Columbus, 215, 216
Cordillera Cantábrica, 9
Córdoba, 10-13, 15, 24-26, 30, 31, 32-37, 39-42, 44, 46, 49-59, 61, 62, 64, 67, 68, 71, 73-79, 81-104, 106-116, 119, 120, 122, 127, 130, 133, 135, 139, 144, 147-149, 154, 159, 161, 162, 164, 171, 174, 175, 177, 179, 183, 207, 242, 247, 250
Corral del Carbón, 196, 197
Count Julian, 21
Covadonga, 25, 29, 30
Crete, 42, 50
Cristo de la Luz, 110
Cuenca, 135, 156

Damascus, 18, 20, 23-26, 29, 31-34, 36, 38, 40, 49, 113, 114
Daroca, 62, 76, 120, 147
Dénia, 120, 122, 123, 133, 144, 147
Despoblado, 244
Dhu l-Nun, 135, 137
Dioscorides, 88, 90
Don Juan de Austria, 227-230
Duero, 9, 39, 43, 61, 63, 77, 79, 93, 100, 121
Duke of Lerma, 232, 234

Ebro, 9, 23, 33, 39, 55, 63, 64, 78, 119, 146, 238
Egypt, 17, 18, 42, 199
El Cid, 128, 139, 144, 145, 155, 175
Elche, 23, 36
Elvira, 58, 68, 130, 133, 135, 171
Enrique II, 200
Enrique III, 206
Enrique IV, 208
Estepona, 208
Eulogius, 52, 53
Évora, 155

Farax Aben Farax, 226
Faro, 58
Fatimids, 69, 72-74, 83, 94, 103, 112
Felipe II, 222, 227, 229, 231,

232
Felipe III, 232, 234, 244
Fernán Gonzaléz, 82, 93
Fernando, 177-180, 186, 188, 208, 209, 211, 213, 216, 219, 221, 226
Fernando de Talavera, 216
Fernando II, 155
Fernando III, 171, 172, 174-180
Fez, 42, 74, 104, 130, 149, 162, 165, 166, 174, 180, 182, 196, 200, 216, 241, 242, 243, 247
France, 25-27, 238, 244
Francisco Jiménez de Cisneros, 216
Franks, 14, 33, 34, 39, 41, 44, 45, 50, 68
Fraxinctum, 89

Galera, 212, 229
Galicia, 29, 42, 43
Garci Fernández, 95
Gaul, 13, 14, 19
Genalguacil, 228
General Ghalib, 74, 93, 99, 101, 102
General Hashim, 54, 56, 57
Generalife, 195
Germanía, 221, 230
Gerona, 44
Gibralfaro, 189, 192, 202, 211
Gibraltar, 10, 19, 21-23, 25, 152, 182, 183, 186, 188, 191, 192, 202, 207, 238, 248
Giralda, 155, 156
Giraldo Sempavor, 155
Gormaz, 61, 77-79, 93, 95, 112
Granada, 58, 59, 114, 118, 121, 130, 133, 135, 140, 141, 143, 144, 148, 174, 176-180, 182, 184-189, 191, 192, 196, 198-202, 205-219, 225-227, 229, 230, 238, 245, 250
Great Mosque, 34-37, 40, 49-51, 83, 85, 87, 90-94, 96, 103, 106-108, 155, 161, 162, 175
Greek, 88, 90, 140
Guadalete, 22, 23
Guadalevín, 116
Guadalhorce, 56, 71
Guadalquivir, 10, 11, 25, 32, 41, 46, 59, 60, 79, 83, 96, 101, 103, 114, 127, 140, 152, 168, 170, 174, 175, 179, 199
Guadiana, 12, 150, 161, 163
Guadix, 177, 182, 188, 196, 210-213
Gutierre de Cárdenas, 214
Guzmán the Good, 185

Hafsids, 172, 199
Hall of the Ambassadors, 191, 214
Hama, 127
Hammudids, 112, 128, 130, 133
High Atlas, 142, 146-149, 163
Hisham I, 38, 39, 40, 44
Hisham II, 97, 99, 102, 108-113, 116, 118, 119
Hispania, 11-16, 20, 28, 37, 62
Hornachos, 239, 243
Huelva, 118
Huete, 156

Iberian Peninsula, 9-11, 14, 16, 19-21, 24-26, 38, 47, 55, 60, 62, 143, 146, 147, 150, 162, 170, 172, 177, 199, 203, 207, 214-216, 222, 247, 250
Ibn Abi Amir, 97, 98-104
Ibn al-Ahmar, 176-180, 182
Ibn al-Khatib, 192, 196, 202
Ibn al-Qitt, 64
Ibn Hafsun, 56-60, 69, 71-73, 83, 90
Ibn Hud, 174, 175, 177, 178
Ibn Mardanis, 150, 154, 155, 156, 172, 175
Ibn Marwan, 54, 55, 57, 58, 75
Ibn Shaprut, 82, 88
Ibn Tashufin, 142-145, 149
Ibn Tumart, 147, 149, 162, 163
Ibn Yasin, 141, 142
Ibn Zamrak, 202
Ibrahim bin Hajjuj, 60, 61, 71
Idris II, 42
Idrisids, 94, 99, 112, 130
Ifriqiya, 19, 21, 22, 30, 71, 72, 84, 103, 104, 145, 148, 150, 152, 166, 172, 203
Íllora, 210
Íñigo Arista, 44
Inquisition, 215, 222, 230, 232
Iraq, 17, 18
Islam, 17, 29, 33, 36, 39, 40, 46, 48, 52-54, 61, 64, 72, 83, 96, 102, 113, 138, 141, 143, 144, 147, 149, 172, 215, 222, 237, 247
Itálica, 12

Jaén, 39, 49, 63, 135, 147, 165, 170, 177-179, 183, 188, 200, 207
Jaime I, 174, 175, 180
James Douglas, 187, 188
James Joyce, 164
Játiva, 122, 130, 144
Jerez, 180
Jerusalem, 43
Jews, 13, 16, 17, 18, 51, 136, 138, 164-166, 215, 232, 248
Jimena, 145
Jimena de la Frontera, 205
John of Gorze, 89
Jordan, 26, 27
Junquera, 78

Kairouan, 19, 42, 58, 60, 72, 162, 165, 166
King Louis of Aquitaine, 44
Koran, 17, 18, 79, 95, 149
Koutoubia Mosque, 154, 162
Ksar el-Kabir, 184

La Carolina, 169
La Guardia de Jaén, 63
La Nora, 127
La Vall d'Alcalá, 174
Lake Janda, 22, 24
Lamtuna, 141, 142
Lanjarón, 219, 225, 227
Las Navas de Tolosa, 162, 163, 168-170
Láujar, 219, 228
Lecrín, 222, 226
León, 75, 76, 77, 79, 82, 83, 92, 106, 119, 120, 121, 128, 133, 152, 155, 166, 174, 177
Leovigild, 14-16
Lepanto, 230
Levante, 111, 121, 122, 143, 144, 147, 150, 154, 156, 175, 179
Libya, 17, 19, 20
Lisbon, 44, 46, 144, 159, 231
Loja, 210, 211
Lorca, 23, 25, 143, 144, 145
Lower March, 36, 45, 54
Lucena, 201, 207, 209

Madinat al-Zahra, 81-92, 101, 108, 112, 133, 179, 203
Madrid, 15, 88, 89
Maghreb, 29, 30, 51, 60, 71, 73, 84, 89, 93-95, 103, 104, 113, 128, 130, 135, 138, 141, 143-145, 147, 152, 154, 160, 162, 163, 166, 170-172, 179, 183-186, 189, 196, 199, 207, 214, 216, 244, 245, 248
Mahdi, 72, 111, 112
Mahdya, 73, 152, 162
Maimonedes, 164-166
Majorca, 160, 166, 175
Málaga, 11, 12, 56, 71, 84, 128, 130, 133, 135, 144, 147, 178, 179, 181-184, 189, 192, 199, 202, 207, 209-212, 228, 231
Maliki, 40, 51, 141, 149, 177
Marina Alta, 174, 236, 244, 245
Marinids, 172, 180, 182-186, 188, 189, 196, 199, 200, 202
Marques de los Vélez, 227
Marques de Mondéjar, 227
Marrakech, 142, 145, 147, 149, 150, 152, 154, 155, 159-162, 164, 166, 170-172, 174
Masmuda, 149
Mecca, 16, 17, 40, 43
Medina, 17, 18
Medinaceli, 82, 93-95, 108
Meknes, 150
Melilla, 73
Mérida, 11-13, 25, 35, 36, 39, 45, 54, 64, 144, 174
Mértola, 58, 118, 147
Meseta Central, 100, 168, 170
Mgoun Gorge, 148
Middle Atlas, 149
Middle March, 36, 93
Mihrab, 92-96, 98
Minorca, 176
Moclín, 210
Mojácar, 207, 209, 212
Monteagudo, 172
Moriscos, 137, 215, 219, 220, 222, 223, 225-238, 241-245, 247, 248, 250
Morocco, 19, 21, 41, 42, 55, 60, 74, 94, 99, 141, 142, 146, 147, 149, 162, 174, 239, 240, 241, 243, 247, 248
Morón, 118, 130
Mozarab, 43, 45, 51, 52, 60, 61, 63, 67, 71, 72, 84, 89, 111, 136, 138
Muawayia, 18, 20
Mudéjars, 180, 216, 218, 219, 221, 245, 250

255

Muela de Cortés, 236
Muhammad bin Hajjuj, 71
Muhammad I, 40, 53-57, 63, 64
Muhammad II, 182-186
Muhammad III, 186
Muhammad IV, 188, 189
Muhammad IX, 207
Muhammad V, 192, 196, 199, 200, 202, 203
Muhammad VI, 196, 199
Muhammad VII, 203, 206
Muley Hacén, 207, 209, 210
Murcia, 23, 45, 49, 57, 116, 122, 127, 143-145, 147, 148, 154, 156, 170, 172, 174, 176, 179, 180, 227, 238, 244, 248
Musa bin Fortun bin Qasi, 39
Musa bin Nusayr, 19, 21
Muwallad, 39, 46, 48, 53, 54, 56, 58, 59, 62, 63, 67, 89, 113

Narbonne, 21, 25, 33, 44, 45
Nasrid, 10, 18, 159, 176, 177-183, 186-189, 195, 200, 202, 203, 205, 207, 208, 210, 211, 214
Navarra, 78, 79, 82, 93, 106, 108, 120, 135, 170
Niebla, 46, 115, 118
Normans, 150, 152
North Africa, 14, 17, 19-21, 25, 26, 27, 31, 39, 40, 47, 56, 58, 60, 69, 71, 73, 74, 88, 93, 102-104, 109, 112, 130, 133, 135, 139, 145, 160, 162, 166, 211, 214, 216, 220, 234, 235, 243, 247, 248, 250
Nuño González, 182

Olvera, 203
Oran, 149, 214, 220, 237, 245
Order of Calatrava, 163, 166
Order of Santiago, 161, 243
Ordoño I, 53
Ordoño II, 76-78
Ordoño III, 82
Ordoño IV, 82, 83, 93
Orgiva, 227
Osma, 77-79, 112
Ottoman Empire, 222
Oviedo, 43, 52-54, 63

Pamplona, 44, 52, 55, 78, 79, 82, 108
Papal States, 230
Paper manufacture, 130
Parias, 119-121, 135, 139, 143, 144, 177
Pass of Despeñaperros, 161, 170
Pechina, 67, 68
Pedro I, 192, 196, 198, 199, 247
Pelayo, 29, 30, 32, 42
Peñón de Frigiliana, 228
Pepin, 33

Picos de Europa, 29
Poitiers, 26
Poley, 58, 59
Pope Innocent III, 166
Pope Paul V, 233
Porto, 9
Portugal, 11, 150, 160, 166, 181, 189, 200, 215, 231, 232
Prophet Muhammad, 16, 133
Pyrenees, 9, 13, 24, 25, 29, 33, 45

Qasr Amra, 26-28
Queen Isabel, 127, 213, 216
Queirola, 245

Rabat, 161, 162
Rabi bin Zayad, 84, 89, 90
Raimundus, 140
Ramiro II, 78, 79, 82
Real Alcázar, 198, 199, 247, 250
Reales Atarazanas, 48
Reconquista, 29, 30, 54, 62, 63, 160, 166, 175, 176, 179, 180, 203, 208, 215, 216, 244, 250
Reina, 161
Renaissance, 140, 250
Rif Mountains, 19, 149, 240, 241, 248
Rio Salado, 189
Roderic, 21-24, 26
Roman, 9, 11-20, 22, 25, 27, 28, 35-38, 41, 43, 47, 49, 51, 62, 64
Ronda, 56, 116, 118, 130, 147, 181, 185, 186, 188, 199, 201, 203, 204, 206-210
Rusafa, 37
Rute, 200

Sabika, 179, 182, 202
Sabinillas, 231
Sabur, 121, 125
Sagrajas, 143
Sahara, 141, 142
Saint James, 43, 237
Sala Dorada, 232
Saladin, 165, 166
Salé, 239, 243, 247
Salobreña, 200, 203, 206, 207, 214
Sancho Garcés II, 110
Sancho García, 78, 111
Sancho I, 82, 83, 92
Sancho IV, 184, 185
Sanchuelo, 110-113, 122, 123, 130
Sanhaja, 73, 94, 111, 133, 141, 144
Sanlúcar, 238
Santarém, 144, 159
Santiago de Compostela, 43, 106, 107, 175
Serranía de Ronda, 71, 219, 229
Seville, 46, 48, 49, 52, 55, 60,
61, 64, 71, 79, 114-116, 118, 119, 121, 133, 135, 136, 140, 143, 144, 148, 150, 152, 155, 156, 159-162, 166, 167, 170-177, 180, 183, 198, 199, 231, 238, 243, 247, 250
Shia, 72
Sierra Bermeja, 219, 228, 229, 248
Sierra de Espadán, 221
Sierra de Retín, 22, 24
Sierra Morena, 11, 53
Sierra Nevada, 179, 182, 220, 230
Sijilmassa, 141
Silves, 118, 147, 160, 161
Simancas, 79
Sistema Ibérico, 9
Slaves, 46, 50, 57, 86, 87, 99, 100, 106, 111-113, 121-123
Soria, 9, 60
Spain, 215, 216, 221-223, 227, 230-234, 238, 243, 245, 247, 248, 250
Spanish March, 44, 45, 106
Spanish Netherlands, 222
Subh, 97, 98, 101, 103
Suevi, 13, 15
Sulayman, 39, 41
Sunni, 73, 172
Suspiro del Moro, 217
Syria, 17, 18, 30, 31, 36, 37, 127, 137

Tablate, 223, 225, 227
Tagus, 75, 100, 159, 160
Taifas, 112-115, 118, 119, 121-123, 128, 130, 133, 139, 140, 141, 143, 144, 146, 147, 150, 174
Tangier, 20, 21, 73, 142, 184, 185
Tarif bin Malluq, 21
Tarifa, 12, 21-23, 143, 144, 179, 183-185, 189, 207
Tariq bin Ziyad, 20-22, 97
Tarragona, 11, 12
Teba, 187, 188
Teruel, 136, 147, 247, 250
Tetouan, 242, 243, 247
Tin Mal, 149, 162
Toledo, 22-25, 30, 36, 39, 41, 44, 45, 52-54, 75, 76, 79, 100, 110, 111, 114, 115, 119, 120, 123, 133, 135-140, 143-146, 156, 161-163, 166, 185, 210, 216
Torre de Espantaperros, 150, 152, 162
Torre del Oro, 152, 162
Tortosa, 120, 122, 123, 133
Toulouse, 14, 25
Trastámara, 200
Tremecen, 172, 183, 185, 199

Tripoli, 150, 162
Trujillo, 52, 155
Tuchibi, 76, 79, 94, 102, 119, 120
Tudela, 46, 63, 64, 76, 78
Tudmir, 23, 44, 57
Tunis, 150, 160, 172
Tunisia, 17, 19, 42, 72, 150, 166, 245
Turks, 223, 225, 230, 231

Úbeda, 170, 200
Uclés, 146
Umayyad, 18, 19, 27-29, 31-34, 37, 39, 40, 42, 45, 47, 49, 51, 53, 56-58, 64, 67, 68, 71, 73, 83, 86, 90, 91, 94, 97, 102, 104, 110-114, 116, 118-130, 139, 226, 242, 247, 250
Upper March, 36, 40, 62, 63, 76, 119
Uqba bin Nafi al-Fihri, 19
Uthman, 18

Valdepuentes Aqueduct, 86
Valencia, 25, 39, 40, 44, 79, 111, 122, 123, 128, 133, 135, 137, 139, 144, 147, 148, 171, 174, 175, 221, 225, 230, 232-238, 244, 248
Vall de Laguart, 233, 235, 236
Válor, 223, 226
Vandals, 13, 14
Vejer de la Frontera, 22
Vicente Turixi, 236
Vikings, 46-48, 55, 60
Visigoth, 9, 13, 14, 16, 21-29, 35, 37, 38

West Africa, 141
Witiza, 21

Yemen, 31
Yusuf I, 187, 189, 191, 192
Yusuf II, 203
Yusuf III, 206, 207

Zahara, 201, 203, 206, 207, 209
Zamora, 64, 67, 83, 106
Zanata, 73, 94, 172
Zaragoza, 14, 23, 25, 33, 36, 39, 44, 64, 76, 79, 94, 95, 103, 119-121, 128, 132, 133, 135, 140, 143, 145-147, 174, 213
Zawi bin Ziri, 111, 133
Zayyanids, 172, 183, 185, 199
Zirid, 135, 141
Ziryab, 51
Zuheros, 171, 172